This book is for parents, grandparents, health professionals and all other caregivers of young children encouraging clear conversations that lead to UNDERSTANDING**CHILDREN**.

This book is the essential guidebook for children 0 to 3 years.

This book is about the special journey that parents have been taking for thousands of years. This journey is filled with the wonder of the nurturing and raising of a child through the early critical years of life.

This book, like a good parent, uses informed guidance, with permission, for the development of this unique caring relationship.

This book identifies questions, clarifies answers, advises on action and expands sources through other books, the internet and helpful contacts.

When you meet anyone who has a new baby, you see in their eyes and hear from their mouths the convincing, joyful message that their baby is the best baby there ever was. With that message also comes the anxiety of newness, vulnerability and not knowing.

It's proper for you to feel your baby is the best, the cutest, the sweetest, the smartest. In fact it's those feelings that create the depth of love
and care necessary in child rearing. This love gets you through the responsibilities, sleepless nights, occasional ill health and seemingly endless diaper changes.

The following is our guidebook to reduce the anxieties of this wondrous journey through the curiosity that leads to questions, answers and actionable suggestions, clearly explained in words, illustrations and diagrams. **RSW**

UNDERSTANDING**CHILDREN**

1 month

Can see, hear, feel, taste and smell at birth. Uses reflexes.

Likes soft, high-pitched voices. Likes to look at faces. Startles at loud sounds.

2 months

Focuses eyes.
Eats every **3 to 4** hours.

Smiles. Reacts to distress by crying.

3 months

Holds head up.

Coos and gurgles.

4 months

Tries to grab with hand.

Wiggles and kicks with arms and legs.
Rolls over (stomach to back).
Sits with support.

Cries different ways for different reasons.
Loves to be touched or held close.
Responds to a shaking rattle or bell and to peek-a-boo games.
Laughs and chuckles.
Shows signs of fear, anger or disgust.

5 to 6 months

Teeth appear.
Rolls over.

Tries to talk to image in mirror.

7 to 8 months

Reaches for cup or spoon when being fed. Drinks from a cup with help. Enjoys some finely-chopped solid foods. Closes mouth firmly or turns head when no longer hungry.

May sleep **11 to 13** hours at night*. Needs **2 to 3** naps a day.

Develops a rhythm for feeding, eliminating and sleeping.

True eye color is established.

Sits alone without support.

Can "rake" objects with hand.

Transfers objects from one hand to another.

Hair growth begins to cover head.

Responds to own name. Recognizes family members' names. Responds differently to family and strangers.

Distressed if a toy is taken away.

Shows fear of falling off high places (table, stairs).

Shows mild to severe anxiety at separation from parent.

Imitates sounds, actions and facial expressions.

Raises arms as a sign to be held.

Likes to be tickled and touched.

9 to 12 months

Enjoys drinking from a cup. Begins to eat finger food. Eats **3** meals a day. Has tripled birth weight and doubled in length. Continues to explore everything by mouth.

Enjoys opening and closing cabinet doors.

Crawls well. Pulls self up to a standing position. Stands alone holding onto furniture for support.

Walks holding onto furniture or with adult help.

Imitates adult actions such as drinking from a cup, or talking on the phone. Responds more to adults than to other infants.

Likes to watch self in the mirror.

Wants parent or caregiver to be in constant sight. Expresses fear toward strangers.

Offers toys or objects to others but wants them to be returned. Points to desired objects.

Pushes away toys, food and other items when she does not want them.

May become attached to a favorite toy or blanket.

* varies greatly

4

INTELLECTUAL DEVELOPMENT

Learning begins at birth.
Recognizes caregiver's voice.

Follows light or objects with eyes.
Recognizes bottle or breast.

Recognizes mother or primary caregiver.

Can use eyes and hands together.

Explores objects with mouth.
Recognizes bottle or breast.

Understands he can reach out to touch objects.

Learns by using all five senses.

Makes noises to show displeasure or satisfaction.

Focuses eyes on small objects and reaches for them. Enjoys dropping objects over edge of chair or crib. Looks for a ball rolled out of sight.

Babbles as if talking.

Says first word. Says da-da and ma-ma or equivalent. Imitates animals.

Dances or bounces to music.

Interested in picture books.

Plays pat-a-cake.

Likes to place objects inside one another.

Pays attention to conversations.

Claps hands, waves goodbye, if prompted.

Source: Used by permission of Lesia Oesterreich, Iowa State University Extension.

IDEAS FOR CAREGIVERS

Help your baby develop a sense of trust and security by responding to his cries. Feeling secure encourages him to try new things. Be consistent so he will know what to expect.

Place your child in new places and new positions so that she can see her surroundings from different angles.

Hold and cuddle your baby when feeding him. This is very important in the development of his sense of self-worth and security. It's also a great stress releaser for adults.

Respect your baby's natural schedule. Most will settle into a routine for eating, sleeping and soiling diapers, but each baby is different. Some eat more often. Some need longer naps.

Expose your baby to bright colors and a variety of objects.

Provide an environment rich with sound. Help your child to recognize common household sounds such as the vacuum, the radio, a clock or the doorbell.

Provide opportunities for your child to experience different smells. Lemon, vanilla and apple juice are wonderful kitchen smells. Outdoors, let them smell flowers and grass.

Give older babies a variety of tastes and temperatures. For instance, try cold sherbet, warm oatmeal, mashed peaches or chopped cooked carrots.

Face your baby when you talk to him so he can see and smile with you.

Ages & Stages

Newborn to One Year

Throughout the first year, your child will grow at a tremendously fast rate. In fact, by the end of the first year, he will have tripled in birth weight and his length can be expected to double. By his first birthday, he will probably be crawling and may even be taking his first steps!

The most essential ingredient for your child's healthy development is a warm, responsive, and dependable adult caregiver. Try to spend lots of time holding, cuddling, and playing with your child. You will be richly rewarded with babbles, smiles and squeals of laughter.

Items in this chart represent baseline averages that most children reach at specified ages. If you are concerned about delays in any area, you might want to talk to your pediatrician about a formal developmental assessment.

13 to 18 months

PHYSICAL DEVELOPMENT

Stands alone, sits down.

Walks without help. Enjoys carrying small objects while walking, often one in each hand.

Gestures or points to indicate wants. Likes to push, pull and dump things. Also likes to poke, twist and squeeze.

Pulls off hat, socks and mittens.

Turns pages in a book. Holds crayon and scribbles, but with little control.

Enjoys holding spoon when eating, but experiences difficulty in getting spoon into mouth.

Can stack two blocks.

Enjoys flushing toilets and closing doors.

Rolls a ball to an adult on request.

Waves goodbye and claps hands.

SOCIAL & EMOTIONAL DEVELOPMENT

Becomes upset when separated from parent. Enjoys being held and read to. Needs reassurance with fears.

Plays alone on floor with toys.

Recognizes himself in a mirror or in pictures.

Imitates others, especially by coughing, sneezing or making animal sounds.

Likes an audience and applause.

Begins to need set limits.

> Encourage play in front of safe mirrors. Talk and make funny faces together.
>
> Have a variety of simple picture books. Get your child to point to things as you name them and share her delight.

19 to 24 months

PHYSICAL DEVELOPMENT

Walks well.

Walks up steps with help.

Takes steps backwards.

Likes to run but can't always stop and turn well.

Can stack two to four blocks.

Helps wash hands.

Bends over to pick up a toy without falling over.

Drinks with a straw.
Feeds himself with a spoon.

Tosses or rolls a large ball.

Enjoys sitting on and moving small-wheeled riding toys.

Opens cabinets, drawers and boxes.

Begins to gain some control of bowels and bladder, but complete control may not be achieved until around age **3.**

(Boys often do not complete toilet training until age **3 1/2.**)

SOCIAL & EMOTIONAL DEVELOPMENT

Likes to imitate parents' actions.

Begins to show signs of independence. Says "no."

Is generally unable to remember rules.

Enjoys exploring and gets into everything.

Needs constant attention.

Has difficulty sharing. Is very possessive.

Tries to do many things independently.

Finds it difficult to wait and wants things right now!

Gets angry sometimes and has temper tantrums.

Often gets physically aggressive when frustrated. Might slap or hit.

Acts shy around strangers.

Refers to self by name. Uses the words "me" and "mine."

Learns that anger and despair pass.

Understands and follows simple one-step directions.

Says **8 to 20** words you can understand. Looks at person talking to her.

Will say "hi" or "bye" if reminded. Uses expressions such as "uh-oh."

Asks for something by pointing or using one word.

Identifies objects in a book.

Plays peek-a-boo.

Likes to take things apart.

Use diaper time to point to and name her nose, ears, arms, toes…

Talk frequently to increase language skills and encourage cooperation.

Encourage bouncing, swaying and wiggling by dancing to music.

Has a rapidly growing vocabulary including names of toys.
Uses **2- to 3-**word sentences. Echoes single words that are spoken by someone else.

Talks to himself and jabbers expressively.
Uses the words "please" and "thank you" if prompted.

Shows preferences between toys. Likes to choose between two objects.

Hums or tries to sing. Enjoys singing familiar songs.

Listens to short rhymes or fingerplays such as "Itsy Bitsy Spider."
Enjoys looking at picture books.

Likes simple pretend play such as wearing hats and talking on the phone.

Dance with your child to music with different rhythms. Give her a simple instrument such as a rattle or an oatmeal box drum.

Encourage dressing up by providing a full-length mirror on the wall and a box of "pretend" clothes—caps, scarves and old shoes.

Enjoy some "floor time" each day. Crawl around together or roll a ball back and forth.

Review baby-proofing. Increasing growth and mobility mean that children can reach unsafe heights. Get down on your knees and look at things from a child's point of view. Put toxic items such as paint, detergent, medicine and vitamins in high cupboards.

Make a junk box of items that are fun to feel and squeeze. Include an old sock, margarine tubs, tissue paper to crumple, measuring cups, an egg carton and paper cups. (Items smaller than a half-dollar can cause choking.)

After 18 months, language development seems to explode. Children will be learning new words at a very rapid rate, so talk to your child about everything. Read simple books together every day. Choose books that are made of cardboard or have cloth pages. Stories that have familiar objects in them are best. Encourage your child to turn the pages.

Make a scrapbook out of a small sturdy photo album that has pictures of objects and people your child knows.

Expand your child's language by adding to what he says. If he says "kitty," you can can say "yes, the kitty is little and soft."

Play a simple game of recognition. Place three familiar toys in front of your child and say "give me the…". See if he tries to find it and give it to you.

One-year-olds are delightful. At this stage your baby is developing a real personality and will reward you with laughter, funny faces and affectionate hugs. **Growth at this time is still rapid, but height and weight gains are not as dramatic.** As growth decreases, appetite decreases and your child may eat less.

By 18 months, children are truly on the go.
A greater sense of independence begins to develop as your child starts to walk, run and climb with greater skill. And you'll notice that at this age your child needs the freedom and encouragement to explore and make choices as well as clear limits and boundaries to follow.

Items in this chart represent baseline averages that most children reach at specified ages. If you are concerned about delays in any area, you might want to talk to your pediatrician about a formal developmental assessment.

Source: Used by permission of Lesia Oesterreich, Iowa State University Extension.

AGE This is a guide—babies differ!	PHYSICAL DEVELOPMENT	SOCIAL & EMOTIONAL DEVELOPMENT

25 to 30 months

Physical Development

Can jump in place and walk on tiptoes. Walks up and down steps putting both feet on each step. Can walk backwards.

Holds pencil with thumb and forefinger.

Can zip and unzip.

Can pull off own clothes.

Helps to put things away.

Toilet training is in progress.

Builds towers of **6 to 8** cubes.

Drinks from a cup without spilling.

Social & Emotional Development

Initiates own play activities.

Wants routines to be "just so" and does not like changes in routines.

Has a hard time waiting. Cannot delay gratification.

Has a hard time sharing things.

Has established a place in the family and knows own sex.

Observes other children at play and joins in.

31 to 36 months

Physical Development

Puts on shoes but cannot tie laces.

Tries to catch a large ball. Can throw the ball overhead and kick a ball forward.

Can stand, balance and hop on one foot. Pedals a tricycle.

Climbs up and down a small slide by herself.

Can jump over a 6-inch barrier.

Can feed self with spoon and fork.

Can use toilet independently.

Can brush teeth and wash hands.

Is interested in handling food and cooking procedures.

Avoids simple hazards.

Social & Emotional Development

Begins associative play activities.

Names or points to self in photos.

Joins in nursery rhymes and songs.

Likes praise.

Has greater impulse control.

Dawdles.

Shows sympathy, modesty and shame.

HOW TIME CHANGES THE PROPORTIONS OF YOUR CHILD'S BODY

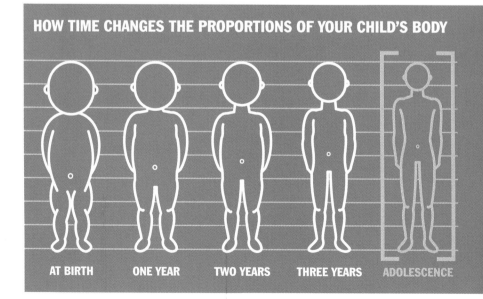

AT BIRTH   ONE YEAR   TWO YEARS   THREE YEARS   ADOLESCENCE

INTELLECTUAL DEVELOPMENT

Often calls self by own name.

Speaks **50** or more words, has a vocabulary of **300** words. Uses phrases and **3- to 4-**word sentences.

Understands and asks for "another."

Can point to and name own body parts when asked.

Talks so that **75 to 80%** of his speech is understandable. Uses **3- to 5-** word sentences.

May stumble over words sometimes—this is not usually a sign of stuttering.

Verbalizes toilet needs.

Uses plural and increases use of verbs. Begins use of adjectives and prepositions.

Vocabulary of **900 to 1,000** words by **3** years. Uses verbal commands.

Gives full name when asked. Asks "What's that?"

Childhood is a time of rapid changes in the proportions of your child's body. At birth your child's head is about a quarter of her total body length. As she grows, the relative size of her head becomes smaller and her limbs become longer.

[Final adult size is reached in adolescence. At this point her head will be only one-eighth of her total height.]

IDEAS FOR CAREGIVERS

As your child gets older, reinforce skills and teach new ones with engaging activities.

Improve abstract thought.
Enhance this skill with games that require organizing and matching colors, shapes, faces and feelings with sets of toys, cards or other objects that go together.

Promote hand-eye coordination.
Try stringing large buttons or beads on a shoelace. Teach your child to throw, catch and kick.

Encourage an interest in reading and writing.
You can both give him books to read and read all sorts of things to him—newspapers, grocery lists, poetry. Point out important words on pages, packages and street signs. Make sure there's always plenty of paper and crayons available.

Introduce numbers.
Count objects of interest like cookies, cups, napkins, dolls. When possible, move one at a time while you and your child count them.

Explore science.
Explain why and how things work with the help of reference books and simple experiments like magnetic attraction or freezing water. Let your child play with toys that come apart.

Stimulate creativity.
Provide ample opportunity for your child to express himself through art, music and theatrics.

Source: Colorado Division of Child Welfare Services.

Ages & Stages
Two Years to Three Years

The toddler is full of wonder and spends a lot of time watching, observing and imitating.
At this age your child is interested in perfecting his motor skills. It's common for him to spend a whole morning going down a slide or riding a tricycle. During this time, help his impulse control along by providing choices, setting limits and showing connections between actions and consequences.

Items in this chart represent baseline averages that most children reach at specified ages. If you are concerned about delays in any area, you might want to talk to your pediatrician about a formal developmental assessment.

What are percentiles?

The best way to understand the term is with an example: Your baby is in the 65th percentile for length if she is taller than 64 out of a hundred normal babies of the same sex and birthday as hers. Of course, she's shorter than 35 of the 100.

Ideally, your baby should follow the percentile curves on the growth charts shown here.

Where your child is on the percentile rankings (90th, 50th, etc.) is not as important as having her positions track along the curves consistently from birth to age three. After infancy, the length percentile is referred to as the height percentile.

When should I worry?

If your baby's percentile changes suddenly. If he's been in the 50th percentile for weight and drops to the 15th, your doctor will need to know why.

Birth weight matters less than you might think.

The average U.S. newborn weighs **7lb., 7oz.** and is **20 in.** long. Studies have shown that genetics (height of both parents), not birth weight determine your child's adult size.

GIRLS' LENGTH-FOR-AGE PERCENTILES

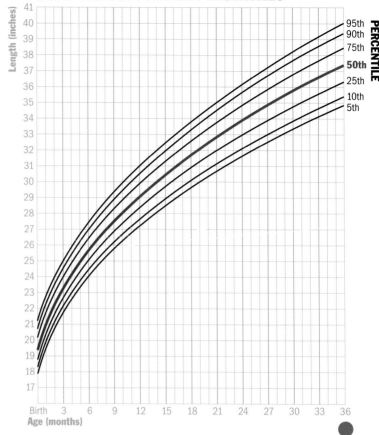

GIRLS' WEIGHT-FOR-AGE PERCENTILES

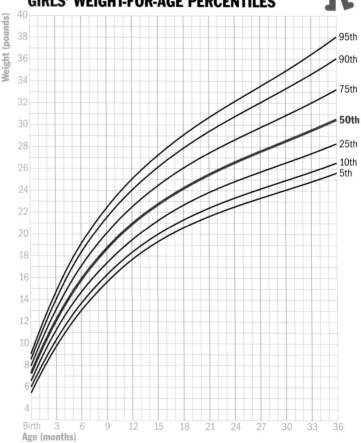

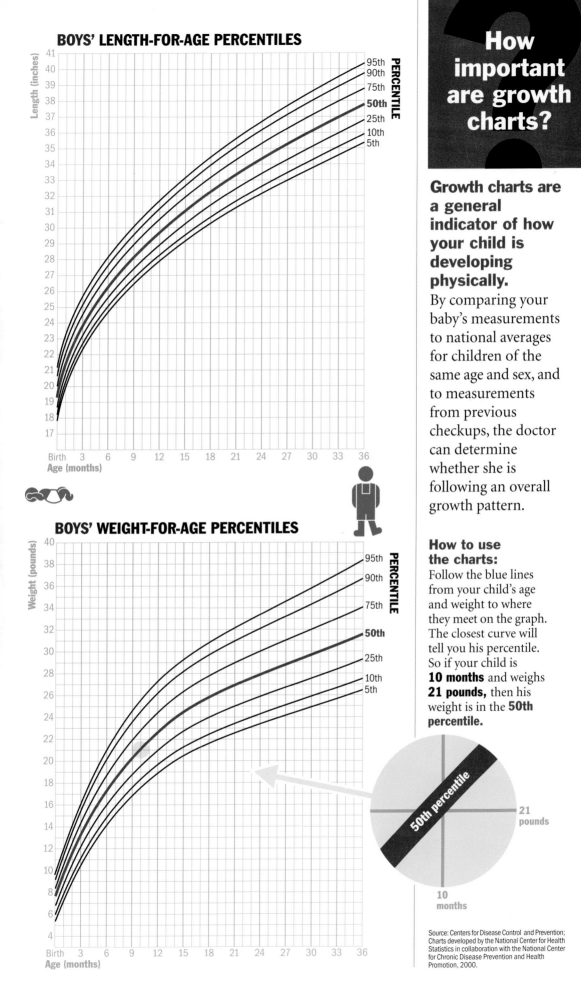

BOYS' LENGTH-FOR-AGE PERCENTILES

Length (inches)

95th
90th
75th
50th
25th
10th
5th

PERCENTILE

Birth 3 6 9 12 15 18 21 24 27 30 33 36
Age (months)

BOYS' WEIGHT-FOR-AGE PERCENTILES

Weight (pounds)

95th
90th
75th
50th
25th
10th
5th

PERCENTILE

Birth 3 6 9 12 15 18 21 24 27 30 33 36
Age (months)

How important are growth charts?

Growth charts are a general indicator of how your child is developing physically.
By comparing your baby's measurements to national averages for children of the same age and sex, and to measurements from previous checkups, the doctor can determine whether she is following an overall growth pattern.

How to use the charts:
Follow the blue lines from your child's age and weight to where they meet on the graph. The closest curve will tell you his percentile. So if your child is **10 months** and weighs **21 pounds,** then his weight is in the **50th percentile.**

50th percentile

21 pounds

10 months

Source: Centers for Disease Control and Prevention; Charts developed by the National Center for Health Statistics in collaboration with the National Center for Chronic Disease Prevention and Health Promotion, 2000.

Pregnancy myths

USA: If a pregnant woman has a lot of indigestion, her baby will have a lot of hair.

SICILY: If she crosses her legs, her cervix will not open easily during labor.

JAMAICA: If she steps over a donkey's rope, the umbilical cord will wrap tightly around the baby's neck.

JAPAN: If she eats sour foods, she will harm the baby's skin. If she eats sweet things, she will slow the baby's bone formation. If she eats spicy foods, she will unsettle the baby's soul.

? Pregnant fathers?

Couvade ("coo – VAHD") **Syndrome:** Phenomenon in which the father feels or exhibits pregnancy symptoms. In some aboriginal communities, men retreat to bed, scream as if in labor and receive nurturing while the mother gives birth somewhere else. In the U.S., fathers-to-be have reported morning sickness, weight gain and food cravings.

Pregnancy and Weight Gain

? How much weight should a woman gain during pregnancy?

If a woman is...	she should gain...
Carrying twins:	35 – 45 pounds
Underweight:	40 pounds
Normal weight:	25 – 35 pounds
Overweight:	not less than 15 pounds

? How fast should she gain it?

A woman should gain about three to four pounds in the first three months and one pound a week thereafter through Month 8. In the last month, the rate of gain should drop to less than a pound a week.

1st trimester	2nd trimester	3rd trimester

(pounds: 0, 5, 10, 15, 20, 25, 30)

(approximations for normal-weight woman)

? How is the weight gain distributed?

In the average pregnancy, most of the extra pounds come not from the baby but from the changes the woman's body undergoes to support pregnancy and lactation.

Baby	=	7.5 pounds
Placenta	=	1.5 pounds
Amniotic fluid	=	2 pounds
Uterine enlargement	=	2 pounds
Breast enlargement	=	2 pounds
Fat stores	=	7 pounds
Increased blood volume	=	4 pounds
Fluid retention	=	4 pounds
Total weight gain	**=**	**30 pounds**

(approximations for normal-weight woman)

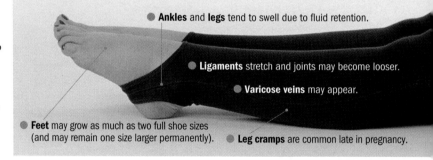

- **Ankles** and **legs** tend to swell due to fluid retention.
- **Ligaments** stretch and joints may become looser.
- **Varicose veins** may appear.
- **Feet** may grow as much as two full shoe sizes (and may remain one size larger permanently).
- **Leg cramps** are common late in pregnancy.

ACTION ITEMS

Coping with pregnancy symptoms

Morning sickness

- Eat several small meals instead of three large ones.
- Keep crackers or dry toast by your bed. Eat them about 20 minutes before you intend to get up.
- Avoid unpleasant smells.
- Drink fluids between rather than with meals.
- Try wearing "pressure-point" (non-medicinal) wristbands sold for preventing seasickness.

Swelling (legs, ankles, feet)

- Elevate your legs or lie down.
- Wear support hose. Put them on in the morning, when swelling is typically down.
- Drink at least eight glasses of fluid daily.

Constipation and hemorrhoids

- Have two glasses of water first thing in the morning.
- Include high-fiber foods in every meal.
- Don't use laxatives unless your doctor prescribes them.
- If you develop hemorrhoids, don't sit for long periods of time. Avoid straining during bowel movements.

Morning sickness: ▪ Who: About 50% of women ▪ What: Ranges from queasiness to frequent vomiting. Occurs any time of day. In severe cases, persistent vomiting requires medical care. ▪ When: Usually ends by Week 12, but for some women, lasts for the duration.

A Total-Body Experience

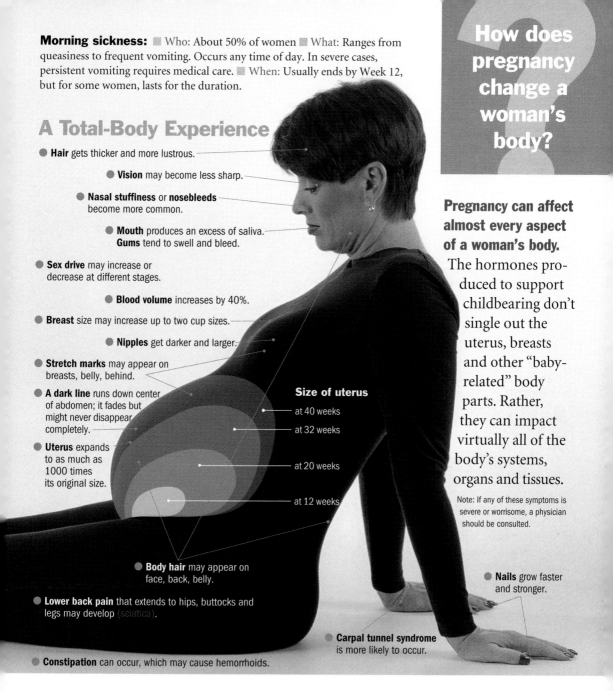

● **Hair** gets thicker and more lustrous.

● **Vision** may become less sharp.

● **Nasal stuffiness** or **nosebleeds** become more common.

● **Mouth** produces an excess of saliva. **Gums** tend to swell and bleed.

● **Sex drive** may increase or decrease at different stages.

● **Blood volume** increases by 40%.

● **Breast** size may increase up to two cup sizes.

● **Nipples** get darker and larger.

● **Stretch marks** may appear on breasts, belly, behind.

● **A dark line** runs down center of abdomen; it fades but might never disappear completely.

● **Uterus** expands to as much as 1000 times its original size.

● **Body hair** may appear on face, back, belly.

● **Lower back pain** that extends to hips, buttocks and legs may develop (sciatica).

● **Constipation** can occur, which may cause hemorrhoids.

Size of uterus

— at 40 weeks
— at 32 weeks
— at 20 weeks
— at 12 weeks

● **Carpal tunnel syndrome** is more likely to occur.

● **Nails** grow faster and stronger.

How does pregnancy change a woman's body?

Pregnancy can affect almost every aspect of a woman's body. The hormones produced to support childbearing don't single out the uterus, breasts and other "baby-related" body parts. Rather, they can impact virtually all of the body's systems, organs and tissues.

Note: If any of these symptoms is severe or worrisome, a physician should be consulted.

Assembling a low-stress, low-cost maternity wardrobe

● Borrow, borrow, borrow!

● Search your husband's or a male friend's closet. Men's dress shirts, vests and T-shirts (if overly large on you) can work well with maternity pants.

● Buy a few simple, flattering, solid-color maternity separates that you can wear frequently. Use jewelry, scarves and other accessories to break the monotony.

● Purchase these "must-haves" at a maternity store:
  ● Maternity or nursing bra
  ● Leggings
  ● Jeans

Resources and information

www.babycenter.com
www.childbirth.org
www.pregnancytoday.com

What to Expect When You're Expecting
Arlene Eisenberg et al.

Planning for Pregnancy, Birth, and Beyond
The American College of Obstetricians and Gynecologists

Mayo Clinic Complete Book of Pregnancy & Baby's First Year
Robert V. Johnson, editor

? How long is the average pregnancy?

The average length of a baby's development—from conception to birth—is 38 weeks. But because it's usually difficult to pinpoint the exact conception date, many doctors use a 40-week model based on the woman's last period. A normal, full-term pregnancy can last anywhere from 37 to 42 weeks.

What a difference two days makes!

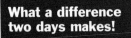

■ Day 24 to Day 26
Arm buds appear.

■ Day 31 to Day 33
The brain grows by 25%.

? Do babies "go to the bathroom" in the womb?

By month three, the baby begins to sip small amounts of amniotic fluid and excrete driblets of urine back into his amniotic sac. (The urine is sterile and therefore does not contaminate the amniotic fluid.) The baby also produces tiny amounts of solid waste, which accumulate in his intestines until sometime after birth.

Months 3 and 4
Constant motion

The baby swims, flips, turns and stretches, seeming to enjoy the ample space it has to exercise its developing muscles. It rarely stops moving for more than five minutes. Despite the vigorous activity, the mother probably won't feel any movement until Month 5.

■ **Hiccups:** The baby begins to hiccup frequently. This helps get the diaphragm in shape for breathing after birth.

4 months
10 cm
(4 inches)

3 weeks
.25 cm

1 day
.015 cm

Month 2
Body formed

The body's main structural components—facial features, limbs, vital organs—are completely formed. About one inch in length, the embryo (now fetus) is clearly a baby-in-miniature.

■ **Brain development:** The baby produces an average of 250,000 neurons per minute throughout its nine-month gestation.

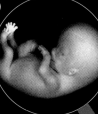

2 months
3.1 cm
(1 1/4 inches)

Month 1
Cells teeming

Dividing gradually at first, the fertilized egg (zygote) explodes with activity, proliferating wildly and migrating to the areas of the "body" where cells will organize according to highly specialized functions.

■ **Lingering sperm:** In Week 1, as the fertilized egg meanders toward the uterus for implantation, a few dozen sperm still writhe around the egg's perimeter.

7 weeks
1.8 cm

ACTION ITEMS Interacting with baby before birth

By months five and six, you can communicate with your baby, especially by appealing to her senses of hearing and touch:

● Talk to and read to your baby frequently. She will know her mom's voice well by the time she is born. With enough conversation directed her way, she can hear dad's voice also.

● Play your favorite music for her. Studies have indicated that babies can "remember" music they heard repeatedly in utero as late as one year of age.

● Engage her in a tapping game. When you feel the baby kick or move at a certain spot on mom's abdomen, gently tap in the same place. You may soon have a playful "back-and-forth" going.

● Provide calming touch. If the baby seems restless, you can soothe her by gently stroking mom's abdomen.

TIP
Even though muffled by mom's womb, sounds from the outside do reach baby. Avoid unpleasant noise where possible, and create an ambiance you want for your child.

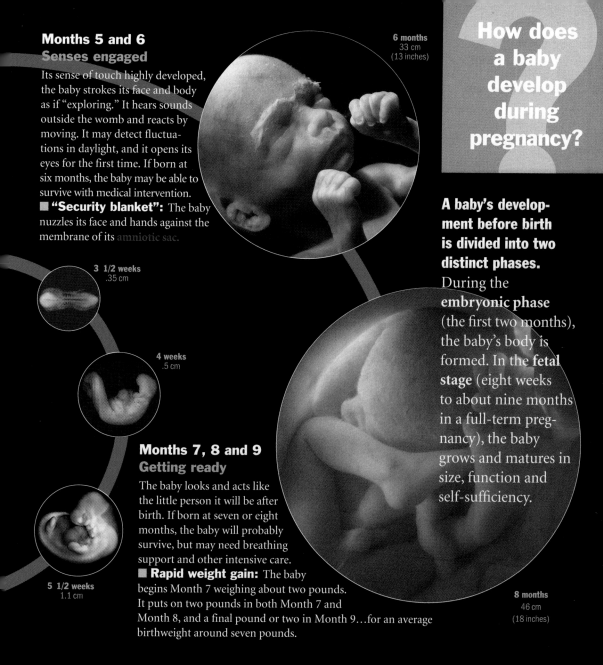

Months 5 and 6
Senses engaged

Its sense of touch highly developed, the baby strokes its face and body as if "exploring." It hears sounds outside the womb and reacts by moving. It may detect fluctuations in daylight, and it opens its eyes for the first time. If born at six months, the baby may be able to survive with medical intervention.

■ **"Security blanket":** The baby nuzzles its face and hands against the membrane of its amniotic sac.

3 1/2 weeks
.35 cm

4 weeks
.5 cm

5 1/2 weeks
1.1 cm

6 months
33 cm
(13 inches)

Months 7, 8 and 9
Getting ready

The baby looks and acts like the little person it will be after birth. If born at seven or eight months, the baby will probably survive, but may need breathing support and other intensive care.

■ **Rapid weight gain:** The baby begins Month 7 weighing about two pounds. It puts on two pounds in both Month 7 and Month 8, and a final pound or two in Month 9…for an average birthweight around seven pounds.

A baby's development before birth is divided into two distinct phases. During the **embryonic phase** (the first two months), the baby's body is formed. In the **fetal stage** (eight weeks to about nine months in a full-term pregnancy), the baby grows and matures in size, function and self-sufficiency.

8 months
46 cm
(18 inches)

Black-and-white photography by Kohei Shiota, M.D., Kyoto University.
Color photography from Lennart Nilsson/Albert Bonniers Forlag AB, *A Child is Born*, Dell Publishing.

Take stress seriously

Babies in utero act differently when the mother is stressed or upset. During pregnancy, try to reduce or eliminate those stress-inducing factors that may be within your control. Exercise, meditation and relaxation techniques such as deep breathing can help relieve tension.

Stress management has longer-term benefits as well: you can decrease your risk for early, long and painful labor. More importantly, you will be better prepared to deal with the challenges of parenting.

Resources: babies in utero

A Child is Born
Lennart Nilsson

Beginning Life
Geraldine Lux Flanagan

The Visible Embryo
www.visembryo.com

How Your Baby Grows
www.modimes.org/mama

Pregnancy calendar
www.babycenter.com/pregnancy-calendar/

What are the risks of Down syndrome?

The risk of Down syndrome, a chromosomal disorder that causes mental retardation, increases dramatically with the mother's age. (Age is not sole risk factor.)

Mother's age:	Risk of Down syndrome is 1 in:
20	1,667
25	1,250
30	952
31	909
32	769
33	625
34	500
35	385
36	294
37	227
38	175
39	137
40	106
41	82
42	64
43	50
44	38
45	30
46	23
47	18
48	14
49	11

Screening vs. Diagnosis

Screening tests: Reveal only the possibility of problems with baby; often a good "starting point"

Diagnostic tests: Determine the existence of problem with a higher degree of certainty

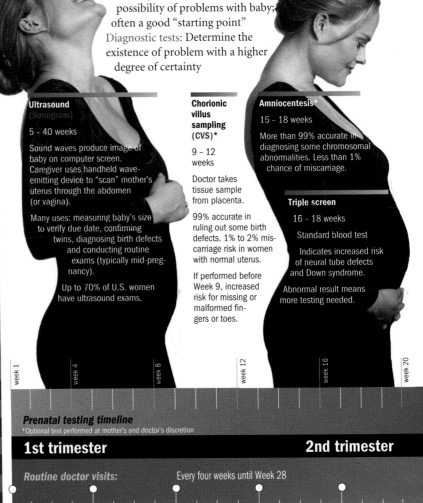

Ultrasound (Sonogram)

5 - 40 weeks

Sound waves produce image of baby on computer screen. Caregiver uses handheld wave-emitting device to "scan" mother's uterus through the abdomen (or vagina).

Many uses: measuring baby's size to verify due date, confirming twins, diagnosing birth defects and conducting routine exams (typically mid-pregnancy).

Up to 70% of U.S. women have ultrasound exams.

Chorionic villus sampling (CVS)*

9 - 12 weeks

Doctor takes tissue sample from placenta.

99% accurate in ruling out some birth defects. 1% to 2% miscarriage risk in women with normal uterus.

If performed before Week 9, increased risk for missing or malformed fingers or toes.

Amniocentesis*

15 - 18 weeks

More than 99% accurate in diagnosing some chromosomal abnormalities. Less than 1% chance of miscarriage.

Triple screen

16 - 18 weeks

Standard blood test

Indicates increased risk of neural tube defects and Down syndrome.

Abnormal result means more testing needed.

week 1 | week 4 | week 8 | week 12 | week 16 | week 20

Prenatal testing timeline
*Optional test performed at mother's and doctor's discretion

1st trimester   **2nd trimester**

Routine doctor visits: Every four weeks until Week 28

Routine doctor visits: ▪ First visit: Complete history and physical; due date estimated. Tests may include: Blood and Rh typing, anemia, rubella, Tay-Sachs disease, sickle-cell anemia, drug use, sexually transmitted diseases. ▪ Every visit: Urine tests for diabetes and pregnancy-induced high blood pressure (preeclampsia). ▪ Month 3 visit and thereafter: Baby's heartbeat monitored.

ACTION ITEMS   Choosing your health care provider

Start by asking friends, nurses or childbirth educators for their recommendations.

If you are not pleased with your current gynecologist (or other provider of well-woman care), this is the time to change. Do not feel a sense of obligation to a health care provider with whom you are not completely satisfied.

Determine your options. If you have special medical conditions (e.g., diabetes), you may need a professional who delivers in a hospital setting. If your history is less complicated, you may want to consider additional options, such as a certified nurse-midwife who works in a birthing center.

Phone screening:
Questions for the office staff

- Where did the health care provider train? What are her credentials?
- How many other providers are in this practice?
- How likely will it be that the one I've chosen will attend my delivery?
- At which facilities (hospital, birthing centers) does she deliver?
- What are the fees for all prenatal visits and delivery? When are payments due?
- Could I briefly interview (at no cost) the person I've chosen?
- How long are the routine office visits? How long of a wait (if any) should I expect when I have a scheduled visit?

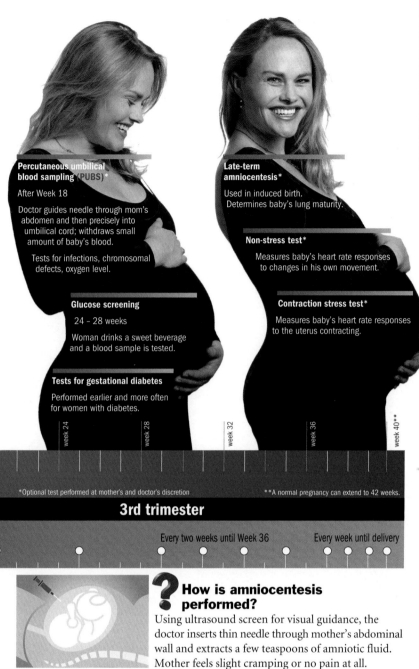

Percutaneous umbilical blood sampling (PUBS)*

After Week 18

Doctor guides needle through mom's abdomen and then precisely into umbilical cord; withdraws small amount of baby's blood.

Tests for infections, chromosomal defects, oxygen level.

Glucose screening

24 – 28 weeks

Woman drinks a sweet beverage and a blood sample is tested.

Tests for gestational diabetes

Performed earlier and more often for women with diabetes.

Late-term amniocentesis*

Used in induced birth. Determines baby's lung maturity.

Non-stress test*

Measures baby's heart rate responses to changes in his own movement.

Contraction stress test*

Measures baby's heart rate responses to the uterus contracting.

week 24 | week 28 | week 32 | week 36 | week 40**

*Optional test performed at mother's and doctor's discretion

**A normal pregnancy can extend to 42 weeks.

3rd trimester

Every two weeks until Week 36   Every week until delivery

? How is amniocentesis performed?

Using ultrasound screen for visual guidance, the doctor inserts thin needle through mother's abdominal wall and extracts a few teaspoons of amniotic fluid. Mother feels slight cramping or no pain at all.

Today a pregnant woman can learn a tremendous amount about the health of her baby. Most tests ultimately reassure parents. In some cases, less-than-conclusive results place parents in the position of having to make some very difficult decisions. And in still other cases, results give parents the option of having their baby undergo a surgery, blood transfusion or other treatment while still in the womb. A word of reassurance: the vast majority of babies are born healthy.

Getting to know you:
Questions for the health care provider

- How can I reach you in case of emergency? Can I call even if I have less urgent questions?
- Which type of childbirth classes do you recommend?
- Will you be the person attending my delivery? If not, who would be there in your place?
- How much time do you usually spend with a woman during labor?
- What advice do you give your patients about managing labor pain? How do you feel about epidurals and other medications?
- What percentage of your deliveries are cesarean sections?

Money matters:
Questions for your insurance company

- What is the coverage for prenatal care?
- Can I choose whichever health care provider and facility I want? If not, what are my choices?
- Will I have to pay a deductible when I go to the hospital to deliver?
- How long of a hospital stay is covered for a normal delivery?
- Am I covered for any treatments or emergency care I might need during my pregnancy?
- Are there any treatments that are not covered?
- Am I covered for childbirth education classes?
- Will my baby's costs after delivery be covered? For how long?

What's different about prenatal vitamins?

Prenatal supplements contain recommended doses of folic acid and other nutrients important in pregnancy. They also have safe amounts of vitamins A and D, which can harm mom or baby in overly high doses.

Is caffeine safe?

Some studies conclude that moderate levels (300 to 400 mg, the amount in three or four cups of coffee) won't hurt mom or baby. However, recent data suggest that even one to two cups of coffee daily may double the risk of miscarriage. Higher amounts have been linked with low birthweight.

Other caffeine facts:

- It stays in a pregnant woman's system for about 18 hours—five times longer than when she's not pregnant.
- It does reach and circulate through the baby's body.
- It can inhibit iron absorption.
- It can worsen heartburn and sleep problems.

Can diet affect a woman's labor?

Like marathon runners, pregnant moms can fuel up for the big event by "carb-loading"—eating a carbohydrate-rich diet—in the two weeks prior to the due date.

Nutritional heavy-hitters	Folic acid 800 mcg (micrograms)	Protein 60 grams
Why it's important	● Helps prevent **neural tube defects*** like **spina bifida** ● Helps build red blood cells * Abnormal formations of brain, spinal cord or their coverings	● Promotes baby's **brain development** ● Essential for cell-building ● Develops mother's uterus and breasts
Where it's found	● Dark-green leafy vegetables ● Citrus fruits ● Prescribed vitamins ● Over-the-counter supplements	● Milk, cheese, eggs ● Meat, poultry, fish ● Tofu, soy products ● Beans ● Nuts
Food for thought	For best protection against defects, women should begin taking folic acid (800 mcg) daily before trying to conceive.	High-protein supplements (drinks, powders) can be harmful during pregnancy; protein should come from food. 

What about exercise?

For most women, moderate exercise is safe and even recommended. Some women with medical conditions or a history of pregnancy complications are advised not to exercise. A pregnant woman should never exercise to lose weight. ■ Benefits: Overall wellness; possibility of easier labor; easier to get back in shape after baby. ■ Best bets: Brisk walking, swimming, stationary bicycling, yoga. ■ To avoid: Downhill skiing, horseback riding, high-impact aerobics.

ACTION ITEMS Food safety during pregnancy

Foods to avoid

- **Raw or undercooked meat or eggs** (*Risk:* Toxoplasmosis, salmonella poisoning)
- **Foods preserved with nitrates** such as hot dogs and smoked meats (*Possible risk:* Nitrates convert to nitrites, which are associated with cancer)
- **Soft, unpasteurized cheeses** such as Brie and Camembert (*Risk:* Bacteria)
- **Unpasteurized milk** (*Risk:* Listeriosis, a bacterial infection)
- **Unpasteurized or fresh juices** (*Risk:* Salmonella, *E. coli*)
- **Raw sprouts** (*Risk:* Salmonella, *E. coli*)

- **Certain seafoods:**
  - **Raw or undercooked fish and shellfish** (*Risk:* Parasites)
  - **Freshwater fish** from polluted body of water or unknown source that could be polluted (*Risk:* PCBs and other toxic chemicals). Farm-raised fish are generally safe.
  - **Large saltwater fish** such as swordfish, tuna, king mackerel, tilefish and shark (*Risk:* Mercury)

Calcium 1200 mg	Iron 30 mg	Fluids 8 cups or more
Crucial in building baby's **bones**	Helps increase volume of mother's red blood cells (which deliver oxygen to baby) • Decreases risk of premature delivery	Develops baby's circulatory system • Alleviates mother's constipation and other pregnancy discomforts
Dairy • Whole grains • Leafy vegetables • Egg yolk	Fortified cereals and breads • Green leafy vegetables, beans • Meat, poultry, fish • Prescribed supplements	Water • Milk • Juices • De-caffeinated drinks
Getting adequate calcium during pregnancy may lower a child's risk for high blood pressure as an adult.	Iron from supplements is absorbed better if pills are taken between meals and with a fruit juice high in vitamin C.	Drinking extra fluids (more than the 8-cup minimum) actually reduces fluid retention.

A pregnant woman does need slightly higher levels of some nutrients. But in general, she should eat what all of us should eat: a well-balanced diet that's high in vegetables, fruits and grain products and low in fat and sugar.

Food guide pyramid for pregnant women

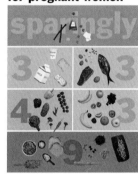

Numbers denote minimum servings pregnant women should have daily.

? What ever happened to "eating for two"?

The average woman needs only

300 calories extra per day

during pregnancy. That's a yogurt and a banana; a tuna sandwich; or a granola bar.

Other precautions

- Buy organic produce whenever possible.
- Wash all other fruits and vegetables thoroughly to rid them of pesticides and chemicals. Peel off skins that have been waxed (e.g., cucumbers, apples).
- Be vigilant about keeping kitchen sanitized. Wash all food-preparation tools in hot soapy water and dry immediately. Avoid using wooden cutting boards, spoons, bowls. Keep towels and sponges clean and dry.

TIP
Limit fresh tuna to one serving a month. Canned tuna, however, contains much less mercury; two cans a week is safe.

About 4 million babies are born in the U.S. each year. About 300,000, or 7.5%, of those babies are low birthweight.

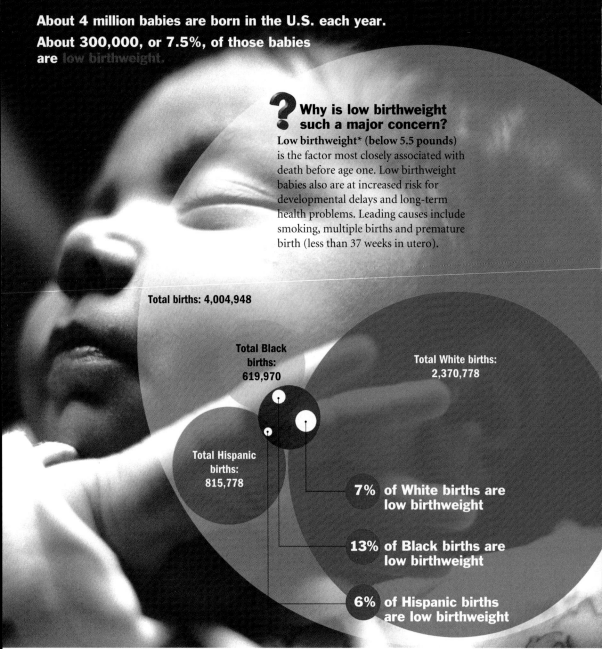

? Why is low birthweight such a major concern?

Low birthweight* (below 5.5 pounds) is the factor most closely associated with death before age one. Low birthweight babies also are at increased risk for developmental delays and long-term health problems. Leading causes include smoking, multiple births and premature birth (less than 37 weeks in utero).

Total births: 4,004,948

Total Black births: 619,970

Total White births: 2,370,778

Total Hispanic births: 815,778

7% of White births are low birthweight

13% of Black births are low birthweight

6% of Hispanic births are low birthweight

*The average weight of a child born at full term is 7.5 pounds. (US)

ACTION ITEMS   What about alcohol consumption?

? I drank alcohol on a few occasions before I learned that I was pregnant. Could this have harmed my baby?

Many women go into their first prenatal exam with this question weighing heavily on their mind—most leave the visit feeling reassured. A few drinks in the early weeks of pregnancy are unlikely to have harmed the baby. However, a woman should stop drinking as soon as she discovers that she is pregnant.

? Having a glass of wine with dinner is okay, isn't it?

Experts now believe that even moderate alcohol consumption—defined as one or two drinks a day or occasional binging on five or more drinks—can increase the risks for miscarriage and other complications. Moreover, there is growing evidence linking moderate drinking with a phenomenon known as **fetal alcohol effect**, a less severe problem than **fetal alcohol syndrome** but still characterized by developmental and behavioral problems as the child grows.

A Day of Births, U.S.: Every **8 seconds** a baby is born. ▉ Every **60 seconds** a baby is born to a teen mother. ▉ Every **2 minutes** a low birthweight baby is born. ▉ Every **3¹/₂ minutes** a baby is born with a birth defect. ▉ Every **hour** three babies die. ▉ Every **24 hours** 406 babies are born to mothers who received late or no prenatal care. Calculations by the March of Dimes Perinatal Data Center

What are the chances of having an unhealthy baby?

Causes of infant death
Infant deaths in 1999: About 28,000

%	Cause
43%	Other (bacterial infection, et al.)
20%	Birth defects
16%	Low birthweight and short gestation
9%	Sudden infant death syndrome (SIDS)
5%	Maternal pregnancy complications
4%	Respiratory distress
3%	Accidents (unintentional injuries)

U.S. Ranks 27th in Infant Mortality
Deaths per 1,000 live births

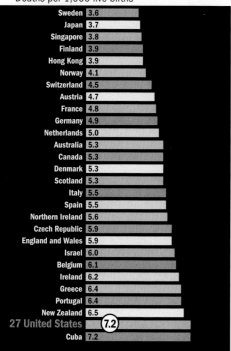

Country	Deaths per 1,000
Sweden	3.6
Japan	3.7
Singapore	3.8
Finland	3.9
Hong Kong	3.9
Norway	4.1
Switzerland	4.5
Austria	4.7
France	4.8
Germany	4.9
Netherlands	5.0
Australia	5.3
Canada	5.3
Denmark	5.3
Scotland	5.3
Italy	5.5
Spain	5.5
Northern Ireland	5.6
Czech Republic	5.9
England and Wales	5.9
Israel	6.0
Belgium	6.1
Ireland	6.2
Greece	6.4
Portugal	6.4
New Zealand	6.5
27 United States	(7.2)
Cuba	7.2

Mom's risky behavior, baby's increased risks

Alcohol
Even one drink per day can increase risks of miscarriage, stillbirth, childhood leukemia, multiple deformations, permanent facial alterations, learning delays and behavioral problems.

Cigarettes
Increased risk of SIDS (sudden infant death syndrome) and low birthweight.

Marijuana
More difficult pregnancy and labor for mom; respiratory distress for baby at birth.

Cocaine
Risk of infant stroke at birth, excessive crying; later behavioral problems.

The vast majority of babies are born perfectly healthy. Of the problems that do occur, many stem from genetics or random chromosomal abnormalities, and are well beyond the control of the pregnant woman. Other problems, however, are direct consequences of the mother's risky behavior during pregnancy.

Parental leave: laws and loopholes

Maternity leave:
Employee benefit. Employer dictates duration and pay.

Short-term disability:
Leave granted for medical conditions, typically with partial pay. Company must treat pregnancy the same as other conditions.

Family and Medical Leave Act (FMLA):
Federal law giving eligible employees the right to 12 weeks of unpaid leave. Applies to fathers and mothers alike.
Employee's rights :
  ▪ Eligible if working for public agency or for a private company with 50+ workers.
  ▪ Must be restored to original job or equivalent.
  ▪ Employer maintains health benefits during leave.
Employer's rights :
  ▪ Can require employee to use paid vacation and sick time as part of 12-week leave.
  ▪ Can demand reimbursement for health care premiums paid during the leave period if employee fails to return.
  ▪ Can refuse to take back staff whose return will cause economic injury and who also are within top 10% of payroll.

❓ How soon do women return to work?

One study showed that 75% of women returned to full-time work by the time their babies were six months old. In a survey of Harvard law, medical and business school graduates, 94% said they returned to work before their first child reached six months.

Pregnancy's impact on relationships

Employer and coworkers
Woman may face real (albeit unspoken) suspicions about commitment to job, timing of maternity leave, plans to return to work. Boss worries about lost productivity during leave; colleagues wonder if they'll be picking up the slack.

Other children
School-age children, who can comprehend the impending shift in family dynamics, may need reassurance. Toddlers, less perceptive of time, need help preparing. Change will be most difficult for first-born. Try to set aside special time to spend together.

Doctor, midwife, other caregiver
Woman works with health care provider as a "partner" in her prenatal care.

Woman herself
Pregnancy is a period of transition, so mixed feelings (elation, anxiety) are normal. "Juggling act" begins, as woman tends to needs of her partner, children, employer, extended family and the baby she's carrying— often while fighting morning sickness, fatigue and other pregnancy symptoms.

ACTION ITEMS   Preparing your KIDS for a new baby

1. Show your child photos and videos of himself as a newborn.

2. Visit friends who have babies.

3. Have your child "practice" by holding a doll. Teach her gentleness and proper support of the doll's head.

4. Ask if your hospital or birthing center offers sibling preparation classes.

5. Have your child buy a gift to give the baby. Have a gift "from baby" on hand as well.

TIP
Give children age-appropriate roles in the new baby's care. A toddler can get a diaper or toys; a school-age child can select outfits or help you dress baby.

A global take on maternity leave. ▪ Most other developed nations give women between two and six months' leave at 80% to 100% of their previous earnings. ▪ Even developing countries offer two to four months at 60% to 100% of previous earnings. ▪ The US has no laws providing paid maternity leave. ▪ Some states are proposing legislation that would provide access to unemployment benefits during the 12-week unpaid leave allowed through the **Family and Medical Leave Act (FMLA).**

Parents and in-laws
Grandparents-to-be may assume more a prominent role in couple's lives, especially if they'll be needed to help with child care.

Spouse/partner
Relationship begins to shift from couple-focused to baby-focused. Major issues to be negotiated: division of child care and household tasks once baby arrives; financial impact of mother's hiatus from work; choosing godparents/legal guardians; naming baby.

Best friend
Pampered pet enjoys status as "baby" of the family. But his behavior may change once infant arrives. No matter how well they seem to get along, never leave Fido unattended with your baby.

A pregnancy (especially the first one) reverberates through a woman's life. Her relationships change. The people closest to her perceive her differently, interact with her on new levels or need more attention from her. And she begins to see herself in a whole new light.

How old are most women when they give birth?
Percent distribution of births by mother's age and race (2000)

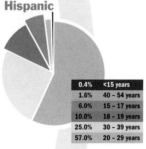

White

1.0%	<15 years
2.0%	40 – 54 years
3.0%	15 – 17 years
7.0%	18 – 19 years
35.0%	30 – 39 years
52.0%	20 – 29 years

Hispanic

0.4%	<15 years
1.6%	40 – 54 years
6.0%	15 – 17 years
10.0%	18 – 19 years
25.0%	30 – 39 years
57.0%	20 – 29 years

Black

1.0%	<15 years
2.0%	40 – 54 years
7.0%	15 – 17 years
12.0%	18 – 19 years
23.0%	30 – 39 years
55.0%	20 – 29 years

Source: National Vital Statistics Report, Vol. 49, No.5, July 24, 2001.

Preparing your BOSS for a new baby

? When should I tell my boss I'm pregnant?
You should talk to your employer before you are visibly pregnant. If you wait until you are already showing, or if the grapevine reaches the boss before you do, your credibility as a team player could be undermined. If you suspect your boss will react to the news negatively, you may want to wait until your second trimester; by this time, your risk of miscarriage will be much lower, and you will have already proven that you can remain productive while pregnant. You may also want to time your announcement strategically, by waiting until after a performance review or the successful completion of a major assignment.

? What should I do if I'm not ready to go back to work when my maternity leave ends?
You may want to propose some alternatives to your employer or supervisor:

- **Flextime:** You work the required number of weekly hours but determine your own schedule.
- **Meal-break flexibility:** By giving up the standard lunch break, you come into work an hour later or leave an hour earlier.
- **Telecommuting:** You work from home one or more days a week.
- **Job-sharing:** You and another employee split job responsibilities, as well as pay and benefits.
- **Part-time work:** Your hours are reduced for specified amount of time or indefinitely.

Objective: To have a meaningful labor and delivery experience.

Rules: Know your options and determine your preferences.

Wild card: Almost any plan can be reversed in the throes of labor.

1 Where?

start

Hospital
Physician or certified nurse midwife (CNM)
Monitors, medications and emergency facilities on hand.

Birthing Center
Certified nurse-midwife
Home-like suite may include whirl-pool, birthing chair, kitchen, other amenities. Often part of hospital for quick access to emergency care.

Home
Physician or CNM should be present. A car should be on "standby" in case of emergency. The ultimate in low-intervention birthing.

Caregiver Choices

Obstetrician: Physician specializing in pregnancy and childbirth

Family practitioner: Physician with specialty training in primary care, including obstetrics

Certified Nurse-Midwife (CNM): A registered nurse with specialty training in low-risk pregnancy

the baby game

5 The Big Moment

Who cuts the cord—and when?
Dad? Mom herself? Caregiver? Do you want to cut it right away—or wait about five minutes, when the cord stops pulsing? (Some people believe that getting all of the placental blood will supply baby with more oxygen while it is learning to breathe on its own.)

Baby's first stop?
You can request that baby be placed on your chest immediately, giving you some "bonding time" and a chance for your baby to nurse before routine tests begin.

Cord Blood Banking: A Biological "Insurance Policy"?

What: Newborn's blood from umbilical cord and placenta is collected at delivery and frozen.

Why: Abundance of stem cells, which could help baby (or even another family member) in case of future illness.

Cost: $300 – $1,000 for collection; $100 – $150 yearly storage fee Or you can donate to a public collection bank.

ACTION ITEMS — Creating a "birth plan"

Several months before birth, some expectant mothers begin drawing up a "birth plan"—a document that outlines their preferences for the management of labor, delivery and postpartum care. Birth plans are not written in stone, of course. The health of mother and baby during labor override any previously stated preferences.

TIP
With a birth plan on record, the mother shouldn't have to communicate her wishes while in labor, or if caregivers change at the last minute.

Sample birth plans

www.babycenter.com

www.birthplan.com

www.childbirth.org

Emergency Consideration
If you need an emergency C-section, will the hospital allow your husband/support person to come into the O.R. with you? Ask your caregiver.

Lights, Cameras, Action?
Decide ahead of time how much you'll want to see (or not see) a year from now. Check with facility about camera and lighting policies.

2 Who Will Be There?

- Spouse/baby's father
- Mom
- Sister
- Other kids
- In-laws
- Best friend
- **Doula***
- Two or more people**

* **Doula** (pronounced "DOO-lah"): a non-medical person trained to comfort and support women during labor and childbirth, especially helpful if the mother doesn't have good support. Studies show that doula care can shorten labor and decrease need for C-section.

** If you wish to have several people present, consider a birthing center or home birth.

3 Childbirth Classes

Lamaze:
Special breathing techniques; mental focus on external object. Open to pain medications during labor.

Bradley:
Normal breathing; inward focus on self. Pain medications discouraged. 12 two-hour classes usually required.

Hospital or birthing center:
Methods taken from a range of birthing approaches.

4 Pain Relief

I want to go "natural"
- Massage
- Acupressure
- Water: Jacuzzi, shower, bath

Bring on the meds!
- Epidural (blocks regional nerve paths)
- "Walking" epidural (permits mobility)
- I.V. pain killers (e.g., Demerol)

Go to the Head of the Class
Childbirth classes help fathers feel more involved in the pregnancy—especially if they have been unable to attend doctor visits. Ask if your classes offer a special "dad's only" session.

C-sections and Pain Relief: What You Should Know

- Cesarean deliveries account for about 23% of births in U.S.
- Epidurals are used for many C-sections. (Mom stays awake.)
- General anesthesia, which is faster-acting, is used in emergency C-sections. (Mom is asleep.)
- Medications for incision pain will not enter the first breast fluid baby drinks (colostrum). But once regular breast milk comes in fully a couple days later, you should not take any pain meds without consulting your doctor.

Women have an amazing array of choices in "designing" their childbirth experience—from the practitioner and type of pain relief right down to the lighting and background music.

Birth plans address issues great and small

- Your own clothes vs. hospital gowns
- Music and dimmed lights
- Clear fluids vs. ice chips for hydration
- Continuous vs. intermittent monitoring of baby
- Medical vs. non-medical pain relief
- Position for pushing
- Episiotomy* vs. natural tearing
- Emergency contingencies
- Shared vs. private hospital room (Note: Insurance may not fully cover private room.)

*Episiotomy: An incision made during delivery to widen the vaginal opening

Other resources

- Support during labor
  DONA (Doulas of North America)
  www.dona.com

- Breast-feeding support
  La Leche League
  www.lalecheleague.org

- Childbirth education
  The Bradley Method
  www.bradleybirth.com

  ICEA (International Childbirth Education Association)
  www.icea.org

  Lamaze International
  www.lamaze-childbirth.com

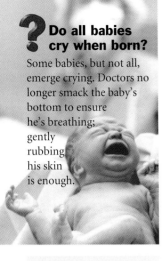

? Do all babies cry when born?

Some babies, but not all, emerge crying. Doctors no longer smack the baby's bottom to ensure he's breathing; gently rubbing his skin is enough.

Epidural Facts

Epidural anesthesia relieves the pain of labor and child-birth; it numbs the lower half of the woman's body. A thin plastic tube is inserted into the lower back, and the anesthesia is delivered through the tube. Pain relief can range from partial to complete.

In 1997, **52%** of women giving birth in high-volume obstetrical units received epidural anesthesia during labor. In low-volume hospi-tals, the rate was **25%**.

Some hospitals now offer patient-controlled epidurals. By pressing a button, the woman can increase—or limit—the amount of pain medication she receives. The apparatus is programmed to prevent overdosing.

Four types of labor

10 cm						
8 cm	**Fast Labor**					
6 cm	A few hours;					
4 cm	contractions					
2 cm	start suddenly, intensify quickly					
0						

Time in hours: 2   4   6   8   12

Countdown to labor

Signs that labor isn't far away:

Lightening and engagement
Baby drops or settles into pelvis; two to four weeks before labor (in first births; much later in subsequent births)

Nesting
Mother has strong impulse to clean house; one or two days before labor

Mucus plug dislodges
During the pregnancy, a thick plug of mucus formed at the cervical opening. As cervix begins to dilate, plug is released; several days before labor or at onset

Bloody "show"
Pink or blood-streaked mucus discharged; usually within 24 hours of labor

Backache
Onset of labor and throughout labor

Waters breaking (rupture of membranes)
From onset of labor to birth

Contractions begin

Fully dilated cervix*

10 cm

Transition
10 cm
8 cm

Active Labor
7 cm
5 cm
4 cm

Early Labor
3 cm

Stages of labor

Stage 1
Cervix dilates

Early labor: 3 cm
Mild contractions, 30 to 45 seconds, up to 20 minutes apart

Active labor: 4 - 7 cm
Strong contractions, 45 to 60 seconds, two to five minutes apart

Transition: 8 - 10 cm
Intense contractions, 60 to 90 seconds, one to three minutes apart

Stage 2
Pushing and delivery
Slightly weaker contractions, 60 to 90 seconds, three to five minutes apart. Some-times powerful, almost uncontrollable urge to push

Stage 3
Delivering the placenta
Mild contractions

ACTION ITEMS How can labor be made easier?

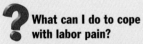

? What can I do to cope with labor pain?

In the early stages of labor, focus on making yourself comfortable: shift positions, take a warm shower, walk around, and rest as much as possible. As labor progresses and contractions intensify, try to relax between contractions. You may also find relief—and even a surge of ener-gy—by visualizing the little one you are about to meet!

? What can I do to help my wife or partner during labor?

Relax her, pamper her, cater to her every need. Give her back massages. Feed her ice chips to keep her lips and mouth moist. As contractions intensify, do breathing techniques along with her, put a cool cloth on her forehead if she's hot, get blankets if her legs are cold. Most of all, give her lots of positive reinforcement.

2	3	4
Average Labor 1st birth: 12-14 hours Later births: eight hours Early labor proceeds at steady pace	**Plateaued Labor** Contractions stop advancing after early labor but can be "nudged" back into action with walking, nipple stimulation, medications	**Slow-to-Start Labor** Up to 24 hours; contractions occur without pattern for hours or even days before becoming regular
14 16	18 20	22 24

What happens when a woman goes into labor?

Typical newborn's head*

11 cm

Each labor is unique. The intensity of pain a woman experiences depends on factors both physical and emotional— from the baby's size and position inside the uterus to the woman's expectations and anxiety level.

A Near-Perfect Fit
It seems mom and baby are designed to work in tandem during birth. Mom's **cervix** (opening of the uterus) stretches to accommodate baby. And baby's head, the skull bones of which have not yet fused together, can mold to fit through mom's birth canal.

* Approximate diameter based on average head circumference (baby weighing 7.5 pounds); photograph actual size

What if we're en route but the baby won't wait?

Delivering the baby on the way to the hospital is extremely rare. But it's nice to know you could handle the situation, just in case…

1. Pull over to the side of the road and put hazard lights on. Call 911 if you have a cell phone.

2. Help the mother onto a flat surface (e.g., car's backseat). Place a coat or blanket under her head and buttocks for support.

3. To help the head deliver: As the top of the baby's head emerges, ask the mother to pant, not push. Apply gentle counter pressure to prevent the head from popping out suddenly. Let the head emerge gradually; NEVER pull it.

4. To help the shoulders deliver: Hold the head gently in two hands and press it downward very slightly. Ask the mother to push while you are doing this. As the upper arm appears, lift the head carefully, watching for the other shoulder to deliver. Once both shoulders are out, the baby should deliver quickly.

5. Wrap the baby in blanket, towel or other covering. Place baby on mother's abdomen or breast (if cord is long enough). Do not cut the cord.

6. Don't pull the placenta out. If it arrives on its own before help arrives, wrap it in towels or newspapers and keep it elevated above baby's level.

7. Once the delivery is complete, go straight to the hospital.

Optimal Alertness:

The baby is more alert during the first 1 1/2 hours of life than he is for the next few weeks. The "quiet alert" state is the best time for parent-infant bonding. Baby can sustain prolonged eye-to-eye contact.

❓ Hard-wired for survival?

Newborns may have deeply ingrained abilities for feeding and bonding.

- If placed on the mother's abdomen immediately after birth and allowed to stay there undeterred, some babies will perform a "breast crawl," first inching up the mother's chest, then locating the breast and then beginning to suckle—completely on their own.

- When the infant first suckles or just licks the nipples, the mother's body releases a hormone (oxytocin) that speeds up uterine contractions and reduces bleeding.

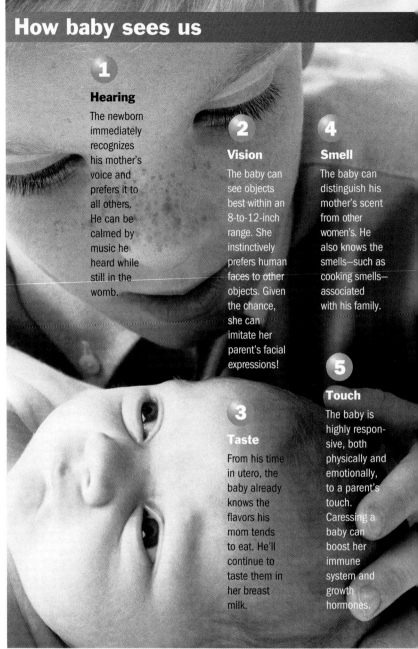

How baby sees us

1 Hearing

The newborn immediately recognizes his mother's voice and prefers it to all others. He can be calmed by music he heard while still in the womb.

2 Vision

The baby can see objects best within an 8-to-12-inch range. She instinctively prefers human faces to other objects. Given the chance, she can imitate her parent's facial expressions!

4 Smell

The baby can distinguish his mother's scent from other women's. He also knows the smells—such as cooking smells—associated with his family.

3 Taste

From his time in utero, the baby already knows the flavors his mom tends to eat. He'll continue to taste them in her breast milk.

5 Touch

The baby is highly responsive, both physically and emotionally, to a parent's touch. Caressing a baby can boost her immune system and growth hormones.

Photo: Harry Sieplinga, HMS Images/Getty Images.

ACTION ITEMS

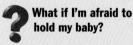

Caring for baby in the first weeks

❓ What if I'm afraid to hold my baby?

Newborns are not as "breakable" as they may seem. As long as you adequately support your baby's body—especially the head and neck—she should be fine.

The real challenge is learning to lift and lower your newborn without startling her. (Having spent months in the womb, she may be frightened by the sensations of soaring upward or free-falling through the air.) Instead of picking her up quickly, slide your arms underneath her and keep them there for a moment before lifting her. When putting her down, hold her close as you lower her, and wait a moment before freeing your hands.

❓ When is it safe to let visitors hold the baby?

Because the newborn's immune system is not highly developed yet, he is especially vulnerable to germs in the first month of life. However, you can safely allow family and friends to hold baby by establishing a few basic ground rules.

Baby's visitors should:

- always wash their hands first.
- hold the baby for only short periods of time.
- avoid coughing or sneezing near him.
- avoid skin-to-skin contact if they have a rash or open sores.

- **Birthmarked:** Salmon patch—reddish blotch on forehead, eyelid or base of skull, usually in Caucasian babies. Mongolian spots—grayish-blue pigmentation on buttocks, back or thighs, usually in babies of Asian, African or Southern European descent; fades away within a few years.

- **Big-headed:** Disproportionately large head equals chest in circumference. Head may also be (temporarily) "cone-shaped" from squeezing through mom's pelvis. Nose and chin may appear flattened.

- **Blue-eyed:** Nearly all Caucasian babies start with blue eyes.

- **Fuzzy:** Fine hair called lanugo may cover shoulders, back, forehead before shedding within a week. Skin may also have yellowish coating called vernix caseosa.

Even within the very first minutes after birth, the baby exhibits a tremendous ability to "meet" and interact with her parents.

- **"Lactating:"** Baby's nipples (in both boys and girls) may excrete small quantities of white "witch's milk"; from exposure to pregnancy hormones.

- **Well-endowed:** Testicles and vulva are temporarily enlarged from exposure to mother's hormones.

Photo: Barros & Barros, Getty Images.

Poked and Prodded and Tested (Oh my!) What's in store for baby in the minutes and hours after birth. ■ **Apgar test:** Assesses baby's color, muscle tone, breathing, heartbeat and "grimace" reflex. Baby receives "Apgar scores." ■ Eye drops: Guard against venereal disease exposure in birth canal (regardless of mother's history). ■ Clamped cord: Purple dye prevents infection. Shrivels in one week, falls off within three. ■ Vitamin K shot: Promotes blood clotting.

How can I be sure my baby is warm enough?

Feel the baby's arms, trunk or back of the neck. (Don't use her hands or feet as your gauge; they are typically cooler.) If the baby feels cool, simply add another layer of clothing.

A good rule of thumb is to dress baby in one more layer than you need to be comfortable yourself. In cool weather, always put a hat on her. But be careful not to overdress her (a common parental mistake); if she is overheated, she could lose fluids.

Which burping position is best?

It all depends on the baby and your comfort. Here are three common positions:

- **Baby on your shoulder.** Support his bottom with one hand while you pat and rub his back with the other.

- **Baby on your lap, facedown.** Position the baby with his stomach on your one leg and his head on the other. Hold him in place with one hand while you pat with the other.

- **Baby sitting up on your leg.** With baby leaning slightly forward, place your hand under his armpit and support his chest with your forearm. Pat and rub with the other hand. Be careful not to let his head flop backwards.

29

How long 'til I get my old body back?

Many women can get back to their pre-pregnancy weight within four months. Some experts, however, say four to nine months is more realistic. For some breastfeeding moms, the last few pounds stubbornly persist until baby is weaned. Barring a C-section or other complications, women can gradually resume exercising as soon as they feel ready.

Do we fail our new mothers?

Many cultures have time-honored, firmly established traditions of supporting the mother in the weeks following childbirth.

In England, midwives visit the new mother at home for ten days.

In China, mother and baby remain isolated for 40 days, with family members attending to their needs and excusing the mother from her normal responsibilities.

In Sweden, mothers get 15 months of maternity leave with full pay.

Physical Reality

Not all women experience these aftereffects. Just as each woman's pregnancy is unique, so is her recovery from childbirth.

Hair loss
Seems worse than it is. Thicker, hormone-fed pregnancy hair falls out quickly and dramatically until normal rate of hair loss resumes.

Breastfeeding complications
Sore nipples
Plugged ducts
Infection (mastitis)

Sore, swollen breasts
Occurs two to four days after birth, when milk comes in fully. Pain subsides with regular breastfeeding. For women who bottle-feed, pain is usually gone within 36 hours.

Unwanted pounds
The average woman who had a healthy weight gain comes home with about 13 to 23 leftover pregnancy pounds. (About 12 pounds are shed at birth.)

Stretch marks
On abdomen, breasts, behind, elsewhere

"Elimination" discomforts
Constipation:
Results from stretched abdominal muscles

Hemorrhoids:
May have developed or worsened with pushing during delivery

Bladder control:
Uncontrollable urination
Difficulty urinating

"Battle wounds"
Sore incision
(episiotomy* or C-section)

Afterbirth pains: Caused by uterus shrinking back to normal size**

Vaginal discharge (lochia): Uterus sheds leftover lining; usually lessens in two weeks and goes away by six.

Uncomfortable (or unsatisfying) sex
Stretched vaginal muscles
Painful intercourse (often due to vaginal dryness)
Lowered libido

Bigger feet
May stay a half or whole size larger—permanently.

What really causes sagging breasts?

Breastfeeding gets an unfair rap here. The real culprit: not wearing a bra supportive enough during pregnancy.

* Episiotomy: An incision made during delivery to widen the vaginal opening
** Breastfeeding helps the uterus return to normal size more quickly.

ACTION ITEMS
Making the first weeks easier

1. Before baby arrives, anticipate the need for postpartum pampering. Knowing that you may feel stressed, tired and in baby's constant demand, use the time before delivery to stock up on a few comfort items: scented lotions or soaps, frozen or easy-to-prepare meals, healthy snacks, a favorite magazine, soothing music.

2. Sleep when the baby sleeps. At the very least, lie down to get some rest, or sit down for a relaxing activity. Don't use these precious opportunities to do housework.

3. Take sleep deprivation seriously. If you find yourself functioning poorly and becoming increasingly miserable, do whatever you need to in order to get ample rest—even if it means hiring someone to watch the baby while you sleep.

4. Ask for help (and quickly accept all offers). Delegate the cleaning, laundry and errands to family and friends so that you can focus on your priority task: caring for your baby.

5. Establish time limits for visitors. Set a clear 15- or 30-minute visitation policy.

6. Get outside. Isolation tends to heighten anxiety and depression. Visit with friends, stroll with other mothers or join a support group.

Emotional Reality

What does a woman experience after childbirth?

Elated, frustrated
Joyful about the birth

Sad about loss of her "old" life

Insecure about mothering ability

Doesn't "know" baby yet; still learning baby's cues

Lonely, bored
Away from job and coworkers

Home alone

Partner back to work

Feeling unattractive
Weight to lose

Old clothes still don't fit

Little time or energy for "beautifying"

Lack of sexual desire

Feeling down

"Baby blues"
80% of women

Starts two to five days after delivery

Lasts up to a week

Resolves on its own

Postpartum depression
10 – 15% of women

The blues continue beyond two weeks, or depression appears one to four months after birth

Can last beyond a year

Treatable with hormone therapy, antidepressants and/or psychotherapy

Postpartum psychosis
Very rare: Less than 0.2% of women

Symptoms include hallucinations, thoughts of harming self or baby

Emergency attention required

Anxious about ability to juggle many responsibilities competing for her attention:
Newborn

Other children

Husband or partner

Cooking

Cleaning

Visitors

Pets

Job...

Tired
Sleep-deprived

Feeding newborn every two to three hours

In the days and weeks after delivery, the mother can experience great joy, but she may also face overwhelming challenges. Plummeting hormones, chronic sleep deprivation and caring for a brand-new baby can take their toll—physically and emotionally.

Thoughtful gifts for the new mom

- Cook a homemade meal and store it for freezing.
- Tape her favorite television shows for later viewing.
- Send her flowers one month after delivery (after the initial floral frenzy has wilted and gone).
- Hire a housekeeper.

Resources for postpartum depression

Depression After Delivery
800.944.4773

Moms Online
www.momsonline.com
(search for "baby blues")

Mothering the New Mother
Sally Placksin

BabyCenter
www.babycenter.com

Postpartum Support International
www.chss.iup.edu/postpartum

Infant massage basics

A growing body of research makes a strong case for infant massage. Babies who are massaged cry less, gain weight better, go to sleep more easily, make better eye contact, and have lower levels of stress hormones (among other benefits).

Presented here are just a few infant massage strokes.* But technique is not critical. The most important thing is that parents have frequent, sustained, skin-to-skin contact with their babies.

* The massage strokes illustrated on this page are appropriate for healthy infants over two months of age.

High-Touch Care for Preemies In a University of Miami study, premature infants who were massaged gained 47% more weight, showed greater alertness, and were discharged from the hospital about a week earlier than preemies who were not massaged. Preemies also fare better with kangaroo care, a method of skin-to-skin contact in which the baby (in diaper and hat only) is held closely to the mother's or father's bare chest for 30 minutes or longer.

Low-Tech Touch for Moms in Labor

Touch and massage are important tools for doulas, individuals trained to support women during labor and childbirth. Data suggest that using doulas (pronounced DOO-lahs) yields significant results:

- Shorter labor
- Less pain
- Less need for epidurals
- Reduced C-section rates

Chest
Criss-cross

With your hands flat on baby's chest, gently rub one hand diagonally toward the opposite shoulder and then back to your starting point, alternating from one hand to the other in rhythm.

Leg Massage
Light wringing

Place both hands around baby's leg. Use a light wringing motion while gently sliding your hands up and down baby's leg.

You can also use the two milking strokes on the legs.

Foot Massage
Bottom, top and toes

Start by massaging the bottom of the foot, running your thumbs from heel to toe. Then gently squeeze each toe one-by-one. Finish by bringing your thumbs across the top of the foot, going from ankle toward the toes.

ACTION ITEMS
Infant massage: Tips for parents

Setting Up

- Choose a soft surface for baby to lie on, such as a bed or a blanket on the floor.
- Massage works best if baby is naked, although you can keep a diaper on if preferable. Keep the room warm enough for baby to stay comfortable.
- Items to have on hand: baby oil, a diaper, a small pillow (which may be helpful during back massage)
- Wear comfortable clothing.
- Play soothing background music if you'd like.
- Contact a local infant massage therapist if you feel you need one-on-one instruction.

Getting Started

- Lay baby on his back.
- Sit at baby's feet. Choose a position that is comfortable for you. Examples: cross-legged; sitting on your feet; legs extended in a wide "V" that surrounds baby on each side.

Age Guidelines*

During the first two months of life, when baby's sensory-motor system is still developing, use only a very simple massage: general stroking of the face, limbs and back. After two months, baby will likely prefer more complex strokes. You can continue massage for as long as you and your child enjoy it—through the first year and beyond.

*Note: For a preemie in a hospital intensive care unit, consult baby's health care providers before attempting massage.

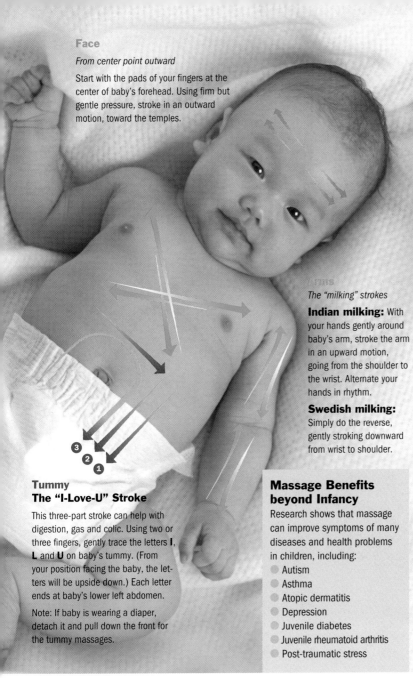

Face
From center point outward

Start with the pads of your fingers at the center of baby's forehead. Using firm but gentle pressure, stroke in an outward motion, toward the temples.

Tummy
The "I-Love-U" Stroke

This three-part stroke can help with digestion, gas and colic. Using two or three fingers, gently trace the letters **I**, **L** and **U** on baby's tummy. (From your position facing the baby, the letters will be upside down.) Each letter ends at baby's lower left abdomen.

Note: If baby is wearing a diaper, detach it and pull down the front for the tummy massages.

Arms
The "milking" strokes

Indian milking: With your hands gently around baby's arm, stroke the arm in an upward motion, going from the shoulder to the wrist. Alternate your hands in rhythm.

Swedish milking: Simply do the reverse, gently stroking downward from wrist to shoulder.

Massage Benefits beyond Infancy

Research shows that massage can improve symptoms of many diseases and health problems in children, including:

- Autism
- Asthma
- Atopic dermatitis
- Depression
- Juvenile diabetes
- Juvenile rheumatoid arthritis
- Post-traumatic stress

Why is touch so important?

Close physical contact is biologically essential to a baby's health. In addition to strengthening a baby's relationship with her parent, touch promotes physical growth and increases alertness. It may even improve the baby's immune functioning. Massage is just one of many ways that a mother—and other important people in a baby's life—can employ the power of touch.

Technique

- You can start the massage on any area of baby's body.
- Massage one area completely before moving on to the next area.
- Use pressure than is gentle, yet firm. Stroking that is too light may actually be unpleasant for baby. (However, do not apply strong pressure; deep muscle penetration is for adult massage only.)
- Do not apply pressure to the area over baby's heart.
- Repeat each stroke several times. You can use different strokes on any one area of the body, as long as baby enjoys them all.
- Talk, sing and make eye contact with baby during the massage.

Reading Baby's Cues

- Don't be discouraged if baby dislikes certain strokes. Like adults, infants have their individual preferences. Start with baby's least sensitive areas, and introduce new strokes as he adapts.
- If baby seems resistant to massage, simply try again later or on another day.
- Most important of all: There is no single, "perfect" way of doing infant massage. Do what is most enjoyable for you and your baby.

To Learn More

Johnson & Johnson Pediatric Institute
877.JNJ.LINK (877.565.5465)
www.jjpi.com Booklet and video available

Infant Massage : A Handbook for Loving Parents
Vimala Schneider McClure

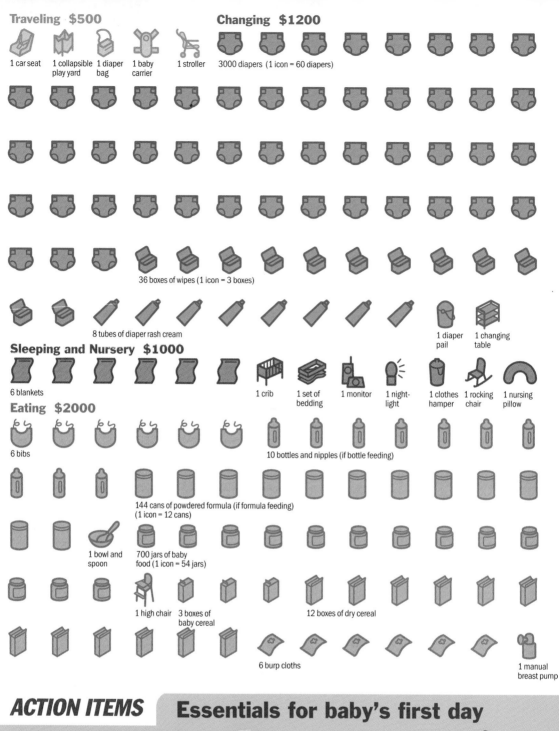

Traveling · $500

1 car seat | 1 collapsible play yard | 1 diaper bag | 1 baby carrier | 1 stroller

Changing $1200

3000 diapers (1 icon = 60 diapers)

36 boxes of wipes (1 icon = 3 boxes)

8 tubes of diaper rash cream | 1 diaper pail | 1 changing table

Sleeping and Nursery $1000

6 blankets | 1 crib | 1 set of bedding | 1 monitor | 1 night-light | 1 clothes hamper | 1 rocking chair | 1 nursing pillow

Eating $2000

6 bibs | 10 bottles and nipples (if bottle feeding)

144 cans of powdered formula (if formula feeding) (1 icon = 12 cans)

1 bowl and spoon | 700 jars of baby food (1 icon = 54 jars)

1 high chair | 3 boxes of baby cereal | 12 boxes of dry cereal

6 burp cloths | 1 manual breast pump

ACTION ITEMS

Essentials for baby's first day

Congratulations on your little bundle of joy! All is well, and you're ready to go home.

The question is, do you have what you need? There are some essentials, and then there are extras. Make sure to stock up on the essentials for baby's first day (and weeks) home... you'll be glad you did.

1 Car seat

2 Diapers (at least 70 disposable or 90 cloth) and wipes

3 Bottles (3 to 10) and formula (if not breast feeding)

6 Receiving blankets (4 to 6)

7 Washcloths and mild soap

8 Stroller

What products do I need for my baby's first year?

Year 1

It's no secret: small baby, big commitment. If you're a new parent, prepare to be stunned. First-year expenses for first-time parents can approach

$10,000 for 1 baby.

Here's an estimate of the types and quantities of products you might need.

Health and Hygiene $250

- 3 sets of towels, hand towels and washcloths
- 1 baby bath
- 12 bottles of baby shampoo/wash
- 2 thermometers (rectal and ear)
- 1 jar of petroleum jelly
- 1 pack of cotton swabs
- 1 toothbrush
- 1 nasal aspirator
- 1 nail clipper
- 1 pair of baby scissors
- 1 comb & brush
- 1 pack of cotton balls
- 1 bottle of rubbing alcohol
- 12 bottles of baby lotion
- 5 bottles of baby medicine

Clothing $2000

- 24 sleepers (1 icon = 6 for each stage)
- 36 one-piece outfits (1 icon = 9 for each stage)
- 1 winter hat
- 6 hats
- 36 pairs of socks (1 icon = 9 for each stage)
- 2 snowsuits/jackets
- 10 shirts
- 10 pairs of pants
- 5 pairs of shoes (3 soft soled, 2 walking)

Odds & Ends $1000 and up

- 3 pacifiers
- 1 baby swing
- 3 teething rings
- 1 portable phone
- Books
- Toys

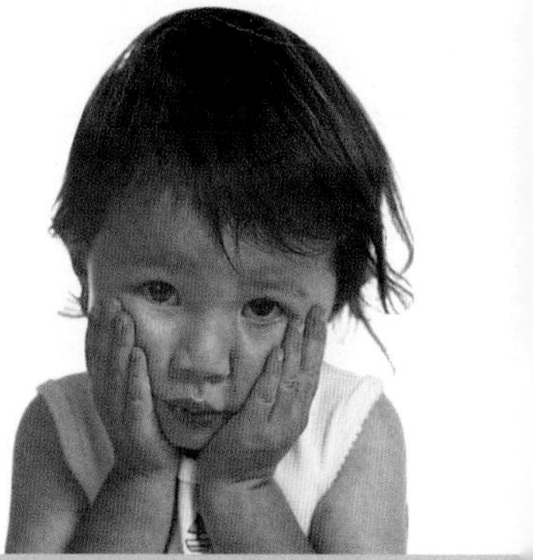

Photo: Reven Wurman

TIP

Cloth diapers make excellent burping and changing cloths. Buy a pack, even if you're using disposable diapers.

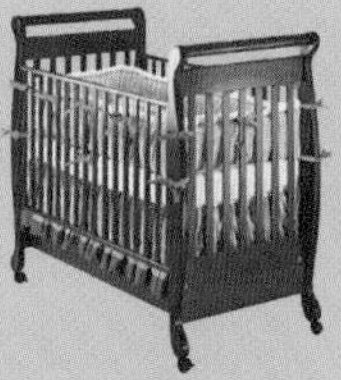

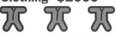

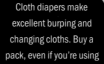

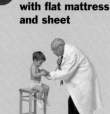

4 **Bassinet or crib with flat mattress and sheet**

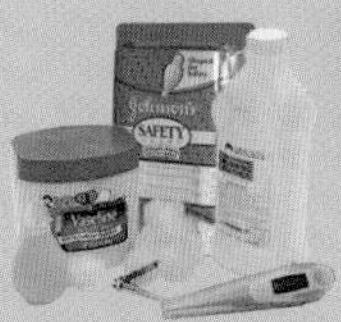

5 **Thermometer, nasal aspirator, nail clippers, cotton balls, rubbing alcohol and petroleum jelly**

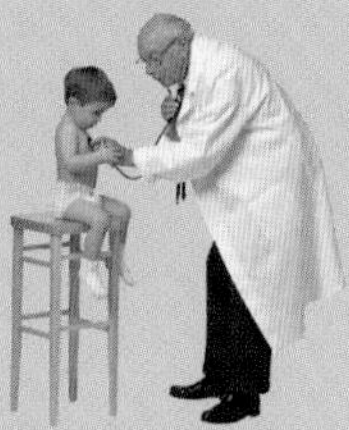

9 **Pediatrician**

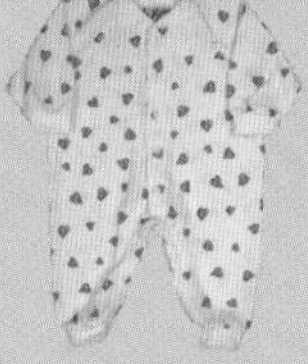

10 **Sleepers, one-piece outfits and socks (at least 6 of each)**

Extras to make parent's life easier

- Monitor
- Rocking chair or glider
- Bouncy seat and/or baby swing
- Changing table
- Nursing pillow
- Bottle/wipe warmers
- Bath tub
- Portable phone
- Baby carrier

? Is there a shortcut?

Yes. Keep everything in the car—except for the diaper bag, Teddy and baby. You don't have to keep re-packing your car for each and every errand around town.

Camera, because you never know when you'll have a great photo op.

Car seat choices

Infant-only

- For use from birth up to 20 pounds
- Rear-facing
- Can double as infant carrier, feeding chair or rocker
- May attach to specially designed strollers

Carrier, sling or backpack, for short trips away from the vehicle when the stroller would be too much.

Favorite toy, for comfort.

Convertible or Infant Toddler

- For use from birth up to 40 pounds
- Start rear-facing, convert to front-facing after 20 pounds and one year old
- Five-point harness fits infants best

Blanket, for warmth or security. Or both.

Umbrella, for a rainy day.

Forward-facing

- For use from 20 pounds and one year old to 40 pounds
- Cannot be used rear-facing
- Some models convert to booster seats (may be used with children over 40 pounds)

Booster Seat

- For use from 40 pounds and three years old up to 80 pounds
- Used with vehicle's lap and shoulder belts
- High-back booster recommended if vehicle has low seat back

ACTION ITEMS

Just buying a car seat isn't enough to protect your child in an accident.

Proper selection and installation are key. No one car seat is the "safest." And a higher price doesn't always mean a better product.

Avoid used seats. When possible, buy new. Manufacturers improve car seats frequently.

Car seat basics

What to look for

- Easy installation
- Proper restraints (adjustable 5-point safety harness is safer)
- Belt adjustment from the front using raised belt slots
- Machine-washable detachable cover
- Well-padded seat with plenty of head and back support

What to do

Up to at least **20 lbs.** and one year

Over **20 lbs.** and one year

Determine which way the car seat should face based on your baby's weight and age. It's safest to keep your child rear-facing as long as possible.

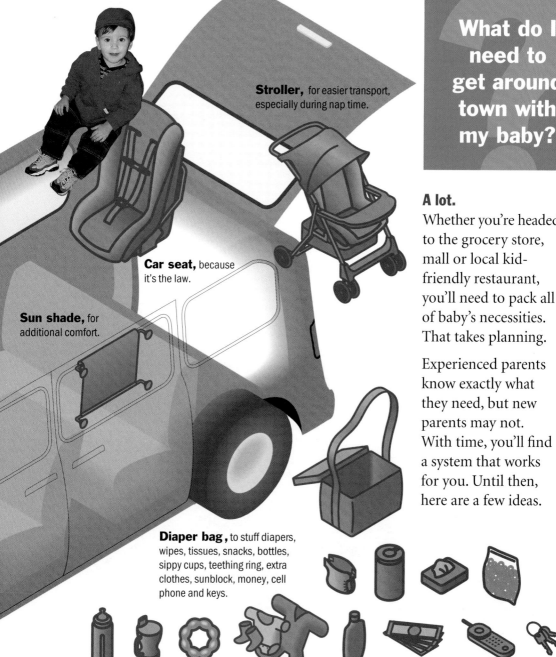

Stroller, for easier transport, especially during nap time.

Car seat, because it's the law.

Sun shade, for additional comfort.

Diaper bag, to stuff diapers, wipes, tissues, snacks, bottles, sippy cups, teething ring, extra clothes, sunblock, money, cell phone and keys.

A lot.

Whether you're headed to the grocery store, mall or local kid-friendly restaurant, you'll need to pack all of baby's necessities. That takes planning.

Experienced parents know exactly what they need, but new parents may not. With time, you'll find a system that works for you. Until then, here are a few ideas.

TIP

To have your car seat installation inspected by a certified child passenger safety specialist, visit www.nhtsa.com for a list of local inspection stations.

Not all car seats are the same. After purchasing, it is imperative that you read your car seat and vehicle manuals for complete installation instructions.

Install the car seat where it fits the most securely. The center of the back seat is the safest place for children to ride.

Thread the vehicle's seat belt through the correct car seat slots.

Attach a locking clip (standard with most new car seats) to the lap and shoulder belt to keep the harness straps in place. Make sure your car seat is secure and does not move more than an inch forward or sideways.

❓ What should I do first?

First, don't panic. It's easy to feel overwhelmed thinking about all the trouble kids can get into. Fortunately, you can childproof your home in phases. You have time to plan and prepare.

First Phase—Newborn

Newborns are vulnerable to the environment. Heat, cold and germs are serious dangers to consider at this phase.

Second Phase—Infant

Infants begin to become mobile. They are crawling and much more dangerous to themselves. A new level of awareness is required on the part of Mom and Dad.

Third Phase—New Toddler

Toddlers can not only sit up, they can stand up, too. Turn your back for a second, and they're down the hall, up the stairs or on top of the coffee table...a whole new world of dangers.

Fourth Phase—Active Toddler

And away they go! Active toddlers have complete mobility to go from room to room and floor to floor. You need a complete line of defense to protect your child from common household hazards.

1 Install safety latches on cabinets and drawers to help deter curious crawlers. Automatic-closing latches are more effective.

2 Keep a protective shield over oven dials when not in use.

3 Cordless phones are a handy way for you to follow your child around the house.

4 Place safety gates at tops and bottoms of stairs and in doorways. Fixed gates, that can be opened and closed with one hand, are safest.

5 Install safety latches on toilets. Automatic-closing latches are more effective.

ACTION ITEMS

More accidents occur in the bathroom and kitchen than in any other room in the house.

Get on your hands and knees and scope out the territory from a baby's point of view. See any open cupboards? Sharp edges? Dangling cords? You may be surprised at what you find.

Bathroom safety

- Keep all sharp objects and electrical products out of reach.
- Put locks on toilet and cabinets.
- Store bathroom cleaners in locked areas.
- Place a non-slip mat on the floor and in the bathtub.
- Install a hook-and-eye lock high up on the outside of the door. Keep it latched when not in use.
- Put a rubberized guard over the bathtub spout to protect your child's head.
- Keep all medications, vitamins, make-up and toiletries safely out of reach.

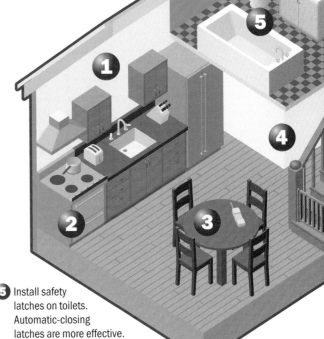

Find the hidden dangers.

6 Bookshelves look like a jungle gym to a toddler. Use L-brackets to secure large objects that can topple over easily.

7 Install a smoke detector on every level of the house and in every sleeping area. Test the detector twice a year and replace batteries when needed. Install carbon monoxide detectors if you have gas or oil heat or an attached garage.

8 Keep first-aid supplies on hand and learn infant CPR.

9 Use a bumper pad to prevent head injury and to prevent your baby's arms or legs from getting caught in the crib rail.

If Murphy's Law is true, he must have been a parent. If anything can go wrong, it will.
Each year, about 2½ million children are injured or killed by hazards in the home. Many of these hazards can be prevented by using simple child safety devices. Though the best childproofing is adult supervision, safety devices go a long way in keeping your child safe.

10 Use cleats to keep dangling cords on drapes and blinds out of reach. Install window guards so windows open wide enough for air flow, but not enough for a child to climb or fall out.

12 Outlet covers for unused electrical outlets are a must. And make sure they can't be removed to become a choking hazard.

11 Use corner bumpers on sharp-edged furniture to help prevent injury when your toddler falls.

Kitchen safety

Find the hidden dangers.

- Avoid tablecloths and placemats. They—and their contents—can be pulled easily.

- Use the back burners of a stove when cooking.

- Keep children out of the kitchen when the oven is on.

- Store kitchen cleaners in locked areas.

- Place hot foods, sharp objects and electrical products out of reach.

- Move pet food and water to a different location. The food can be a choking hazard and the water a drowning hazard.

The cost to childproof a standard three-bedroom home could run approximately

$694.

Set hot water heaters at no more than 120 degrees Fahrenheit and install anti-scald devices.

Also, post a list of emergency numbers next to each telephone. Program these numbers into your phone for complete flexibility.

Getting started...

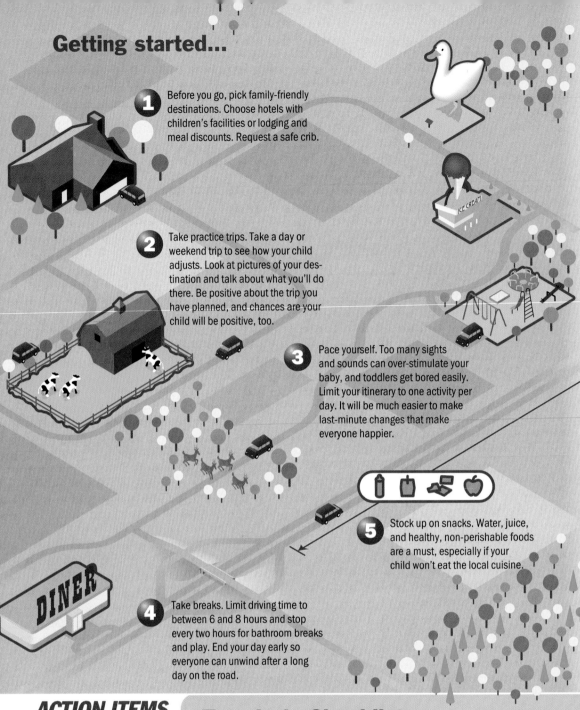

1. Before you go, pick family-friendly destinations. Choose hotels with children's facilities or lodging and meal discounts. Request a safe crib.

2. Take practice trips. Take a day or weekend trip to see how your child adjusts. Look at pictures of your destination and talk about what you'll do there. Be positive about the trip you have planned, and chances are your child will be positive, too.

3. Pace yourself. Too many sights and sounds can over-stimulate your baby, and toddlers get bored easily. Limit your itinerary to one activity per day. It will be much easier to make last-minute changes that make everyone happier.

5. Stock up on snacks. Water, juice, and healthy, non-perishable foods are a must, especially if your child won't eat the local cuisine.

4. Take breaks. Limit driving time to between 6 and 8 hours and stop every two hours for bathroom breaks and play. End your day early so everyone can unwind after a long day on the road.

ACTION ITEMS

The goal is to get by with the barest minimum while still remaining comfortable.

Start your packing a week before leaving. Here's a checklist of things you should consider taking for your infant or toddler.

Traveler's Checklists

Checklist for infants

- Diapers (One for each hour you'll be in transit plus extra, diaper rash ointment, wipes and lotion)
- Food/Formula (Take extra in case of travel delays.)
- Blankets (One for comfort, shade and warmth, one for lying down, one for burping)
- Clothes (One to two outfits per day, plus extras. Don't forget socks and hats.)
- Collapsible play yard
- Collapsible or lightweight stroller/baby carrier
- Car seat
- Medicines/toiletries
- Plastic bags for soiled diapers, clothing and shoes
- Electrical outlet covers

Photo: Reven Wurman

40

Much later...

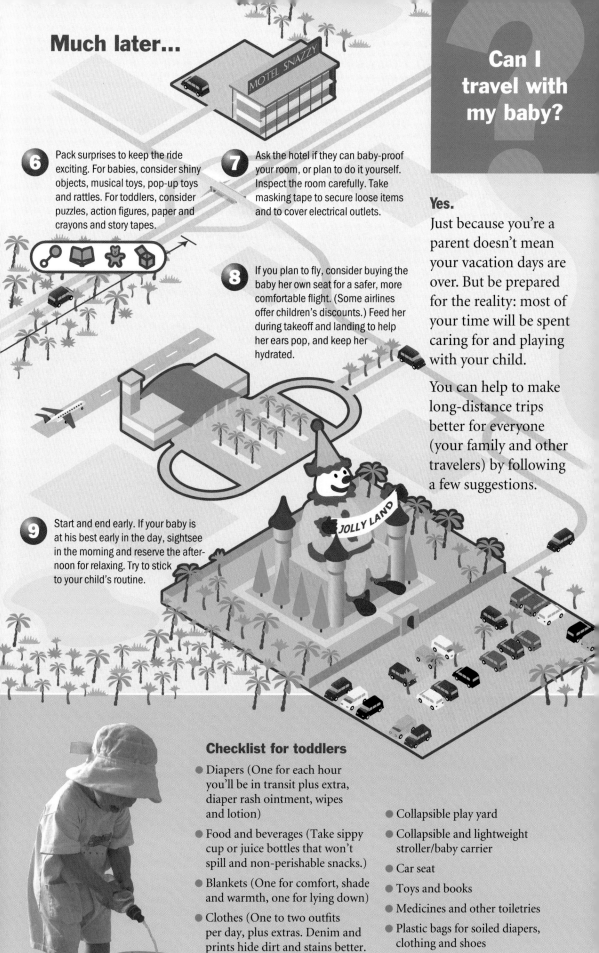

6 Pack surprises to keep the ride exciting. For babies, consider shiny objects, musical toys, pop-up toys and rattles. For toddlers, consider puzzles, action figures, paper and crayons and story tapes.

7 Ask the hotel if they can baby-proof your room, or plan to do it yourself. Inspect the room carefully. Take masking tape to secure loose items and to cover electrical outlets.

8 If you plan to fly, consider buying the baby her own seat for a safer, more comfortable flight. (Some airlines offer children's discounts.) Feed her during takeoff and landing to help her ears pop, and keep her hydrated.

9 Start and end early. If your baby is at his best early in the day, sightsee in the morning and reserve the afternoon for relaxing. Try to stick to your child's routine.

Yes.

Just because you're a parent doesn't mean your vacation days are over. But be prepared for the reality: most of your time will be spent caring for and playing with your child.

You can help to make long-distance trips better for everyone (your family and other travelers) by following a few suggestions.

Checklist for toddlers

- Diapers (One for each hour you'll be in transit plus extra, diaper rash ointment, wipes and lotion)
- Food and beverages (Take sippy cup or juice bottles that won't spill and non-perishable snacks.)
- Blankets (One for comfort, shade and warmth, one for lying down)
- Clothes (One to two outfits per day, plus extras. Denim and prints hide dirt and stains better. A bathing suit may also come in handy.)
- Collapsible play yard
- Collapsible and lightweight stroller/baby carrier
- Car seat
- Toys and books
- Medicines and other toiletries
- Plastic bags for soiled diapers, clothing and shoes
- Electrical outlet covers

❓ What do I need to know?

Babies are big business. Each year thousands of baby products are introduced, reintroduced, recalled and discontinued, all to keep up with an increasing market and savvy parents. From concept to cradle, baby products have complex life cycles and are subject to safety testing and monitoring. And there's more to the story.

Baby products are a

$6.02 billion

annual business.

Source: Juvenile Products Manufacturers Association

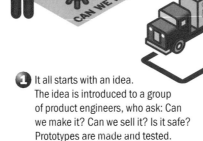

1 It all starts with an idea. The idea is introduced to a group of product engineers, who ask: Can we make it? Can we sell it? Is it safe? Prototypes are made and tested. Ultimately one will pass all of the tests and will be approved for production.

2 The product is mass-produced. Quality checks during production remove outwardly flawed products.

3 The product is distributed to contracted companies in the marketplace. Consumers buy the product on the Internet, off of television, from a catalog or in a store.

4 Consumer groups test the product and compare it with its counterparts. These groups are typically advocates for the public and are not affiliated with specific manufacturers.

5 Consumer groups release their research, typically in print, on the Web and on television. Consumer reporters use the findings as part of local news or talk show segments.

6 Some consumers read the published findings. They determine if they want the product, or have the product and want to know more about what they purchased. Is there something they need to know?

ACTION ITEMS

Before you buy... 👁 Consumer advocate

"Buyer beware" doesn't mean what it used to.

Nowadays, you are not alone. There are countless resources that you can consult to determine if the baby products you buy are reliable and safe.

- Think about the type of product you want and any specific features you feel are important.
- Ask your friends and neighbors about particular products or brands.
- Consult *Consumer Reports, Good Housekeeping* or an equivalent, objective publication to see how products rank.
- Consult government and national organization Web sites, depending on the product you're buying. You can get a good idea of brands to stay away from, brands that are highly rated and the best products for your child's development. For example:

| www.nhtsa.com   National Highway Traffic Safety Administration |
| www.momshelpmoms.com/babysafety.html |
| www.kidshealth.org/parent/firstaid_safe/home/products.html |
| www.babycenter.com |
| www.parentsplace.com |
| www.babiestoday.com |
| www.childsafetystore.com |

7 Other consumers buy the product and give it directly to their children, the ultimate litmus test. Usually the product is satisfactory. Sometimes it's defective.

8 Consumers report defects to the manufacturer. If enough complaints arise, the manufacturer will recall or completely discontinue the product. The manufacturer offers an alternative for disappointed consumers, be it a repair kit, refund or new product.

9 Separate consumer groups monitor the product's recalls, defects and discontinuation. They release their research, typically in print, on the Web and on television. Consumer reporters use the findings as part of local news or talk show segments.

10 Savvy parents monitor the product carefully as well, to ensure that it continues to be highly rated and safe for their children.

Where do baby products come from?

Good question. Sometimes knowing a product's history helps you make better decisions. Be it a car, food, or your baby's stroller, staying informed before and even after the purchase is smart. And when it comes to your baby's safety, knowledge is power.

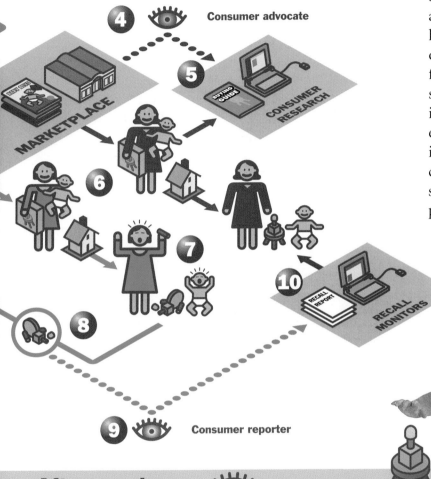

4 Consumer advocate

5 CONSUMER RESEARCH

MARKETPLACE

6

7

8

10 RECALL REPORT RECALL MONITORS

9 Consumer reporter

After you buy... Consumer reporter

- Fill out a product warranty or registration card if one is provided. Companies use these items to inform you when a product is defective.

- Keep an eye out for potential dangers. Make sure your baby is supervised when handling any product, especially one for the first time.

- Consult government and national organization Web sites, depending on the product you bought. You can learn about recalls and what to do if you have a defective product. For example:

  www.nhtsa.com National Highway Traffic Safety Administration
  www.cpsc.gov Consumer Product Safety Commission
  www.jpma.org Juvenile Products Manufacturers Association
  www.consumer.gov/children.htm FirstGOV for Consumers
  www.pueblo.gsa.gov Federal Consumer Information Center
  www.safekids.org National Safe Kids Campaign
  www.safetyalerts.com
  www.consumerreports.org
  www.goodhousekeeping.com

Diapering

How much will your baby's diapers cost?

It is estimated that your baby will require **8,000** diapers from birth until toilet training is complete. The average baby will be in diapers for about **2½ years,** using fewer diapers as he gets older.

Disposable
Disposables get more expensive per diaper as your child gets older.

Cloth
Diaper services usually charge by the week or month and provide up to **70 diapers a week.**

The estimated cost of cloth diapers from a service and disposable diapers is virtually identical, about

$2,250

from birth until toilet training is complete.

Before you diaper

- **Never** leave baby alone on changing table.
- Lay baby on his back on a flat, stable surface.
- If using disposable, unfasten tabs and fasten them back on themselves.
- Gently grasp baby by ankles and lift bottom.
- Fold dirty diaper in half under baby.

If your baby's a boy

Wipe away excess poop from genital area with corner of diaper and baby wipe, **covering penis** *with a clean cloth to prevent any urine from spraying up if he pees.*

If your baby's a girl

Use baby wipe or wet cloth to clean front. **Wipe from front to back** *to help minimize possibility that bacteria will get into her vagina, from her bottom.*

- Exchange diapers and follow directions at right depending on what type of diaper you have chosen to use. The clean diaper's top half should go under baby's bottom.
- To avoid chafing, try not to bunch diaper between baby's legs.
- **For newborns,** avoid covering umbilical cord stump (special newborn disposable diapers have notches cut out).
- **For boys,** be sure to tuck penis down so urine will flow down into diaper.
- Toss soiled diaper in trash or diaper pail. Wash your hands thoroughly.

Disposable

Open diaper with the tabs facing out.

Place diaper under your baby's backside.

Prevent the adhesive tabs from touching other parts of the diaper or your baby until you are ready to secure them.

Pull the tabs so that the diaper fits snugly but without constraining your baby's mobility or causing discomfort.

And now: swim diapers!

Disposable swim pants can be worn at the beach or pool. Both disposable and waterproof, they have snug fitting elastic legs that keep water out and, presumably, baby's urine and poop in. Some even come with a decorated, reusable fabric cover.

Tip on diaper wipes

If your baby has sensitive skin, avoid commercial diaper wipes containing alcohol, fragrance, or other chemicals. Use soft tissue or cotton balls instead.

ACTION ITEMS

How can I prevent diaper rash?

The best defense against diaper rash is a dry bottom.

 Change your baby's diaper as soon as possible after it becomes wet or soiled.

 Clean your baby's genital area thoroughly after each bowel movement and allow it to air dry.

3 Coat your baby's bottom with a thin layer of protective ointment especially made for baby skin. Cornstarch is a time-honored and safe remedy for treating diaper rash, but its effectiveness is unproven.

4 It's okay to use petroleum jelly as a barrier, but it's not particularly effective since it rubs off easily and is not water-soluble.

Cloth using pins | Cloth using wrap

Version 1 | Version 2

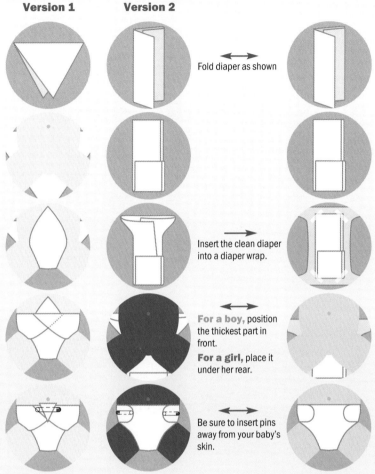

Fold diaper as shown

Insert the clean diaper into a diaper wrap.

For a boy, position the thickest part in front.
For a girl, place it under her rear.

Be sure to insert pins away from your baby's skin.

Cleanup for cloth

Dump any poop inside soiled diaper into toilet. Put used diaper in diaper pail, and close lid tightly. If you're not using a diaper service, wash diapers in separate load and **use soap, not detergent** (soap is made of natural substances, detergent is synthetic). Use hot water, double rinse, and avoid fabric softeners or antistatic products, as they can irritate baby's sensitive skin.

Sources: BabyCenter.com, Dy-dee.com, Webhome.idirect.com, Babysupermall.com.

Are cloth diapers from a diaper service better for the environment?

- Reusable products with a long life span are a better environmental choice than single-use products with a short life-span.

- Commercially laundered diapers use **half** the energy of home-washed and a **third** of the energy used to manufacture disposable diapers.

- Disposable diapers consume **10 to 20 times** more raw materials than cloth diapers.

- Disposable diapers contribute **over seven times** as much solid waste as reusable cotton diapers.

And what about for your child?

- Many disposable diapers contain chemicals and perfumes to which your child may be allergic.

---

5 Don't secure diapers so tightly that there is no room for air to circulate. Plastic pants, diapers, and clothing must fit somewhat loosely to let your baby's bottom "breathe."

6 Avoid disposable diapers and detergents with fragrances. They may cause your baby to develop a rash or skin irritation.

7 Breastfeed your baby as long as you can. No one knows exactly why, but diaper rash is less common among breastfed babies than among those who drink formula.

Breastfeeding

How milk flows from you to your baby

As your baby sucks, sensory impulses are transmitted to your hypothalamus gland, which instructs your pituitary gland to release a hormone called oxytocin into your bloodstream. This hormone stimulates the outer muscle walls of the alveoli (clusters of sacs) to contract, forcing the produced milk into the ductules (pathways to your nipple) and down to your milk pools.

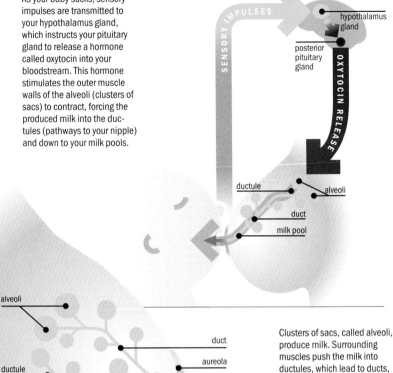

BRAIN

SENSORY IMPULSES

hypothalamus gland

posterior pituitary gland

OXYTOCIN RELEASE

ductule

alveoli

duct

milk pool

alveoli

ductule

duct

aureola

nipple

milk pool

Clusters of sacs, called alveoli, produce milk. Surrounding muscles push the milk into ductules, which lead to ducts, which widen into milk pools just behind the aureole. When your baby sucks, your milk is drawn through the 15–20 tiny holes in your nipple and into his mouth.

How much does formula cost per year?*

Ready-to-feed:

$1,871

Concentrate:

$1,639

Powder:

$1,435

*Based on an estimate of **14,500 ounces** (453 quarts) of formula per year.

How much does a breast pump cost?

Renting an electric breast pump:

$390 per year

Buying an electric mid- to high-quality breast pump:

$100-650

Source: nmchc.org.

ACTION ITEMS   How do I get my baby to nurse?

Breastfeeding entails more than popping your baby onto your breast and letting nature take its course. For many first-time moms, nursing is a mystery. How exactly do you do it without pain? What's the correct way to get your baby to latch on to ensure breastfeeding success? Follow these six simple steps:

1 Tickle the edge of your baby's mouth with your finger or nipple to encourage your child to latch on.

2 Wait until his mouth opens wide and then insert the nipple squarely into it.

3 Make sure your baby gets a large mouthful of the breast, encircling most, if not all of the aureole.

4 The best latch-on position is when your baby's mouth is opened against your breast.

5 As your baby nurses contentedly, hold him close so he feels secure and not tempted to "hold on" with his mouth.

6 Relax and enjoy the time together.

Successful breastfeeding can be a pleasant experience for both of you, but be patient. It doesn't always happen right away.

Football

As the name suggests, position your baby at your side and tuck her under your arm (on the same side that you're nursing from) like a football. She should be facing you with her nose level with your nipple and her feet pointing toward your back.

Support your baby's shoulders, neck, and head with your hand. Guide her to your nipple, chin first. Don't push her toward your breast so much that she resists and arches her head against your hand. Use your forearm to support her upper back.

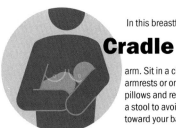

Cradle

In this breastfeeding position you cradle your baby's head with the crook of your arm. Sit in a chair that has armrests or on a bed with pillows and rest your feet on a stool to avoid leaning down toward your baby. Hold her so that she's lying on her side with her face, stomach, and knees facing you. Tuck her lower arm under your own. Rest her head in the crook of your arm on the side of the body she's nursing from. Extend your forearm and hand down her back to support her neck, spine, and bottom.

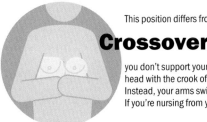

Crossover

This position differs from the cradle hold in that you don't support your baby's head with the crook of your arm. Instead, your arms switch roles. If you're nursing from your right breast, use your left hand and arm to hold your baby. Rotate her body so her chest and tummy are directly facing you. With your thumb and fingers behind her head and below her ears, guide her mouth to your breast.

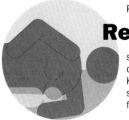

Reclining

Place pillows behind your back, neck, and shoulders for support, and place one between your bent knees. Keep your back and hips in a straight line. With your baby facing you, draw her close and cradle her head with the hand of your bottom arm. If your baby needs to be higher and closer to your breast, place a small pillow or folded blanket under her head. She shouldn't strain to reach your nipple, and you shouldn't have to bend down toward her.

Source: BabyCenter.com.

Why breast is better

- Babies and mothers were designed for breastfeeding.
- Breastfeeding may reduce the risk of allergies, asthma, infections, and a host of other illnesses in babies.
- Breastfeeding helps protect mothers from many diseases and assists them in regaining their figures quickly.
- Breastfeeding is less expensive.

Why formula is fine

- Some women simply can't nurse due to medical reasons. Other women choose not to breastfeed because of scheduling inconveniences.
- Formulas contain the necessary nutrients for normal growth development.

Tip on formula:

Choose high iron-fortified formula.

Breastfeeding support

If you need help with breastfeeding or are looking for more information, contact a lactation consultant or visit one of these helpful websites.

La Leche League International
www.lalecheleague.org

La Leche League International's mission is to help mothers worldwide to breastfeed through mother-to-mother support, education, encouragement, and information, and to promote a better understanding of breastfeeding as an important element in the healthy development of the baby and mother. Their website, which includes a product catalog, offers a kaleidoscope of valuable breastfeeding information on everything from nutrition and diet to medical concerns and weaning.

Breastfeeding.com
www.breastfeeding.com

Through a healthy mix of information and inspiration, this advocacy site will show you why breastfeeding is good for you, your baby, and the planet. The website is a nursing mom's primer offering a wealth of facts and figures, support and attitude. It provides expert answers to most conceivable breastfeeding questions and offers sound advice on a host of other breastfeeding topics such as techniques, health maintenance, and product selection.

Source: BabyCenter.com.

47

Circumcision

Circumcision involves removing the foreskin, which shields the head (the glans) of the penis.

Circumcision around the world

The U.S. is the only country in the world that circumcises the majority of its male newborns for non-religious reasons.

More than 90% of circumcisions in the U.S. are for non-religious reasons.

More than 80% of the world's male population is not circumcised.

Circumcision in Britain has been on the decline since the creation of the British National Health Service in 1948 and currently stands at **less than 1%**.

 Jewish people practice circumcision regarding it as an important religious ritual.

 Ritual circumcision is also practiced by **Muslims.**

Ritual circumcisions are practiced by the **Aborigines** in Australia and by other people throughout the world.

The circumcision rate in the U.S. has remained constant between 1994 and 1997 at about **60%**.

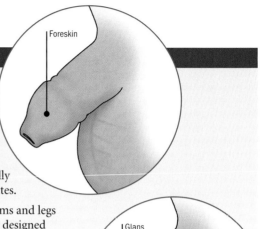

Foreskin

The Procedure

Hospital-based circumcision is usually done early in the morning. The morning feeding is delayed until after the procedure, which usually takes less than 15 minutes.

Typically, the baby's arms and legs are restrained on a tray designed just for this purpose. The penis and surrounding area are cleansed and an anesthetic may be injected into the penile shaft. The injection stings but blocks further pain. To remove the foreskin, the physician uses a clamp designed for newborn circumcision or a specially designed plastic ring.

After removal of the foreskin, the end of the penis (glans) appears red and sore. Usually an ointment, such as petroleum jelly, is applied. A strip of gauze is loosely wrapped around the glans to keep it from sticking to the diaper. If the plastic ring is used, it will remain on the end of the penis until the edge of the circumcision has healed, usually within a week.

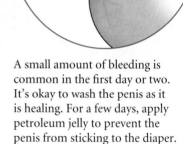

Glans

A small amount of bleeding is common in the first day or two. It's okay to wash the penis as it is healing. For a few days, apply petroleum jelly to prevent the penis from sticking to the diaper.

ACTION ITEMS

Frequently asked questions

 When should we talk to our pediatrician about circumcision?
Because of religious, social and medical concerns, it's wise to talk this one through with your physician early. You might want to bring it up when you first choose your pediatrician during your seventh or eighth month of pregnancy. If you decide to circumcise, ask your doctor about the use of an anesthetic to relieve pain and when the procedure should be performed.

 When should a circumcision be done?
Talk the issue through with your doctor and spouse before the baby arrives—it's an emotionally charged issue for some parents and not to be confronted when you're fatigued after giving birth. Delaying a circumcision until your baby is older than a few months may be traumatizing.

What do we need to know about circumcision?

The American Academy of Pediatrics (AAP) states that the choice is best left up to parents who should make a decision based on possible health benefits and risks, as well as cultural, religious, and ethnic traditions. In 1999, the AAP stated that the benefits of circumcision are not significant enough to recommend it as a routine procedure.

Why you should Pro

- In the United States, circumcision is generally a simple, rapid operation with preventive health benefits.
- Overall, a baby is less likely to get a number of infections and diseases if he is circumcised. Foreskin infections are common in uncircumcised boys between the ages of one and four, and although the chance is small, uncircumcised boys under a year old are 12 times more likely to get urinary tract infections. Many boys do not clean under the foreskin thoroughly; as boys hit puberty, smegma (a cheesy substance) builds up, with odor and even infection. A circumcised penis is easier to keep clean.

Why you shouldn't Con

- Choosing whether or not to circumcise your son is a personal decision unless he has a medical condition.
- Cleanliness alone isn't a good reason to choose circumcision. Parents can easily teach their son how to thoroughly wash his genitals. Careful cleaning should ensure a boy won't develop an infection of the foreskin.
- Most uncircumcised boys never develop medical complications, but bleeding and infection is a risk for an infant who is circumcised.
- Uncircumcised men have a less than one percent greater risk of penile cancer than those who are circumcised.
- Don't be concerned that your son won't fit in with his peers. Forty percent of American male babies are uncircumcised and circumcision is much less common worldwide.

Does it hurt?

Yes!

For many years, newborns were circumcised without anesthesia, because the prevailing view was that newborns don't feel pain. We now know this is not true, but anesthesia has been used—by some physicians—only in recent years. If you are considering circumcision for your child, the AAP **strongly recommends** that the doctor use **anesthesia,** such as a dorsal penile nerve block which blocks the pain and has been proven effective and safe.

Sources: BabyCenter.com, Vix.com, Mayoclinic.com, Circumcision.org, Parenthoodweb.com.

How should I care for my baby's circumcised penis?
You need do little more than normal bathing, but for both circumcised and uncircumcised baby boys, it's best to avoid bubble baths, as they can be drying and irritating to penile tissue. For the first few days after a circumcision, the penis may look quite red, and you may notice a yellowish secretion. This is not a cause for alarm as both indicate that the penis is healing normally. Though circumcision sites rarely get infected, signs of an infection include persistent redness, a swollen penis tip, crusted yellow sores that contain fluid on the end of the penis, irritability, poor feeding, or a fever. If you notice any of these signs, call your doctor immediately.

How should I care for my baby's uncircumcised penis?
When bathing an uncircumcised baby boy, it isn't necessary to retract the foreskin. Actually, you won't be able to for several months or even years—it takes this long for the foreskin to separate from the penis. When the foreskin has separated and can be retracted safely (your doctor will tell you when), you'll need to retract it occasionally to cleanse the end of the penis underneath. Very gently and quickly, wipe off the white, waxy substance known as smegma that appears on the head of the penis. Once your son is out of diapers and showering or bathing solo, you'll need to teach him how to do this so he can wash his penis by himself.

Source: BabyCenter.com.

Toilet Training

What are some ways to reward my child?

Keep track of her successes with stickers and a calendar or chart. **Give her a sticker** every time she makes a successful trip to the potty or has an accident-free day.

If stickers alone are not enough of a thrill, you can **offer an additional reward,** such as a long-coveted toy, when she accumulates an agreed-upon number of stickers or has a certain number of accident-free days.

For the ultimate thrill, **put blue food coloring in the toilet bowl water.** Your child will be so amazed and excited when she turns it green, she'll want to do it again and again.

Put some of his books in the magazine rack in the bathroom. For a boy, **try putting a target in the bowl** and watch him go.

For girls
Teach her to sit and wipe

One of the most important things you'll need to teach your daughter is how to wipe properly. She needs to make sure she moves the toilet paper from front to back, especially when she has a BM, to avoid contact between her bottom and vagina that can lead to infection. If this seems too complicated for her to grasp, teach her to pat the vaginal area dry after she pees.

For boys
Teach him to sit first, then stand

Since bowel movements and urine often come at the same time, it makes sense initially to have your son sit for both poop and pee so he learns that both belong in the potty. Also, that way he won't get distracted by the fun of spraying and learning to aim when you need him to concentrate on just mastering the basic procedure.

What can I do if my child says no to the toilet?

"No!" is a great discovery for your two-year old and she'll use it as much as possible. **Let her feel in charge.** Put the potty in a central location and let her go bottomless. She may surprise you. When she does sit, try not to force her to stay until she goes. If she stays for a short moment, goes back to playing and then has an accident, chances are she will understand what has happened and will try not to do it the next time.

To buy a potty—search for "toilet training"

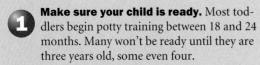
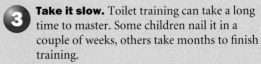
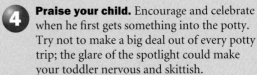

www.babycenter.com   www.babyuniverse.com   www.babystyle.com

www.babyoutlet.com   www.babiesrus.com   www.rightstart.com

ACTION ITEMS   Toilet training tips

Toilet training is not easy but it doesn't have to be taxing. Here's a list of helpful tips to guide you through this often trying process.

Do...

1 **Make sure your child is ready.** Most toddlers begin potty training between 18 and 24 months. Many won't be ready until they are three years old, some even four.

2 **Plan ahead.** Go over the methods of toilet training with your spouse and/or your child's caregiver. Ask the pediatrician, nanny or day-care provider for any advice. Their experience can help with the best plan for your child.

3 **Take it slow.** Toilet training can take a long time to master. Some children nail it in a couple of weeks, others take months to finish training.

4 **Praise your child.** Encourage and celebrate when he first gets something into the potty. Try not to make a big deal out of every potty trip; the glare of the spotlight could make your toddler nervous and skittish.

5 **Be patient.** Virtually every child will have numerous accidents before being able to remain dry all day and night. When she does make a mess, calmly clean it up and get her into dry clothing.

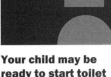
Buying a potty seat

Child-sized potty seat
Some children like having a potty of their own. One that is just their size that can be personalized with their name and decorated with stickers. Your child may be afraid of the adult size toilet. From their perspective the toilet may seem cold and dreadful. Some toddlers feel more secure on a potty where their feet easily reach the floor.

The manufactures wouldn't let this item go without having numerous options and styles as well. The web site list to the left may prove helpful when making a decision.

Attachment seat
The attachment seat fits on adult size toilets. It's portable and is especially helpful in public restrooms. The attachment seat is great for toddlers who are fascinated with the "big potty" and are already comfortable sitting on the toilet. This type of potty will also make the transition to the adult size toilet less of a hassle. Having a stool in the bathroom is important because your child will need to have her feet planted when she is making a bowel movement.

There are many different styles of attachment seats. Some are adjustable, others are cushioned and have handles. There is even a folding one that will fit in the glove box of your car. Check out the web sites listed to the left to see for yourself the many different styles.

Your child may be ready to start toilet training if she:
- Can help pull her pants up and down.
- Is interested in what goes on in the bathroom and imitates others' bathroom habits.
- Makes a physical demonstration when she's having a bowel movement.
- Can and will follow simple instructions.
- Dislikes the feeling of being in a dirty diaper.
- Understands the physical signs that indicate she has to go and can tell you before it happens.
- Has "dry" periods of at least three or four hours.
- Has regular and formed bowel movements.
- Demonstrates a desire for independence and wants to do "big girl" things.

Sources: BabyCenter.com, Rightstart.com.

Don't...

1 Start at the wrong time. Toddlers need routine; change will cause setbacks in their behavior. A new baby due, moving into a new home, or anything else that may disrupt the routine will only make potty training more difficult.

2 Put on the pressure. Be encouraging without being pushy. Let your child take his time to get used to this new process. Stimulate his interest with gentle reminders and stories, but if he turns you down, don't push.

3 Worry about what others say and think. Let others know you're toilet training, and you'll be deluged with advice, much of it outdated or simply misinformed. While there's nothing wrong with culling the best advice from what's offered, you and your child are the only ones who can determine what works best for her.

4 Punish your child. Setbacks are natural, and getting upset and scolding your child will only make him dislike or fear using the potty. If you can, respond to these challenges calmly; otherwise, bite your tongue, count to ten, and try again.

Bathing

Here's what to do to make bathing easy. With any luck, bathtime will become an enjoyable time together.

Brushing baby's teeth

Brand new baby teeth should be cleaned with a wet washcloth or a piece of gauze. At 18 months or when the molars have come in, you can switch to a soft, nylon-bristle child's toothbrush. Using a pea-sized amount of toothpaste, gently brush the teeth on both the outside and inside surfaces twice a day. Brush her tongue as well (if she'll let you) to dislodge the bacteria that can cause bad breath. Replace the toothbrush as soon as the bristles start to look worn or spread out.

Cleaning baby's ears

Never insert a cotton swabs or anything else into your child's ear canal since the eardrum can be easily punctured. Earwax will come out on its own. If you are concerned about a buildup in your child's ear, ask your pediatrician. Clean the outer parts of your baby's ears with a cotton swab or a washcloth and warm water.

- **Assemble all necessary supplies** and take them to the bath area.
- **Fill the tub** with two to three inches of water that feels warm but not hot, about 90 degrees Fahrenheit (32 degrees Celsius).
- Bring your baby to the bath area and **undress him completely.**
- **Gradually slip your baby into the tub,** using one hand to support his neck and head.
- **Pour cups full of bath water over him** regularly during the bath so he doesn't get too cold.

- **Wash him** with your hand or a washcloth from top to bottom, front to back. Wash his scalp with a wet, soapy cloth. Use a moistened cotton ball to clean his eyes and face. Soften dried mucus around the eyes and nostrils several times with a moistened washcloth, then wipe it out.
- **Rinse your baby thoroughly** with a clean washcloth and fresh water.
- **Wrap your baby in a hooded towel** and pat him dry.

Supplies

- A small blanket
- Mild soap
- Washcloth
- Towel
- Clean diaper and ointment
- Suitable clothing

What is Cradle Cap?

Cradle Cap is a harmless scalp condition common in newborns. Its symptoms are flaky, dry skin that looks like dandruff. More severe cases are marked by thick, oily, yellowish, scaling or crusting patches. It usually clears up on its own after several months and tends not to be a problem after a baby is about six or seven months old.

ACTION ITEMS

Tips for keeping bath time safe

Bath time can be fun for you and your baby, but you can't be too cautious. Start early by teaching your baby water safety basics, and keep these 12 safe-bathing tips in mind before you plunge in:

1 **Never leave your baby unsupervised.** If the doorbell or phone rings, and you feel you must answer it, wrap your baby up in a towel and take him with you.

2 **Set your water heater to 120 degrees F.** A child can get deep third degree burns in less than a minute at 140 degrees.

3 **Prepare for bathtime.** Gather everything you need before you start giving the baby a bath so you will not leave the baby unattended.

4 **Wait until the water is finished running.** Never put your baby into a tub when the water is still running because the water temperature could change or the depth could become too high.

5 **Know the right depth for the water.** Two to three inches for newborns and infants up to six months old. Never more than waist-high (in sitting position) for older children.

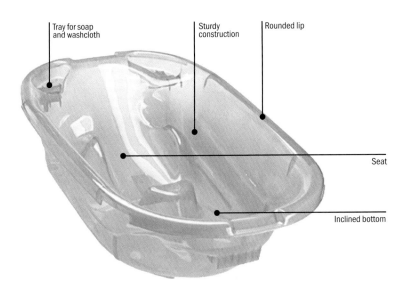

Tray for soap and washcloth

Sturdy construction

Rounded lip

Seat

Inclined bottom

- Until your baby is mobile and getting into messes, a bath isn't necessary more than once or twice a week. Cleaning his genital area after each diaper change and washing his face is fine.

- The umbilical stump will fall off within ten to 21 days. A small wound will remain that takes a few extra days to heal. Until then, sponge baths are better than the tub.

- Wait ten to 14 days before cutting a newborn's fingernails. A membrane under the nail will bleed if cut too soon. Careful filing can help with sharp edges until cutting is possible.

Buying a bathtub

Until your baby can sit up on his own, bathing him in an adult-sized tub can be more trouble than it's worth. Your baby could hit his head on a hard surface or drown if he slips out of your grasp. Use a baby bathtub designed to make washing a safe experience.

Most infant tubs are contoured for comfort and lined with a soft sponge interior. One end is elevated so that water pools around his bottom, not his head. Baby tubs are designed for use in kitchen and other big sinks, which is easier on your back and helps hold your baby in place.

There are many models to choose from. A basic one will do, but manufacturers have come up with a multitude of designs and features.

Sources: BabyCenter.com, 123babyland.com, Americanbaby.com, Cincinnatichildrens.org.

6 Make the bath water comfortably warm. Test the water with your wrist or elbow. Babies require a cooler temperature than you.

7 Soapy bodies are slippery. Always keep a firm hold on your baby after lathering.

8 Use soap sparingly. Soaps, bath oils, and bubble baths can dry out your baby's skin and may cause rashes. They can also lead to urinary tract infections.

9 Shampoo hair at the end of the bath. This will avoid having her sit in shampoo-filled water, which also can lead to discomfort when she urinates.

10 Keep the faucet handles off limits. Even if he can't move them now, he'll be strong enough to do so soon and that could lead to serious injury.

11 Never leave your child unattended. (Yes, it's so important we listed it twice). Children can drown in less than an inch of water—and in less than 60 seconds.

12 Don't rush. Make sure there is enough time for the bath so that you won't be in a hurry.

Wellness check-ups

The information below is for typical wellness visits. Your child's doctor is available whenever necessary; call your pediatrician or bring your child in for a visit whenever you feel there is a problem.

Questions the doctor may ask

Are you having any problems with breastfeeding?

How is your baby sleeping?

When, how, and how often is your baby eating?

How is baby's elimination?

What are your baby's bowel movements like?

What is your baby's crying pattern like?

What sounds does your baby make?

Can your baby roll over one way or sit with support?

How are your baby's motor skills developing?

Does your baby seem ready for solid food?

What games does your baby like to play?

How does your baby react to strangers?

How many teeth does your baby have?

Is your baby standing? Walking?

Does your baby point at objects?

What does your baby say?

How are your baby's social skills developing?

Is your child showing any signs of toilet training readiness?

Are you cleaning your child's teeth and gums?

Has your child been saying "no" a lot or throwing temper tantrums?

Is your child talking a lot?

What new words is your child learning?

Does your child play well with others?

How does your child react when left at school or with someone else?

Source: American Academy of Pediatrics, Center for Disease Control.

Immunizations

Hepatitis B
DTaP or DTP
Hib
Polio
Pneumococcal conjugate
MMR (measles, mumps, rubella)
Chicken pox

Developmental assessment

Height and weight
Vision and hearing
Head circumference
General development and behavior
Sleep, bedtime behavior and routines
Elimination, bowels, constipation
Feeding and nutrition
Skills, new and old

Health and hygiene

Umbilical cord, circumcision
Car seat and home safety
Cradle cap, baby acne, diaper rash
Return to work, child care, transitions
Ear infections, colds, flu, diarrhea, croup
Cuts, bumps and falls
Toilet training

ACTION ITEMS Make doctor's visits less traumatic

1 Don't get there early. We arrive at the doctor's office just in time for the appointment, not early. For that long wait in the tiny examining room, I make sure that I have a favorite toy and a snack/drink. We sing and cuddle and talk about all of the things in the room. I let her touch anything she wants except the dreaded "medical waste can." We even wash her hands in the sink. After the nurse gets the necessary information, we undress, counting toes and fingers and doing the "head, shoulders, knees, and toes" song.—*Glenna*

2 Treat the doctor's staff like friends. When I take my son to the doctor's office he's not scared at all. That's because the people who work there don't wear lab coats or anything like that; they wear normal shirts and jeans. I took pictures of everyone in the office holding either Tyler or Logan and I made a photo album and put their names under their pictures. We look through it the day of the appointment. He knows everybody there and he just loves them.—*Amy*

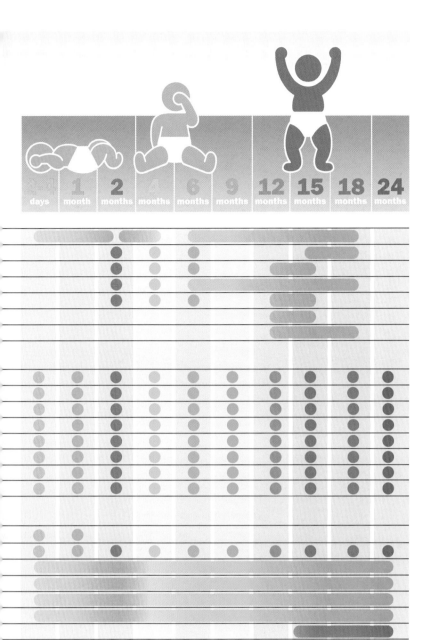

Choosing the right pediatrician for your child

Choosing the right pediatrician is one of the biggest decisions you'll make as a parent. It's more important than you might think: The average new parent and baby visit the pediatrician's office 11 times in the first year for six routine well-baby visits and five other visits. Choose well, and the doctor you pick might treat your child all the way from her first cold to her pre-college physical.

Source: BabyCenter.com.

3 **Make it a family affair.** I have three children, and I try to take them all with me to our family's doctor and dentist appointments. That way, each child is "the patient" less than half of the time, and they can see that the doctor's office is not necessarily a scary place.—*Tracey*

4 **Bring a toy.** Take your baby's favorite toy with you to the doctor. While playing with the toy and sitting on your lap, your child will be preoccupied and comfortable—making it easier for you, your baby, and your doctor.— *Michelle*

5 **Keep the same doctor.** Try to keep the same doctor. That way your child can get to know the doctor (and vice versa) and the surroundings.—*Sunshine*

Source: BabyCenter.com.

Feeding

Food Allergies

6% of babies have food allergies and most don't develop them until they're at least six-months-old and have had time to be exposed to certain foods.

Signs of an allergic reaction or food intolerance:

- Atopic dermatitis or eczema on face, elbows or behind knees.
- Itching and swelling of face, mouth, and lips.
- Hives.
- Watery eyes and runny nose.
- Wheezing or difficulty breathing, loss of consciousness.
- Vomiting or diarrhea.

If your baby passes out or has trouble breathing, call

911.

0 to 4-6 months	4-6 or 6-8 months	6 to 8 months
Liquid *Breast Milk or Formula*	**Smooth** *Single-Ingredient*	**Mushy** *Combination*
All nutrition comes from breast milk or iron-fortified formula until your baby reaches about four- to six-months of age and shows signs that he is ready for solid foods. (See signs at far right.)	Breast milk or iron fortified formula are still the primary form of nutrition. Introduce your baby to solids with single-ingredient cereals mixed with equal amounts of breast milk or formula. Start with one feeding per day and add a second when your baby is eating two to three tablespoons per feeding. When your baby becomes accustomed to spoon feedings, you can begin to add (one-at-a-time to screen for reactions) other single-ingredient smooth or pureed foods like carrots, bananas, sweet potatoes, yogurt, apple sauce and squash.	Most nutrition is still from breast milk or iron-fortified formula. You can now experiment with simple combinations of mashed or pureed foods like cereal with fruit or turkey with sweet potatoes. Other good foods to add at this stage are dark green and yellow vegetables for essential vitamins.

ACTION ITEMS

Feeding tips for baby

1 Don't start your baby on solids earlier than about four months, unless otherwise recommended by your healthcare professional.

2 Remember that breast milk or formula is still your baby's main source of nutrition for the first year.

3 To prevent choking, make sure your baby is sitting up before feeding him solids. Do not feed your child anything that is difficult to chew or swallow like nuts, grapes, popcorn, or uncooked carrots, peas, or corn.

4 Once your baby gets used to eating cereal, slowly start introducing him to other foods.

5 Wait at least three to five days after introducing each new food so you can watch for allergic reactions such as diarrhea, rashes, or vomiting.

6 Don't feed your baby any products containing honey for the first year and no peanut-containing products until he's three-years-old.

8 to 18 months **Soft** *Finger Foods*	**18 to 24 months** **Toddler-Size Pieces** *"Most" Table Foods*	**24 months on** **Self-Feeding** *"Most" Table Foods*
Breast milk or formula will now provide about half of your baby's nutrition. After your baby is one-year-old, you can start giving her whole milk to drink (no low- or nonfat milk until she's two) and begin offering a cup.	By now your baby should be fairly adept at using a cup and be weaned from a bottle.	By two-years-old, your child should be able to eat whatever the rest of the family eats, though you may have to continue to exercise creativity in presentation.
At about eight months, your baby will be ready for easily gummed and digested finger foods cut into safe, bite-size pieces. Try bagels, ripe bananas, soft cheeses, pastas, cooked carrots. She's also ready for ground-up poultry, meat and fish but will not have the molars for chewing until she's 15 to 24 months.	Your toddler can eat the same food as the rest of the family as long as it soft or chopped or mashed into toddler-size pieces. Offer a variety of nutrient-dense foods such as melon, cooked beans, whole grain cereals, and cooked cauliflower.	The good news is that as your child gets older, she'll want to please her parents, which may mean improved table manners and increased willingness to try new foods.
She'll also like (since she's teething) hard foods that dissolve easily like teething biscuits.	Now is the time to get inventive. Most toddlers like dips and spreads, so let them dunk into pureed chickpeas or smear mashed avocados on their toast.	
	He probably won't eat too much in one sitting, so let him eat five to six small "meals" per day.	

Five signs that your child is ready for solid foods (usually between four and six months old)

- Has control of head.
- Can sit up with support.
- Wants to breastfeed more than eight to ten times during a 24-hour period.
- Is getting enough breast milk or formula but is still hungry after feedings.
- Can take food from a spoon and swallow.

Sources: BabyCenter.com, Babybag.com, Beechnut.com, Gerber.com.

7 If your baby is very hungry, prevent frustration by feeding him a little breast milk or formula first. Then switch to a small half-spoonful of food and finish off with more milk.

8 If your baby cries or turns away, do not force the issue. Go back to nursing or bottle-feeding for a week or two, then try again. If this behavior continues after your baby is six-months-old, talk with your pediatrician.

9 Don't feed cereal or other solid foods through a bottle. This might make your baby gag or choke.

10 Don't feed your baby directly from a jar unless you're going to use the whole thing in one sitting. Storing partially eaten food can encourage bacteria growth.

11 Do keep a sense of humor. Early feedings can be unproductive, frustrating, messy—and often hilarious. If you have a camera, now is the time to take some classic shots.

12 Check with your pediatrician to see if and when your child may need a fluoride supplement.

Source: BabyCenter.com.

Illness

An allergy is a physical reaction to a substance in the environment. When a child comes into contact with one of these substances, known as an allergen, either by touching, breathing, or eating it, or having it injected, his body releases histamines to fight it.

Allergies

Chicken pox is an itchy rash that starts as small red bumps which quickly change into thin-walled water blisters on a pink base. The blisters then develop into clear fluid blips, which finally become dry brown crusts in about four days. Highly contagious through touch, sneezing, coughing or even breathing.

Chicken Pox

Asthma is a chronic condition in which a person's airways tend to become inflamed and fill with mucus when exposed to cigarette smoke, a known allergen, cold or exercise. The body reacts with coughing and wheezing.

Asthma

A cold is characterized by a stuffy or runny nose (thick, clear, white, yellow, or green mucus), a cough and sometimes a sore throat. Medicine will not cure the cold faster, but you can help your baby feel better and keep her from getting worse by giving her lots of rest and liquids (breast milk or formula only for babies under six months).

Cold

Symptoms

1	2	3	4	5
Fever Rectal temperature more than 100.4° F	**Diarrhea**	**Cough**	**Breathing problems/ wheezing**	**Congestion/ stuffy nose**

10	11	12	13	14
Rash/ purple spots or sores	**Sore Throat**	**Nausea/ vomiting**	**Crying or fussiness**	**Itchy/watery eyes**

Ear Infection

An ear infection can result when fluid and bacteria build up in the area behind your baby's eardrum. When the eustachian tube is blocked (common during colds, sinus infections, even allergy season), the fluid gets trapped in the middle ear and bacteria growth causes the eardrum to bulge. Symptoms include pus draining from the ear, baby tugging at her ear, fever and irritability.

Stomach Flu

A stomach flu caused by a virus is one of the most common causes of vomiting and diarrhea in a toddler. Avoid spreading germs by insisting that everyone in the house wash their hands thoroughly after changing diapers or using the bathroom.

Pneumonia

Pneumonia is an infection of the lungs that can be caused by bacteria and viruses. The infected child may develop pneumonia after two or three days of having a cold or sore throat. Symptoms may include fever and unusually rapid breathing. The most common type begins suddenly and can be prevented by immunization.

Gastric Reflux

Gastric reflux disease is characterized by frequent stomach eruptions and vomiting. Reflux is exactly what it looks and sounds like—frequent uprisings of stomach fluid—and it makes for a cranky baby who won't eat much and, in the worst cases, wheezes, coughs and gags.

ACTION ITEMS

When should I call the pediatrician?

You're the best judge of whether your baby is really ill, so call if you're worried, no matter what his temperature is. Besides, temperature isn't the only indication of whether his illness is serious. His age is a factor (fever is more serious in babies under three months), and so is his behavior (a high fever that doesn't stop him from playing and feeding normally may not be cause for alarm). Keep in mind that he'll feel hotter if he's been running around than if he's waking up from a nap.

With all this in mind, you should call the doctor if:

 Your baby is younger than three months and has a rectal temperature of 100.4° F (38° C) or higher.

 Your baby is three months or older and has a rectal temperature above 101° F (38.3° C).

 You are worried—no matter what the time or temperature.

Coxsackie causes hand, foot and mouth syndrome and herpangina, with blister-like sores in mouth and throat and on feet and hands. Highly contagious, the virus spreads from mouth to mouth, feces to hand to mouth, or through sneezing or coughing, usually striking in the first two years of life.

Coxsackie
 ① ② ⑨ ⑩ ⑪

Croup is an infection in the upper respiratory tract that swells the trachea and larynx (windpipe and voice box). Children tend to develop a harsh, barking (like a seal) cough. Most cases of croup are caused by the parainfluenza virus (the adenovirus is another offender).

Croup
 ③ ④

Respiratory Synctial Virus (RSV) is the most common cause of lower respiratory tract infections in children worldwide. It is the leading cause of pneumonia and bronchiolitis in infants.

RSV
 ① ③ ④ ⑤ ⑧ ⑨ ⑬

A child shouldn't go to child care if he has any of the following:

- Fever, irritability, lethargy, persistent crying or difficulty breathing
- An upper respiratory illness such as bronchitis or a bad cold
- A gastrointestinal illness, blood or mucus in the stools or vomiting
- Rash if it's linked to an infection
- Bacterial conjunctivitis (pinkeye) or yellow discharge from the eye
- Strep throat or mouth sores that cause excessive drooling
- Untreated head lice

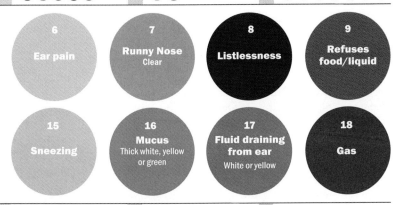

6 Ear pain

7 Runny Nose — Clear

8 Listlessness

9 Refuses food/liquid

15 Sneezing

16 Mucus — Thick white, yellow or green

17 Fluid draining from ear — White or yellow

18 Gas

Whooping Cough
① ③ ④

Whooping cough (also known as pertussis) is a rare bacterial infection that inflames the airways. The pertussis bacteria set up shop in the windpipe, where they bring on a persistent, violent cough. The coughing spell can last for 20 to 30 seconds. Whooping cough is rare and very serious and can be prevented by immunization.

Eczema
⑩

Eczema is an itchy skin rash that can appear on a baby's skin when the child is as young as two months old. It generally shows up on the forehead, cheeks, or scalp and sometimes spreads to the arms or chest. The rash often causes the skin to appear dry, thickened and scaly.

Colic
⑬ ⑱

Colic is a term used to describe persistent crying (usually in the afternoon or evening) in an otherwise healthy baby. If your baby is under five months old and cries for more than three hours a day, more than three days a week for more than three weeks, and there is no medical explanation for the distress, chances are he's colicky.

Symptoms to watch out for

Any of the following symptoms could indicate a more serious problem when coupled with a fever and should be treated by a physician. Page your pediatrician, call 911 or go to the emergency room immediately if:

1 Your baby has lost her appetite, has little energy or is noticeably pale; or you notice other changes in her behavior and appearance.

2 Your baby has small, purple-red spots on his skin that don't turn white when you press on them or large purple blotches; both of these can signal meningitis, an infection of the brain.

3 Your baby has difficulty breathing even after you clear her nose with a bulb syringe.

4 Your baby seems delirious, glassy-eyed, or extremely cranky or irritable; these could signal a serious viral or bacterial illness.

First Aid

How can I tell if an area is infected?

Look for:
- Increased swelling, redness, or tenderness at the site.
- Pus at the site.
- Fever of 100° or higher.
- Red streaks or a feeling of heat emanating from the site.

Who knew?
Longtime favorites such as rubbing alcohol, hydrogen peroxide, iodine and mercurochrome are painful when applied, provide no benefit and may actually cause harm.

Who is Mr. Yuk?
Mr. Yuk was created at the Poison Center at Children's Hospital of Pittsburgh, out of the need to find a symbol to identify lethal substances to young children. Research had shown that the skull and crossbones used to identify poisons had little meaning to young children, especially those who can't read. Mr. Yuk has been adopted by 24 states and the District of Columbia. Mr. Yuk stickers may be available from the Poison Center in your area. (© CHP)

POISON HELP!
1-800-222-1222

Burns (from sun, appliances, liquids, chemicals)

What to do:

Get the child out of danger and away from the source of the burn. Cool the burned area so that damage doesn't continue to occur. Submerge the area in cool water, not ice, for about 20 minutes. If on the face, apply a cool, water-soaked towel. **Do not** break a blister, place butter, grease, lotion or powder on the injury, or use ice.

Call 911 if the burned skin is white or charred or if the burns cover an area larger than the size of his chest, if the injury is from an electrical burn or if the burn is on his face, hands or genitals.

Bites (from humans, insects, animals)

What to do:

Human: Wash the wound carefully with soap and water. If the skin is broken or bleeding, place a gauze pad on the wound and apply pressure. Human bites have a high infection rate, so call your doctor regardless whether the bite is minor or serious.

Insects: For ticks, remove with tweezers by grasping the bug as close to where it's connected to the skin, then gently pull. Wash the bite area and your hands with soap and water. Check the rest of your child's body (scalp, armpits, groin area) for other ticks. **Do not** use petroleum jelly, fingernail polish, a hot match or squeeze the tick. For spiders, wash the site with soap and water and apply ice to reduce swelling.

Animals: Same treatment as human. If the bite is minor, watch closely for signs of infection.

Call 911 if pressure doesn't stop the bleeding, if the biter is known to have HIV or hepatitis C, if your child has been bit by a poisonous spider or scorpion, or if the animal that bit her is wild, foaming at the mouth or acting strangely.

ACTION ITEMS
Keeping your child out of harm's way

1. Don't carry your child and hot food or drink at the same time; keep hot food and drink away from the edges of tables and counters.

2. Don't hold him while cooking at the stove, try to always use the back burners and turn pot handles towards the back.

3. Put safety plugs or outlet covers in unused outlets or block them with furniture. Hide electrical cords behind furniture or use hide-a-cord device. Keep blow dryers, toasters, and other appliances unplugged and out of reach. Cover or block access to hot radiators and floor heaters.

4. Never leave him alone on beds or sofas, in the bouncy chair or high chair, on the changing table, or in any other spot from which he can fall.

5. Use window guards and safety netting on windows, decks and landings. Install gates to block stairways at bottom and top. If railings have openings wider than four inches, block with plastic garden fencing, plexiglas or other material.

Cuts and scrapes

What to do:

Remove any foreign material by flushing with cool running water or with sterilized tweezers. Apply pressure with a clean bandage or towel to stop bleeding, then gently wash with soap and water or antiseptic wash for five minutes. Use antiseptic ointment to reduce risk of infection and cover with a bandage to create the best healing environment. **Do not** use rubbing alcohol, hydrogen peroxide, iodine or mercurïochrome.

Call 911 if bleeding doesn't stop in ten minutes or appears deep enough for stitches. For best results, he should have the stitches within eight hours of receiving the cut, and preferably sooner, to avoid risk of infection or to prevent scarring. For cuts that are deep or are puncture wounds, a tetanus booster may be necessary.

A First Aid kit should contain items to:
- Clean cuts
- Soothe and cleanse skin
- Relieve dry or cracked skin
- Protect wounds
- Cover scrapes
- Relieve stuffy nose
- Reduce pain and fever
- Relieve diaper rash

For example:
- Adhesive bandages in assorted sizes
- Antibiotic ointment, tweezers, Acetaminophen suspension drops, decongestant and fever-reducing drops, nasal aspirator
- Diaper rash ointment, antiseptic wipes, sterile gauze pads

And:
- A First Aid guide
- Your doctor's phone number

Source: BabyCenter.com.

6 Attach corner and edge guards to sharp furniture. Secure furniture that can topple (bookcases, chests of drawers) to the walls. Keep televisions on low furniture, pushed back as far as possible or in a closet with door that can be closed. Secure tall, tippy lamps behind furniture.

7 Keep knives, breakables, heavy pots, and other dangerous items like household cleaners locked up or out of reach. Control access to unsafe areas with safety gates, door locks, and knob covers. Put locks or latches on accessible cabinets and drawers that house unsafe items. Keep trash cans in inaccessible cupboards or use ones with child-resistant covers.

8 Secure your refrigerator with appliance latch. Keep small fingers out of VCRs with a VCR lock. Don't use tablecloths or placemats — he can pull them and what's on them down. Distract him from forbidden places by keeping one cupboard unlocked and filled with lightweight, baby-safe items. Install a lock on the toilet. (He's top-heavy and can fall in and drown.)

Source: BabyCenter.com.

Fever

How to use a rectal digital thermometer

- Lubricate the tip with a non-petroleum lubricant and turn the thermometer on.
- Hold your child on your lap, tummy down and bottom up; or position her on her back as for diaper changing.
- Spread her buttocks with one hand, using the other to grasp the thermometer between your middle and index finger. Gently insert the bulb about one inch into her rectum or until the tip disappears.
- Keep a firm grip on her buttocks. The reading should take 30 seconds to two minutes.

What to avoid:

- Inserting the thermometer can stimulate her bowels, so don't be surprised if she poops when you take it out.
- Don't use temperature-sensitive strips that you place on her brow or under her arm. Pediatricians say they are unreliable.
- Don't use any thermometer that contains mercury.
- Don't use an ear thermometer until she's at least three months old. Because young infants have such narrow ear canals, ear thermometers may not be accurate.

Fever is often the first sign of illness, and your doctor will often ask you to observe and wait for more specific signs to develop. The degree of fever is not always related to the severity of the illness. Your child could have a high fever and only be mildly ill, or she could have a serious infection with a low-grade fever. If she's reasonably alert, taking fluids, and has a temperature you've been able to keep **at or below 102°F/38.9°C** with the recommended dosage of acetaminophen or ibuprofen, your health care provider might advise you to wait before bringing her in.

Call your doctor if your child is **older than three months** and has a temperature of **101°F/38.3 °C or higher.**

Call your doctor if your baby is **younger than three months** and has a temperature of **100.4°F/38°C or higher.**

Call 911
if the fever accompanies:

- Difficulty waking up or listlessness
- Unusually severe or long febrile convulsions
- Stiff neck
- Fresh purple (not red) spots on the skin
- Difficulty breathing that suggests a blocked airway

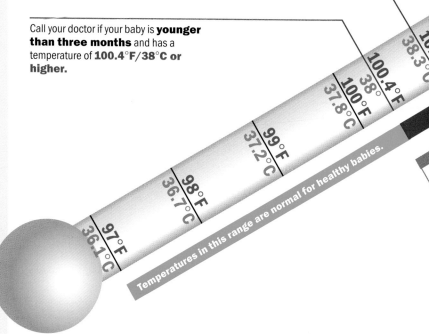

101
38.3°C

100.4°F
38°

100°F
37.8°C

99°F
37.2°C

98°F
36.7°C

97°F
36.1°C

Temperatures in this range are normal for healthy babies.

ACTION ITEMS
At home treatment for mild fevers

1 **Dress your child in loose, lightweight cotton clothing.** Use only a sheet or light blanket for covering. Bundling a baby to "burn out" a fever can cause his fever to rise even higher.

2 **Keep your child's room cool (between 67 and 69°F).** If necessary, place a fan nearby (not directly on him), but far enough away that he can't hurt himself.

3 **Make sure to give your child plenty of fluids** to prevent dehydration, especially if he's vomiting or has diarrhea. He needs plenty of fluids when he's sick. Electrolyte drinks are particularly beneficial. If he's old enough, offer flavored gelatin, ice pops or clear soups.

4 **Give him children's acetaminophen,** such as Tylenol , or ask your physician about using children's ibuprofen (e.g. Advil, Motrin or Nuprin). Follow dosage instructions carefully. Check with your physician first if your he's under three months old.

5 **Try a sponge bath** if the medication doesn't help or if he's vomiting. Sit him in a shallow tub of lukewarm water, and rub his body with a clean, lightly wrung washcloth or sponge one area at a time. Don't dry him off—let the water evaporate and cool his body. Keep the room at about 75° (23.9°C), and keep sponging him until he feels more comfortable. It may take 30 to 45 minutes for the fever to go down.

105°F 40.5°C

104°F 40°C

103°F 39.4°C

102.5°F 39.2°C

102°F 38.9°C

Many childhood illnesses will generate fevers above normal.

According to the American Academy of Pediatrics, a fever is **a rise in temperature above normal,** usually in response to some type of infection.

What causes a fever?

A fever is not what causes him to get sick. It's a sign that his immune system is working properly to fight off **an infection**.

Why does it keep coming back?

A fever will run until your child's body is clear of the infection. This can take as little as two or three days, or as many as five to seven. Fever-lowering medications temporarily bring down body temperature, they don't affect the bug that's producing the infection.

Febrile Seizures

If your child's temperature rises rapidly into this range, she may have a seizure. These "febrile seizures" are usually harmless and are not a forerunner of epilepsy. Signs of a seizure are heavy breathing, drooling, turning blue, rolling back her eyes or shaking her arms and legs uncontrollably. Try to remember how long it lasted (usually between 10 seconds and 3–4 minutes) and call your doctor for an immediate appointment. If she has trouble breathing after the seizure passes or is still drowsy or lethargic an hour later, call 911 or go to an emergency facility.

Roseola

Roseola usually starts with a moderate to high fever and may hover in this range for two to five days (usually three) and then return to normal. Once the fever subsides, a spotty raised rosy pink rash will appear. Like most viruses, there is no specific treatment for roseola, it just needs to run it's course. It occurs between the ages of six months and two years.

Scarlet Fever

Scarlet fever is basically strep throat accompanied by a skin rash and most often strikes children between two and ten. The bacteria that causes it releases a toxin, producing a pink rash that gives the illness its name. Antibiotics are necessary to avoid complications. Call your doctor if she still has a fever of 102°F (38.9°C) or higher 48 hours after starting antibiotics.

Source: BabyCenter.com.

What not to do

1 **Never give your child children's aspirin.** Aspirin has been linked to Reye's Syndrome, a rare but potentially fatal illness.

2 **Never use alcohol.** It can be absorbed through the skin and can lead to more severe complications.

3 **Do not overdress your child.** If your child complains of being cold or is shaking, you can add a layer of clothing. Monitor him closely and take it off as soon as he warms up.

4 **Never restrict your child to bed,** but don't allow him to overexert himself, either.

5 **Never starve a fever.** He needs plenty of calories and liquids.

Skin Care

1 Eczema refers to various forms of skin inflammation accompanied by **itching, dry red patches and small blisters** that burst and make the skin moist and crusty.

2 Infectious rashes include measles, rubella (German measles), chicken pox and scarlet fever have a toxic effect on the skin that produces a **temporary rash.**

3 Chicken pox causes **itchy, fluid-filled blisters** that dry out and form scabs after a few days. Chicken pox may be accompanied by a **fever.**

4 Miliaria is another name for sweat rash or prickly heat, an **itchy rash** resulting from obstruction of the sweat ducts. Infants who can't sweat are especially prone.

Source: Dermnet.com; The Human Body, Dorling/Kindersley.

Epidermis (about 4/1000" thick) The outermost protective layer of the skin, the epidermis helps prevent damage from abrasions and cuts, keeps out bacteria and fungi, and helps preserve the body's water content. In full-term babies, its thickness is similar to adults.

Dermis (about 4/100"– 16/100" thick) Lying directly beneath the epidermis, the dermis contains connective tissue, nerves, blood vessels, lymphatic tissue, sweat- and oil-producing follicles. An infant's dermis is generally thinner than an adult's and is less elastic and resiliant.

Subcutaneous tissue under the dermis helps insulate the body from heat, cold and pressure.

Hair shaft
Pore
Squamous epithelial cell layer
Prickle cell layer
Basal cell layer
Nerve
Oil gland
Hair follicle (root)
Sweat gland
Arteriole
Venule
Subcutaneous fatty tissue
Connective fibrous tissue

Source: Johnson and Johnson

ACTION ITEMS   Six ways to protect your infant's skin

The first step to ensure healthy skin is to prevent skin damage. Here are six easy ways parents can help:

1 Avoid exposure to irritating agents such as harsh detergents and soaps. Infant skin is very sensitive. The chemicals present in many adult products can produce irritation in infants. Harsh adult soaps and shampoos should be avoided in favor of gentle, hypoallergenic washes specifically formulated for infants.

2 Reduce contact with environmental irritants. Substances such as urine, feces and even laundry detergent residue in clothing can cause localized irritation. Protect your child's skin with barrier-forming products like baby oil or petroleum jelly.

3 Maintain the skin's moisture level. Controlling the temperature and humidity of your home, protecting your child from wind, and gently cleaning your child with mild cleansers and shampoos are all ways to maintain the skin's moisture level. Using a specially formulated infant lotion or cream immediately after the bath is another good moisture-preserving step.

Babies' skin issues

Sunburn

Infants sunburn more easily than adults because their skin contains less melanin, a protective pigment. Direct sun exposure should be avoided by infants until they are old enough (six months) to wear a sunscreen. It's estimated that 80% of our lifetime permanent sun damage occurs before we are 18 years old.

Infection and irritation

Infant skin is more vulnerable to infection than adult skin, due in part to babies' relatively immature immune systems. Infant skin is more permeable than adult skin. Therefore, their skin can be easily irritated by some chemicals found in adult shampoos and cleansers, as well as household detergents. Other irritants include saliva, urine and feces. Because infant skin is often wrapped in a diaper, their skin folds can trap perspiration, food and waste materials, possibly promoting skin breakdown.

Hyperthermia

Infants can't sweat like adults until they are about two years old. Since they don't cool off by perspiring, they are at risk for hyperthermia and possibly a rash-like condition called miliaria.

Preterm infants

have special considerations. Their poorly developed epidermis is more permeable to water and fatty substances; they may have increased evaporative heat losses, increased fluid requirements, and increased risk of toxicity from substances applied to their skin. Consult a specialist in infant skin care if your baby is preterm.

Did you know that each square inch of skin contains

65 hairs, **650** sweat glands, **1,300** nerve endings and **9,500,000** cells?

Source: Johnson and Johnson.

In brief, keep your baby's skin clean and moisturized, out of heat and direct sun, and away from irritants and chemicals.

What is scabies?

The itchiest disease your child can get (its name comes from a Latin word meaning "to scratch"), scabies is caused by microscopic parasitic mites that burrow under the skin. It is extremely contagious. Your child will develop a rash of red patches at the hands, wrists, elbows, armpits, navel, nipples, lower abdomen and genitals. Itching is usually most intense at night. Your doctor will prescribe a topical insecticide and may also prescribe a cortisone cream to relieve itching. Even after treatment, your child may itch for up to three weeks and the rash may take up to six weeks to clear up.

Source: BabyCenter.com.

---

4 **Reduce friction.** Friction in the diaper area and in skin folds is uncomfortable for a baby, and constant abrasion can weaken the skin barrier. This makes it easier for irritants and infecting organisms to penetrate. Dressing infants in looser clothing, applying lubricants such as creams, oils, lotions, baby powder or cornstarch baby powder are all good ways to reduce friction.

5 **Minimize changes in the bacterial flora of the skin.** Infant skin, like adult skin, normally has helpful bacteria growing on it. When these bacteria are displaced through irritation or over-cleansing, harmful bacteria and fungi can take hold. Again, use gentle cleansers and changes diapers often to preserve the helpful bacteria.

6 **Avoid exposure to the sun.** Babies should avoid the sun during mid-day hours. A sunscreen with a SPF of 15 to 30 is recommended for daily use on children over the age of six months.

Source: Johnson & Johnson

Some say that in processing language, imaging results show that women use areas on both sides of the brain, while men are more likely to use only the left side.

Because of body size, male brains typically are **10%** larger than female brains.

Girls typically score slightly higher than boys on language and reading tests, while boys out-perform girls slightly in math. It is not known, however, the degree to which genes and socialization contribute to these differences.

Some gender differences may go back to the way our ancestors' brains developed where males were hunters (outdoors/visual/spatial) and women were gatherers (indoors/nurture).

FEMALES
pay attention longer in infancy.

have more acute sensory perception when they're infants.

tend to be somewhat more socially attuned.

tend to perform better verbally and be more emotionally aware.

MALES
tend to out-perform girls in visual-spatial integration.

tend to perform better on tasks like mental rotation of objects.

look at objects for shorter but more active periods as infants.

need more space to play, work.

The **brain** develops very early in embryonic life, earlier than limbs or internal organs.

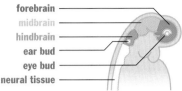

forebrain
midbrain
hindbrain
ear bud
eye bud
neural tissue

embryo at 4 weeks
In the tube of neural tissue at the back of the embryo, three areas (the primary vesicles) develop into the main parts of the brain.

actual size of a 4-week embryo

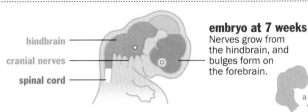

hindbrain
cranial nerves
spinal cord

embryo at 7 weeks
Nerves grow from the hindbrain, and bulges form on the forebrain.

actual size of a 7-week embryo

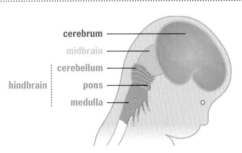

cerebrum
midbrain
cerebellum
hindbrain
pons
medulla

embryo at 11 weeks
One of the bulges on the forebrain becomes the cerebrum; this grows back over the midbrain towards the hindbrain, which has separated into three parts.

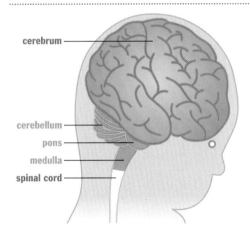

cerebrum
cerebellum
pons
medulla
spinal cord

birth
The cerebrum grows to be the largest part of the brain, and folds appear in the gray matter (the cerebral cortex) which covers it.

The pattern of folds is different in each human being.

By age three, the brain has reached 90% of its adult size, while the body is still only about 20% of full size.

ACTION ITEMS

Want to know more?

Right from Birth: Building Your Child's Foundation for Life

Craig and Sharon Ramey

Child development experts help parents understand the most important practices to enhance a baby's overall development and raise a confident, creative and happy child.

Brain Wonders
www.zerotothree.org

Learn about what happens in infant development at various stages from birth to 18 months. This website addresses areas of child development including brain growth, vision, hearing, touch, crying, breast feeding, emotional, cognitive/learning, coordination and social development.

Brain Connection
www.brainconnection.com

Brain Connection is a fascinating website that features high quality, easy-to-read information about brain development and how people learn. Special features include a research library, animations of brain function and an image gallery on topics including brain anatomy, vision and development.

Here's what's inside your child's **brain:**

the cerebrum
represents **70%** of the brain, and is divided into four lobes:

the occipital lobe
detects and interprets visual images and is active shortly after birth, but does not reach maturity until after preschool.

the parietal lobe
is active from the second or third month for space perception and some aspects of math.

the frontal lobe gradually becomes active at the end of the first year, at the same time as reasoning and speech develop. Skilled movements are controlled by neurons in this part of the brain, which is not fully mature until mid to late adolescence.

the temporal lobe deals with hearing, language and smell. This area also controls memory formation.

the cerebellum
controls your baby's balance and muscle tone. Later, neurons in this area link to other regions of the brain, coordinating smooth and precise movement, and speech.

the brain stem
controls functions vital for survival: breathing, circulation and heartbeat, and reflexes such as swallowing and vomiting. It is completely wired at birth.

the thalamus
sorts, interprets and delivers signals from the sensory systems to the appropriate parts of the cerebrum.

the basal ganglia,
deep in the brain, control basic voluntary movements such as walking.

the corpus callosum is a bundle of nerve fibers that connects the two hemispheres of the brain.

Your baby's brain contains over 100 billion neurons (brain cells) at birth. Each neuron connects through electrochemical structures (synapses) with thousands of others, creating the circuits or architecture that determines who we are.

Most pruning, or streamlining, after birth is the result of stimuli coming from the environment. So the "wiring" of your baby's brain is a work in progress.

At birth, there are ten times as many neurons in the brain as there are stars in the Milky Way.

Source: Your Child from Birth to Three, Newsweek.

From Neurons to Neighborhoods
Jack Shonkoff and Deborah Philips, editors

This book stresses the importance of early child development and provides thought-provoking conclusions and recommendations on four main themes.

- Children are born wired for feelings and ready to learn.
- Early environment matters, and nurturing relationships are essential.
- Society is changing without addressing the needs of young children.
- Interactions among the early childhood disciplines of science, policy and practice are problematic and demand dramatic rethinking.

What's Going On in There? How the Brain and Mind Develop in the First Five Years of Life
Lise Eliot

Explains brain development and its implications for children's emerging motor, emotional, language and other cognitive skills.

In a recent study by Civitas, Zero to Three and BRIO, **1 in 5** future parents and **1 in 5** non-parents believe parents cannot impact a child's brain development until he is one-year-old or more. *Not true.* There is enormous development during that first year.

The brain is so malleable in the first years of life that young children with epilepsy who have had an entire hemisphere surgically removed can still mature into highly functional adults with intensive therapy.

Genes influence behavioral development in the areas of IQ, specific cognitive abilities, academic achievement, mental retardation, personality factors, schizophrenia, affective disorders, delinquent and criminal behavior, and alcoholism.

As a way to understand the difference between **nature** and **nurture,** with regard to your child's brain, imagine the construction of a telephone network:

genes

(the **nature** part) are like engineers who select and develop the different parts of the system—the relay stations, the big trunk lines between relay stations, and the phones themselves…

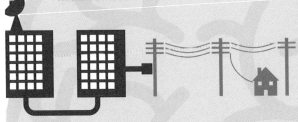

It's easy to see that you need both parts for the system to work.

experience

(the **nurture** part) is like the person from the phone company who fine tunes the wiring between the telephone poles and each individual household. **Experience** monitors that wiring to make sure it works and adapts to any changes that are needed.

ACTION ITEMS

Nurture your child's brain with:

1 Love and affection

Your affection is key to your baby's growth and development. Giving your child lots of love, attention and positive reinforcement helps her feel confident, relaxed and happy and impacts on the development of her intellectual capacity. When she is happy, she can explore, be more open to learning and better cope with stress.

2 A predictable world

Providing routines and consistent responses at bedtime, feeding and bathing gives your baby a sense that the world around him is trustworthy and teaches him that he can depend on you. If your baby knows this, he will spend less energy fussing over his needs and more time learning.

3 Opportunities for fun

Activities that most encourage your child's brain to grow are those that she enjoys. If your child is forced to participate in activities that do not hold her interest, she will tune out. Make learning fun, and your child will grow to love it.

4 The sound of your voice

The newborn brain is especially interested in sounds—the building blocks of speech and language. You can form a deep emotional connection between you and your baby by simply talking to him. It doesn't matter what you say, let your baby hear your voice as much as possible.

❓ Does experience change the actual structure of the brain?

Yes. Brain development **depends on how and how much the brain is used.** The way that each circuit in the brain—sensory, motor, emotional, cognitive—is put together is shaped by the electrical activity in them. But these circuits are not fixed structures (as they are in a computer).

Use it or lose it

Every experience excites certain neural circuits and leaves others inactive. **Those circuits that are consistently excited by experience (positive or negative) are strengthened, while the others that are not stimulated are weakened.** In the words of some neuroscientists, **"cells that fire together, wire together."**

A young child expands her ability to absorb and understand new information as she grows and interacts with people and her world. One way that this happens is through **dendritic growth** in her brain. Dendrites are filaments that branch out from the body of a brain cell. They recieve electrical signals from other brain cells. According to Peter Huttenlocher, a neurologist at the University of Chicago, there are two phases in this development:

1 From birth to age four, dendrites branch and grow, pushing neurons apart and causing the cerebral cortex to become thicker and heavier.

2 Between age four and adolescence, **pruning** of unused circuits causes nerve connections to decrease in density, even though dendrites continue to branch and grow.

Pruning is the process by which inactive brain circuits are removed. This elimination, or streamlining, is a good thing since it allows remaining active circuits to work more quickly.

❓ What roles do nature and nurture play in brain development?

Nature (genes) and nurture (experience) interact at every step of brain development but play different roles.

Genes provide the basic wiring plan. They are responsible for the formation of brain cells and the connections between brain regions.

Experience

fine tunes the architecture of the brain, through a streamlining process which determines which circuits will be kept and which discarded.

Source: Brain Wonders, Zero to Three.

---

5 Understanding and patience

Respond to your baby's fusses or cries, without worrying that you will spoil her. By understanding and answering your baby, you teach her that you care about her and that she can trust you to read her signals. If you are unsure of what your baby needs, don't panic. And, keep in mind that there will be times, such as nap or bedtime, when letting her cry it out may be appropriate.

6 Time to digest what he's learned

Beware of overstimulation. If your child is exposed to a lot of new information about the world without time to digest and process it, he will tune out or break down. Pay attention if he is getting frustrated and let him regroup.

7 Group play

Interacting with peers and other adults meshes perfectly with the natural curiosity of toddlers to explore the world beyond their home and family. It can be helpful if your child interacts with a child slightly more advanced than her, someone who can show her new ways of acting or playing.

8 An enriched environment

Creating an enriched environment means providing everything from good food to stimulating colors, novel challenges, and an enjoyable and stress-free atmosphere with opportunities to explore and learn.

Studies have shown that parental behaviors like talking and giving children choices can positively influence a child's vocabulary and IQ score.

In the 1970s Weisel and Hubel discovered that sewing shut one eye of a newborn kitten prevented normal visual development. When the eye was opened three months later, even though the eye was anatomically perfect, it was unable to see. This finding demonstrated the critical role that early stimulation plays in brain development.

Scientists at the University of Miami have shown that premature babies massaged **15** minutes **3** times a day gained weight **47%** faster than the other preemies who received only standard care.

Learning in the womb
The basic functions of your baby's five senses are developed during pregnancy.

Touch
Skin nerves appear at the **10th week after conception.** By the **6th month in the womb,** the primary somato-sensory cortex—the area responsible for touch perception—can process tactile sensations.

Taste
The more than 5,000 taste buds on the tongue and soft palate appear **7 weeks after conception.** Each bud reacts to one of four tastes: salty, sour, sweet or bitter. While most newborns prefer the taste of sweet things, other tastes that the fetus is exposed to—what the mother is eating during pregnancy—shape those that an older newborn will eventually prefer or reject.

primary somato-sensory cortex

back of head

front of head

taste cortex

primary visual cortex

primary auditory cortex

olfactory bulb

Vision
The visual cortex receives signals from the fetus's eye at **28 weeks after conception,** but neurons along the route from the eye to the processing area at the back of the brain do not mature until several years after birth.

Hearing
The sounds that a fetus can hear in the womb can have a lasting effect. By **28 weeks afer conception** the auditory cortex can perceive loud noises. At birth, a baby will probably know his mother's voice—after all, he's been hearing it for the last three months while in her womb.

A newborn baby can perceive every phoneme (the smallest unit) in the world's languages, but she will lose the ability within one year.

Smell
A fetus can perceive the smell of amniotic fluid **during pregnancy;** at birth it can distinguish its mother's smell from all other smells.

ACTION ITEMS
What can you do for development?

Between **birth** and **2** months

Focus on the eyes

Hold your infant at his optimal seeing distance—about nine to twelve inches from your face—and move your mouth, open your eyes wide, move your head from side to side and up and down so the he can follow it or hang a mobile within his sight range.

Help hearing

Talk to your infant throughout the day. Baby talk is a very natural behavior, and is one of the best ways to encourage the baby to listen to language since he is naturally attracted to the sound, tone and rhythm of your voice. Pretend your baby is talking to you when he coos and gurgles. Expand on what he says, and answer his "questions."

Pay attention to touch

Hold, cuddle, hug and rock your infant in your arms. Massage her back or stroke her head. Pay close attention to the type of touch she likes best.

Between **2** and **6** months

Continue with the above suggestions. Expose your infant to various styles of music. Smile, nod, touch and listen to your baby to help him strengthen his emotional attachments. Talk a lot to him. Read to him. He can now distinguish several hundred different spoken words. It's a time of tremendous physical development. So play with him on the floor, offer simple toys to help him practice his grasp or put a toy just beyond his hands to encourage him to reach.

After birth, different regions of her brain mature at different times. Based on both behavioral and neuroscience research, here are some **windows of opportunity**—the ages at which your child will be most ready to learn specific skills:

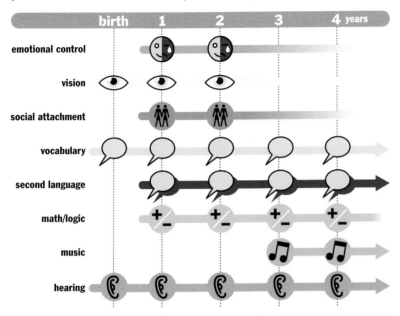

> Your child learns language by hearing you talk. But research shows that only "live" language will help her amass a bigger vocabulary. A baby's brain regards TV as "noise."

There are sensitive periods of time in the development of the brain for learning particular skills or having experiences that will alter future structure or function.

Language and vision are particularly time sensitive. If a baby does not get visual stimulation, his brain will not "learn" to see. By hearing people talk, a baby learns the basic sounds that make up language, long before he is able to speak.

Sources: Neurons to Neighborhoods; BrainLab, Ron Kotaluk; Newsweek.

Synapses in the vision part of the brain multiply enormously between **2 and 4 months**—the same time that babies start to notice the world. This synapse-growth spurt peaks at **8 months** and in this **critical development period** brain cells need visual stimuli to facilitate the proper development of neural connections between eye and brain and within the visual cortex.

When your baby is **3 months old,** her brain can distinguish several hundred different spoken sounds. By **6 months,** this auditory map is different for babies in English-speaking homes vs. babies in Spanish-speaking ones. At **12 months,** your baby will be babbling in the sounds of her own native language. If your child's hearing is impaired, language development will be sidetracked. So, it is critical to test your child's hearing early in his life.

Between **6** and **12** months

Enhance emotions

Shower your baby with warmth and affection to help her feel safe and secure. Easy things, like consistent hugs, kisses, and touching, do a world of good.

Lessons for language

Talk and interact a lot with your child face-to-face so he begins to understand the connection between sounds and words. Talking will follow naturally.

Between **6** and **18** months

Mastering motor coordination

Give your child safe objects and opportunities to practice walking, pushing, pulling, climbing and dumping. Provide "tummy time" to help strengthen her neck, torso and upper body.

Between **6** and **24** months

Stimulate memory

Point to familiar objects and people everywhere—in the park, the grocery store, your child's bedroom, the family photo album—and ask him to identify them. Prompt memories of past experiences by talking about them.

Between **2** and **3** years

Steps toward socialization

Teach your child to get along with others and follow rules by setting—and consistently enforcing—consequences, such as "time outs," for dangerous or inappropriate behavior. Reward positive behavior with praise. Help your child develop independence by encouraging exploration and offering choices while also setting clear limits.

Stress causes chemical changes in the brain and body. Many parts of the body contribute to the management of stress. Among these, interaction between the **limbic system,** the **hypothalamus,** the **pituitary gland** and the **adrenal glands** is of primary importance.

Doctors call this the **LHPA** system.

The system's main function is to alert the brain to potential threats and challenges. Scientists can measure changes in the body by noting the amount of **cortisol** in a child's saliva.

What is cortisol and how does stress affect its levels in the brain?

Cortisol is a steroid hormone produced by the adrenal glands. Together with adrenaline, this hormone is needed for survival by responding to danger and preparing the body for **fight or flight.**

When the danger passes, the brain returns to normal. But if a child is consistently under stress, the levels of these hormones will be consistently elevated, and his brain will lose its ability to return to normal, even when the danger has passed.

When too much cortisol is left in the brain, it reduces the number of synapses (brain connections) in the limbic system. An over-production of cortisol may also affect the workings of the child's immune system, suppress physical growth and affect brain activities such as emotions and memory. **Having a smaller cortex and limbic system means that a child will be unable to regulate his more primitive impulses.**

Many of these effects are muted if the child is raised in a **warm, trusting relationship** with his caregiver. Research shows that elevated cortisol levels are related to the quality of care: children with high cortisol levels live, in general, in poor or even abusive situations, whereas those with low levels enjoy a healthy caregiving environment. In addition, the cortisol levels of this latter group will often remain low even in fairly stressful situations—such as during a doctor's examination.

ACTION ITEMS
Interacting with a stressed child

1 **Educate yourself.** The more you learn about the stress of trauma, its effects and how to cope, the better able you will be to understand your child and interact with him in comforting and nurturing ways. Do not be shy about talking to professional counselors, local agencies or other individuals who deal with similar issues.

2 **Talk about it.** If your child wants to talk about a traumatic event, go ahead and listen. Answer questions and offer comfort. Don't worry if you have no good explanation for the trauma. Your support and attention will do a world of good. You may not want to bring up the topic, but let your child know that you are not avoiding it and that talking about it is okay.

3 **Create a stable world for your child.** Consistent times and routines for meals, school, play and bedtime help your child relax and feel safe. To thrive, he needs to sense that the adults in his world are in control. If you have been touched by the same trauma as your child and feel anxious or out of control, make sure your child understands why and that it will pass.

4 **Set clear rules and enforce them.** Consistency and stability for your child is key. Let her know your expectations for behavior and any consequences for not living up to them. Be sure to consistently, but flexibly, enforce your rules and make good use of positive reinforcement and rewards. Stay away from physical discipline.

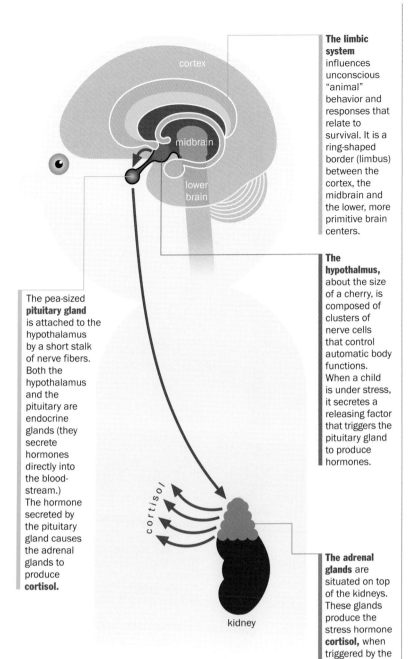

The limbic system influences unconscious "animal" behavior and responses that relate to survival. It is a ring-shaped border (limbus) between the cortex, the midbrain and the lower, more primitive brain centers.

cortex

midbrain

lower brain

The pea-sized **pituitary gland** is attached to the hypothalamus by a short stalk of nerve fibers. Both the hypothalamus and the pituitary are endocrine glands (they secrete hormones directly into the bloodstream.) The hormone secreted by the pituitary gland causes the adrenal glands to produce **cortisol.**

cortisol

kidney

The **hypothalmus,** about the size of a cherry, is composed of clusters of nerve cells that control automatic body functions. When a child is under stress, it secretes a releasing factor that triggers the pituitary gland to produce hormones.

The **adrenal glands** are situated on top of the kidneys. These glands produce the stress hormone **cortisol,** when triggered by the pituitary.

Stress can be defined as the series of neurochemical changes that occur throughout the body and the brain in response to significant threats to physical or psychological well-being.

Research with animals suggests that stressful experiences—such as exposure to violence, abuse, neglect and trauma—can affect the "wiring" of a young child's brain.

Source: Megan R. Gunnar, Institute of Child Development, University of Minnesota.

5 Be watchful of your child's behavior. Signs that a trauma has re-surfaced in your child's thoughts or experiences will reveal themselves through his behavior. Pay attention to what games he plays, the kinds of pictures he draws and whether he withdraws from other children, daydreams or experiences sleep problems.

6 Let other caregivers know what's going on. It is important not only to let other people who play a role in your child's life know about the trauma suffered, but to help them understand how painful the trauma can be and how long it can take to heal. The aim in educating others is to increase the amount of nurturing, patience and support your child receives.

7 Give your child choices and a sense of control. The effects of trauma are often worse for children when they lack the sense that they have control over a situation, since control makes them feel safe and relaxed. By giving your child choices in all types of situations, you can help her regain a sense of control and relieve her anxiety.

Studies have shown that babies fed breast milk have IQs that are **3-8** points higher than formula-fed babies.

Research has shown that a child's capacity for learning is not totally set from birth and can be significantly increased or decreased by how his caregivers interact with him.

Parents' emotional closeness with their baby can strongly influence the child's intellectual development.

Craig Ramey demonstrated that impoverished children, who participated in an early intervention program that exposed them to nurturing and mentally stimulating experiences for **3** years, had **20%** higher IQs than children in the same neighborhood who did not participate.

 Are there different types of intelligence?

Yes. **Intelligence is not limited to what is tested in IQ tests.** Dr. Howard Gardner, of Harvard University, has listed seven types of intelligence:

 social — The ability to notice other people's moods and intentions, and using this knowledge to guide one's actions.

 self-awareness — The ability to know one's own feelings and emotions, and being able to use this to guide and understand behavior.

 math and logic — The ability to recognize what can be done with objects and symbols; knowing how to think abstractly, to identify problems, to ask questions and to come to logical conclusions.

 language — The ability to recognize the sound and meaning of words, and to appreciate how language can be used in different ways.

 spatial — The ability to perceive the visual world and to understand changes in perception of it; to be able to express visual things in a creative way.

 musical — The ability to recognize individual musical notes and phrases; to be able to understand how to combine notes, tones, phrases and rhythms, and knowing about the role emotions play in music.

 physical/manual — The ability to manipulate objects skillfully and to use the body to reach goals or express feelings.

Source: Right from Birth: Building Your Child's Foundation for Life, Craig and Sharon Ramey.

ACTION ITEMS — Create a learning environment

1 **Give your child chances to experiment with new objects and environments.**
Novel experiences not only feed your young child's natural curiosity but also spur the growth of new connections in the brain. Exposure to interesting toys and games stimulates her brain, and as it processes new information, its wiring develops.

2 **Stop an activity when your child starts to turn his head away or fuss.**
When it comes to learning and brain development, beware of too much of a good thing. Avoid overstimulation. Pay attention to your child's cues. Signs like turning his head away or fussing and crying indicate that your child has had enough of an activity and should be given quiet time to rest or digest what he has just experienced.

❓ How can I help my child do well in the classroom?

This is a perfectly natural question for parents to ask. Research points to two factors affecting the growth of your child's intelligence:

1. Parents are the crucial contributors to intellectual development for almost all children. Some research estimates that 50% of IQ is attributed to genes. By age two, many of the intellectual foundations to support a lifetime of learning are in place.

Nurturing has a profound effect on intelligence.

However, there is no study that shows that children who are already in nurturing environments can have their IQ's boosted.

2. No short-term learning program in the first 3 years that concentrates on a single aspect of development has been shown to have lasting benefits. Instead, your child's intelligence is shaped by her experiences over time. Studies with at-risk children show that the compounding of daily experience is the most important factor in shaping a child's intelligence.

Experimental studies in early intervention education for children from low-income families have shown that these programs have been able to boost IQ by as much as 8 points. The 1972-85 Carolina Abecedarian Project found that with these disadvantaged children:

- high-quality preschool programs had positive effects on intellectual and academic achievement.
- as adults, participants reach higher income and education levels and have lower rates of criminal behavior.

Source: Rethinking the Brain: New Insights into Early Development.

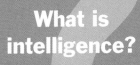

There are currently two major proponents of intelligence theory: the **lumpers** and the **splitters**.

For the **lumpers,** intelligence is defined as a general, unified capacity for acquiring knowledge, reasoning and solving problems.

The **splitters** believe there are multiple, independent intelligences, each guided by its own form of perception, learning and memory.

Source: American Psychologist, Richard Weinberg, PhD.

---

3 Make time for playtime.

While classes like gymnastics or swimming lessons are great influences on your child's development, too many can have diminishing returns. The reality is that safe, supervised play in an unstructured environment can be as beneficial to her development of creativity, reasoning and understanding.

This does not mean that supervised play groups are not valuable. Watching and playing with others—parents, siblings and peers—floods your young child's mind with new ideas. In social settings like play groups, playgrounds, child care programs or even library reading hours, she'll learn to use objects in new ways and to interact in socially acceptable ways.

4 Don't rush to turn on the computer.

Experts suggest waiting until your child is at least three years old before introducing him to the computer, since children younger than three lack the motor skills or attention span to absorb the benefits of computer learning. Also, no research shows that computer activities give young children a head start in school or are more beneficial than spontaneous play or interaction with others. Instead, young children need to play and explore in three dimensions, not in the two-dimensional world of a computer screen.

The brain is separated into two hemispheres, the left and right brain. They control different bodily and mental functions. While the right brain absorbs new information in chunks, the left brain sifts and sorts the information in an organized fashion. Some of their other characteristics are as follows:

The **right brain** is more holistic and controls

Imagination and intuition

Artistic ability

Divergent thinking (*creative, artistic approach, throw out the rules*)

The **left brain** is more analytical and controls

Analytical thinking

Mathematics

Word skills

Convergent thinking (*systematic approach, play by the rules*)

Based on 20 years of experience and observation,

Dr. Lauren Bradway, a speech-language pathologist, has come to the conclusion that children use distinctive learning styles. Her book, *How to Maximize Your Child's Learning Ability,* details her findings:

● the way a child learns in his infancy influences his ability to socialize, and to perform athletically and academically later in life

● every child has dominant ways of absorbing information...

...some learn best through visual stimulation...

...some are more responsive to sound and language...

...and some learn more through touch and motion.

The following is a guide to three learning styles.

❓ Is he a LOOKER?

When he wishes to express himself, he...
- [ ] points to what he wants
- [ ] responds with gestures, not words
- [ ] plays very quietly
- [ ] likes to observe goings on, rather than participate
- [ ] didn't babble until late in his first year

When he plays, he...
- [ ] likes dangling toys, color and motion
- [ ] is visually alert
- [ ] looks at picture books

When he moves about, he...
- [ ] watches his hands while playing
- [ ] reached for objects before 5 months of age
- [ ] likes to explore small objects with his hands
- [ ] likes to pick up and place small pieces, and enjoys puzzles and shape sorters

When he is fussy, he...
- [ ] is quieted by the sight of a familiar face
- [ ] is calmed by a familiar toy
- [ ] is easily distracted by a change of scenery

CHECK ALL BOXES THAT APPLY

ACTION ITEMS
Tips for maximizing learning

Looking

From birth to 12 months

Give your visually-oriented baby lots of interesting things to look at and watch. Hang mobiles, wear bright colors, flip through the pages of colorful picture books or photo albums, make faces in front of a mirror or place him where he can observe family activities.

From 13 months to 3 years

Let your child play with crayons, finger paint, Play-Doh™ and different colored paper. She also will enjoy puzzles or other games that involve matching shapes and sizes. In conversation, whether walking down the street or looking at a magazine, point to different objects and ask her to name them.

Listening

From birth to 12 months

Focus on offering opportunities for listening, such as playing gentle music, talking to your baby, "conversing" with her by imitating her sounds, laughing and by providing her with rattles and other noise-making toys.

From 13 months to 3 years

Converse with your child in adult language, rather than baby talk, so his skills develop. Ask him questions, read him stories and get him into a playgroup where he can talk to and make friends with other children. Also, teach him songs like the ABCs and nursery rhymes and give him children's cassette tapes for listening and singing along.

? Is he a LISTENER?

When he wishes to express himself, he...

- [ ] babbled early and frequently
- [ ] said his first words before age one
- [ ] follows directions easily
- [ ] tries to imitate words spoken by others
- [ ] uses inflection when vocalizing

When he plays, he...

- [ ] likes rattles and noisemakers
- [ ] likes rhymes, songs and finger plays
- [ ] seems to "eavesdrop" on conversations
- [ ] babbles to his toys

When he moves about, he...

- [ ] was slow to sit up, and more interested in babbling
- [ ] is consumed by talking, not walking
- [ ] prefers riding toys that make noise
- [ ] uses toys mainly to create sounds

When he is fussy, he...

- [ ] is quieted by the sound of a familiar voice
- [ ] is calmed by music
- [ ] is easily distracted by a xylophone or a piano

CHECK ALL BOXES THAT APPLY

? Is he a MOVER?

When he wishes to express himself, he...

- [ ] uses gestures rather than words
- [ ] is prone to tantrums
- [ ] shakes his head to indicate "no"
- [ ] grabs at objects and toys impulsively
- [ ] rarely babbles at all

When he plays, he...

- [ ] likes being bounced and tickled
- [ ] likes to be rocked, cuddled and held
- [ ] often kicks at his crib mobile
- [ ] enjoys the swing and bike rides

When he moves about, he...

- [ ] sat without support before six months of age
- [ ] crawled before eight months and walked before age one
- [ ] is very active
- [ ] used riding toys before ten months of age

When he is fussy, he...

- [ ] is quieted by being picked up
- [ ] is calmed by a being held and rocked
- [ ] is easily distracted by a massage or car ride

CHECK ALL BOXES THAT APPLY

Children learn in a variety of ways. Here are a few:

Looking, or visual learning, involves responding to visual stimulation, like motion, color, shape and size.

Listening, or auditory learning, are more has to do with sounds and spoken words.

Moving, or tactile and kinesthetic learning, happens through touch and movement.

Moving

From birth to 12 months

Incorporate touch and chances to use, move and manipulate objects. Massage, bathing, and cuddling provide good opportunities for touch. Games like peek-a-boo and mobiles with rings or other pieces for your baby to reach for will give her the opportunity for movement.

From 13 months to 3 years

Take your child to the playground, the beach or the swimming pool. Give him a tricycle to ride, sand to dig in or a soft ball to kick, throw or catch. Touch is also important, so keep him close with hugs, high-fives, and tickling.

A survey conducted by **Hewitt Associates,** a benefits consulting firm, says that although **only about 10% of U.S. companies offer on-site or near-site child care,** 91% of companies surveyed say they provide some kind of child care assistance, including dependent care spending accounts and resource/ referral services.

Employers are being creative in order to recruit and retain employees. Some are now allowing employees to bring their infants with them to work (usually only until the babies are six months old or just until they start crawling).

A *Newsweek* poll found that **83% of parents surveyed were very satisfied** with their current child care arrangements.

Choosing the right kind of child care is one of the first important issues a new parent faces.

65%

of American women with children under age 6 are in the workforce, compared to 30% in 1970.

Their child care choices follow:

22% are cared for by a parent, including the mother while working from home

21% are cared for by a grandparent or other relative

25% are cared for in organized child care centers

28% are cared for by other non-relatives, including nannies and in-home child care

3% have other arrangements, or no regular arrangements

Source: U.S. Census Bureau

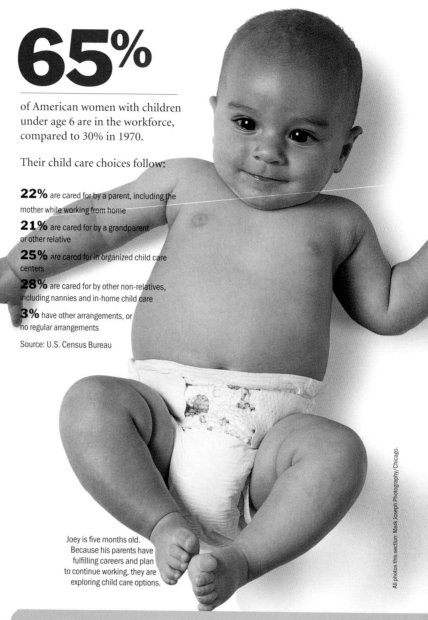

Joey is five months old. Because his parents have fulfilling careers and plan to continue working, they are exploring child care options.

All photos this section: Mark Joseph Photography/Chicago.

ACTION ITEMS — Ask yourself these questions

1. Can you or your spouse afford to stay home with your child?
   It is also important to ask what you'd be happiest doing.

2. How much can you afford to pay?
   Nannies are usually most expensive, in-home child care least.

3. How flexible is your schedule?
   Child care centers and preschools usually have set drop-off and pick-up times.

4. Does your company offer a child care center, allow you to bring your baby to work with you, or let you work at home?
   This benefit allows you to continue working and still be near your child.

5. Do you have relatives nearby that can help?
   Many parents prefer relative care, especially with infants, because they know this caregiver best.

Pros	Cons

Nanny: Parents choose nannies because they believe their children will be safer and feel more secure at home, they find it more flexible and convenient, and if there is more than one child, they find it as economical as centers.

More personalized attention Care at home is more convenient than out-of-home care More flexible than child care centers and home child care situations Children stay in familiar surroundings	Most expensive child care option ($300 to $700 a week) No nanny supervision Playtime with other children must be arranged separately Extensive paperwork and taxes Can leave you in a bind if she quits, is sick or is unavailable

Home child care: Parents like this choice because they want to keep their children in a home-like environment and think their children are happier and healthier in smaller groups.

Nurturing, home-like atmosphere Smaller groups of children than at large centers Less expensive than most other child care ($420 per month for infants, $360 per month for toddlers) Kids socialize with children of same or different ages Usually more flexible pickup/drop-off times than a center	No back-up if provider gets sick Most providers don't have formal training in early childhood education or early childhood development No caregiver supervision Less stringent licensing requirements

Child care center: Parents choose centers because they believe that larger groups, multiple care givers and state inspections make programs safer for their children. Parents also feel that these centers may provide a richer learning environment.

More affordable than nanny care ($330 to $830 per mo.) Reliable (won't call in sick) Ample supervision Kids socialize with children of same or different ages Staff members are trained in early childhood education Licensed and regulated	Teachers care for more than one child; recommended ratios are 1:3 for babies, 1:4 for toddlers Centers that care for infants can be hard to find Kids get sick more often Centers won't provide care for sick children Closed during most holidays Rigid pickup and drop-off times

Relative care: Parents with this option consider themselves lucky, because they believe that relatives will provide more loving care for their child, and their values and child care philosophy will be more aligned.

More personalized care; ratio is 1:1 (for one child) Caregiver has personal interest in your child You often share values with your caregiver Very inexpensive (many relatives refuse payment, but if you choose to pay, aim for at least $5.15 an hour, which is minimum wage)	An emotional minefield; employee-employer relationship is hard to establish with a relative Difficult to separate personal and child care issues Playtime with other children must be arranged separately No caregiver supervision or regulation Older relatives may have a hard time handling toddlers

Stay-at-home parent: There is no substitute for a loving parent. Most experts agree that the best child care option is a parent at home with a child during the first year, as long as they willingly take on the role.

No one truly replaces mom or dad You get to be there for your child's developmental milestones You're assured of loving, attentive care You don't have to explain your rules or parenting philosophy to others You avoid the work/family tug-of-war	Isolation and loneliness, especially for stay-at-home dads who may be looking for other fathers in the same boat Physical and emotional strain on the caregiver Some women suffer a loss of identity in giving up career Playtime with other children must be arranged separately Loss of income and perhaps lifestyle changes

Your finances, your child's needs and your own schedule will determine who cares for your child while you are away. No matter what type of child care you choose, the **quality of care is much more important than the type** of care.

Preschools are licensed and regulated by the same bodies as child care centers, but are usually more curriculum-based. If you have an older toddler or young child (two and a half through five), preschool is definitely an option. The cost is about the same as a center.

TIP

Spend time carefully investigating your child care options, beginning about six months before you need it, if possible. Start early!

6 Would your child benefit the most from group play or from more individualized attention?
During the first year, individualized attention is often best. After that, look for an environment that gives a mix of both.

7 Does your child have health issues or needs that require special attention?
If so, you need to review them with your child's pediatrician and ensure those needs are being met.

8 Do you prefer structured play and activities for your child, or are you comfortable with a more free-form situation?
Some settings are more structured, while others have more flexible schedules. A balance is often best.

Pediatrician **T. Berry Brazelton** and child psychiatrist **Stanley Greenspan** have identified "seven irreducible needs of children," which they say provide the funda-mental building blocks for a person's higher-level emotional, social and intellectual abilities. The first and most basic of these is the need for **consistent nurturing care with one or a few caregivers.** Drs. Brazelton and Greenspan consider this to be far more important than early cognitive training or the use of educational games. If this relationship is absent or interrupted, a child can develop disorders of reasoning, motivation and attachment. Infants, toddlers and preschoolers need these nurturing interactions most of their waking hours.

Source: The Irreducible Needs of Children, T. Berry Brazleton and Stanley Greenspan.

? What is quality child care? Although there are no guarantees, research has shown that the following conditions are necessary for the child care situation to be considered high quality:

Small groups of children
No more than six to eight babies, six to ten toddlers, or 16 to 20 preschoolers, always with at least two adults in each group ensures important individualized attention.

Consistent caregivers
Infants and toddlers especially need nurturing from consistent caregivers to build self-esteem and a sense of security.

Adequate staff compensation
When staff are paid well, they tend to stay in their positions longer.

Low turnover
Low turnover in caregivers prevents children's anxiety about changes in the important adults in their lives.

Active parents
Involved parents help ensure trust, communication and consistency between home and child care.

Education and training
Staff training in child development is critical to higher-quality care, along with clean, safe and stimulating environments.

? What are the results of low-quality child care? It's easy to make child care decisions based on cost and convenience, instead of on quality. But the consequences of inferior child care are serious. Recent studies have concluded that the quality of care in most child care settings is only fair to poor. Only about one in six children is in a high-quality setting. Poor-quality care puts children at risk in these areas:

Language development
Children exposed to a lot of language in reading, singing, and talking develop more neuron connections in the part of the brain that handles language. Children not involved in that kind of verbal stimulation, as can happen when one adult cares for many kids, have skills that are measurably less developed.

Thinking skills
Exposure to language is directly linked with advanced thinking skills, also. These children understand and can solve more difficult problems at a younger age than toddlers in poor-quality settings.

Physical skills
When children have the opportunity to climb, play and run, their brains thrive. Exercise actually caus-es the parts of the brain that control movement to develop more neuron connections. If a child is cooped up in a play yard all day, for instance, her motor development slows down.

Emotional control
Infants raised with inconsistent routines, changing caregivers and stressful envi-ronments are more anxious and more impulsive. They also may be less caring toward others and have fewer problem-solv-ing skills. This lack of healthy emotional experi ences early in life can contribute to a lack of emo-tional control as a child grows older.

For low- and middle-income families with children between the ages of three and five, child care represents the third greatest expense after housing and food. For families with more discretionary income (annual income above $60,600) it represents the second greatest expense after housing. Source: National Women's Law Center

The AFL-CIO in their recent study, *Ask a Working Woman*, reports that nearly half of all women who are married or living with a domestic partner are working opposite shifts from their spouse or partner in order to manage child care.

ACTION ITEMS   Things to check for

Caregiver
- Treats children with respect
- Gets on the child's level physically when speaking to her
- Speaks and listens with respect
- Accepts children's feelings
- Encourages growth and independence
- Provides every child with their own place for sleeping and storing belongings

Safety
- Keeps all equipment in good condition
- Removes potential hazards from reach: cleaning supplies, sharp objects, medications etc.
- Provides a clean and comfortable environment
- Practices good hygiene — hand washing, wiping noses, etc.

Appropriateness
- Provides age appropriate equipment and activities
- Uses appropriate discipline
- Helps children learn how to interact with each other
- Helps children learn how to take care of themselves

Background
- Provides references
- Provides written policies
- Has a daily plan of activities
- Has experience with children
- Has supervision as well as education and training
- Understands and respects differing parenting styles and diversity

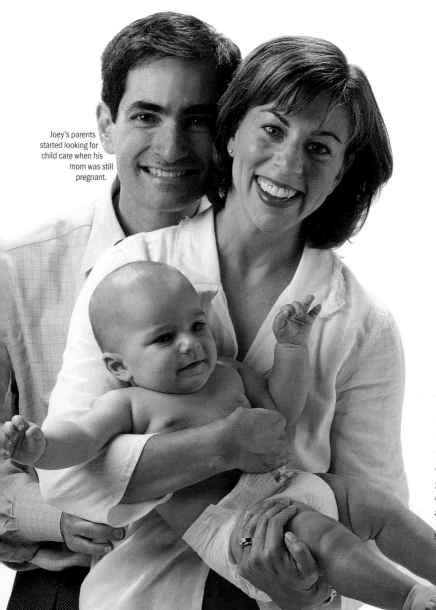

Joey's parents started looking for child care when his mom was still pregnant.

There's no magic formula.

Take your time, do your homework and ask a lot of questions until you find the right situation.

15%

of mothers said that going back to work had been "satisfying." 44% said their feelings vary. So if you have conflicting feelings about going back to work, take comfort in the fact that you aren't alone.

Source: BabyCenter.com.

TIP

When in doubt, keep looking. Your instincts are an important factor in evaluating a child care situation that's right for your family.

Resources for exploring child care

Child Care Action Campaign is a national organization focused on increasing the availability of quality, affordable child care for all families.
330 7th Avenue, 14th floor
New York, NY 10001
212.239.0138
www.childcareaction.org

Child Care Aware (a program of the National Association of Child Care Resource and Referral Agencies) helps parents locate and select child care in their local area.
1319 F Street, NW, Suite 810
Washington, DC 20004-1106
800.424.2246
www.childcareaware.org

National Network for Child Care provides extensive information on child care including state-by-state resources.
www.nncc.org

National Child Care Information Center helps people find quality child care and start their own child care facilities.
800.616.2242
www.nccic.org

81

What is an au pair?

An au pair (means on par or equal) is a visitor to the U.S. on a student visa who lives with an American family for 12 months and cares for their children in order to gain a better understanding and appreciation of American life. Au pairs must be proficient in English, generally have prior child care experience, have a valid driver's license, references and a physician's report. In exchange for room and board and about $250 per week, an au pair works no more than 45 hours per week. Since an au pair is not your employee, no social security taxes are paid.

What is a nanny?

A nanny is a child care specialist who works in a family's home caring for the children, either full-time or part-time. She **may** or **may not** live with the family. A nanny is responsible for the complete care of the children, including tending to the child's basic physical needs, organization of play activities and outings, discipline and intellectual stimulation. She may also plan and prepare meals and do some housework. A nanny is your employee, so social security and other applicable taxes must be paid.

1 million

There are at least nannies working in the United States, but since many are hired illegally, this estimate is certainly low.

Source: International Nanny Association.

Will my child love his nanny more than me?

Parents often worry that a baby or child will become more attached to their nanny than them. Don't worry! Nothing can replace a parent's love, and a healthy, loving bond between caregiver and child not only benefits the baby, but the entire family.

A loving, attentive nanny would provide Joey with a lot of individual attention. Nannies aren't regulated or licensed, though, and if she becomes ill or quits, the parents are left to find alternative care.

ACTION ITEMS
A good nanny interview

1 Experience:
Look for a nanny who has taken care of children before — your kids shouldn't be her first.
- Why are you a nanny?
- How long have you been a nanny?
- How old were the other children you cared for?
- Do you have any formal early childhood development or child care training?
- Do you have CPR and first aid training?
- What would you do if my child were sick or had an accident?

2 Philosophy / Approach:
Make sure the nanny's approach to child care is in line with yours. Ask each person you interview what she likes about the job — you want to be sure that she's a nanny because she wants to be and she's good at it.

- What do you like about being a nanny?
- What about the job could you do without?
- What are your beliefs about child rearing?
- How do you discipline children?
- Have you ever spanked a child?
- How do you comfort children?
- What will my child be doing on any given day?

3 Logistics:
Find out if the nanny can start work when you need her. Plan ahead, if possible, so you can be flexible on the start date in order to wait for someone you really like.
- Why are you looking for a new job?
- What are some of the rules you've followed in other households that you think work well?
- Which rules don't work for you?
- How would you describe your ideal family / employer?

How to ensure a successful relationship with your nanny:

- Write up a contract and a job description.
- Review your child care philosophy with her.
- Review the house rules; revisit them as necessary.
- Make a commitment to touch base every day; in person is best, but by phone or through a written journal or diary will work.
- Develop a back up plan in case your nanny is sick or is on vacation, and let her know what your plan is.
- Discover pet peeves in advance, for both you and her.
- Express your gratitude, and tell her frequently if she's doing a good job.

Signs of a good nanny:

- Your child is happy to see her.
- Your child talks about the fun things they do together.
- She creatively solves problems, and works with you to give your children the best possible care.
- She is on time and reliable.
- She communicates with you about the children's day.
- Your child shows you new projects, sings new songs or teaches you words in your nanny's language.
- Your child is clean and her room is neat. Accidents are infrequent, and she tells you how they happened before you have to ask.

Signs of a bad nanny:

- Your child is not happy to see her, or becomes anxious and withdrawn.
- Your child is in a lot of avoidable accidents.
- Your requests or instructions are not followed.
- She is late or calls in sick often.
- Your child is dirty and unkempt.
- The phone is often busy when you call home.
- Your child seems to have forgotten your household rules.
- Your child has started swearing or using unacceptable language.
- Her stories don't add up.

Learn as much as you can about each candidate.
A good interview is the first step.

5%

of children under age six are cared for by a nanny or au pair in the child's home

Source: US Census Bureau

TIP

Your nanny or au pair needs time with you frequently to talk about your children and your expectations so she can feel good about her job.

- Do you have any pet peeves about parents / children?
- Are you willing to do light chores while the baby is sleeping? Which ones?
- When can you start working?
- Will you ever be available to work evenings or weekends?

4 Additional considerations:
While in your home, each candidate should have a chance to spend a little time with your child. Your observations matter a great deal when you are finally ready to make your choice. It may help to ask yourself the following questions:
- Does she seem comfortable with your child?
- How does your child interact with her?
- Was she pleasant, neatly dressed and groomed?
- While you're at work, will you feel comfortable knowing your child is with her?
- Does she need extra time for travel during the year (to visit family in another country, for instance)?

5 Salary:
Nannies usually charge between $300 and $700 per week (usually about $7 per hour), depending on where you live, how many hours she works, and other factors, including how many children you have.
- What is your salary range?

6 References:
Ask each nanny you're considering for several references, and call them. Ask specific questions and take notes.
- Why is she no longer working for you?
- Would you hire her again? Why or why not?

Waiting until your chiild is asleep to leave

This sounds like a good way to avoid a tantrum, but imagine the terror a young child would feel if he woke up to find himself with a stranger. It might not be as easy to leave when your child is awake, but it will get easier over time. Watching you leave and learning that you always come back is an important lesson.

It's important for a sitter to have emergency information about your children and your house. For a great checklist that you can fill out and leave with your sitters, go to: www.parenting.com/parenting/checklists/babysitter.html

Who can you count on for baby-sitting? Typically, parents think of baby sitters as the teenager down the street. But more and more, moms, older adults and agencies are providing baby-sitting services. Some communities even have baby-sitting cooperatives, where groups of parents take turns caring for each other's children.

Adolescents

Twelve to 13 year olds have limited availability during the week, but usually are available after school and on the weekends. Many adolescent baby sitters have completed the American Red Cross CPR program and can administer simple first aid.

Teenagers

Teenagers and young adults, ages 14 to 18, also have limited time during the week due to their academic/social pursuits. Typically, these baby sitters are available on weekend days and evenings for a few hours. Many have also completed the American Red Cross CPR program and can administer first aid in an emergency or know what steps to take should an emergency arise which they are unable to handle.

Adults

Other parents and adults have greater flexibility and availability during the week and weekends. Generally speaking, care is provided in the baby sitter's home. Unless they are licensed caregivers, these baby sitters are often not trained in CPR; but, they are a mature, experienced and responsible care source and are more likely to use good judgment in crisis/emergency situations.

Agencies

Agencies and centers have greater flexibility during the week and weekend, and operate under a license. Typically their staff is CPR-trained and has a series of checks and balances in place to ensure a safe environment. Additionally, this care source tends to have an established schedule and planned activities. This option tends to be more expensive.

Cooperatives

By definition, a co-op is an enterprise or institution owned and operated by the people who use its services. A baby-sitting co-op is a group of parents who get together and agree to take turns watching each other's children. baby-sitting is free (except for the obligation to return the favor) and usually provided by a friend, but coordination and scheduling may be a challenge.

ACTION ITEMS

Where to find baby sitters

- Your neighbors
- Local high schools
- Local colleges
- Your church or synagogue
- Referral agencies
- American Red Cross
- Neighborhood association newsletters
- PTA, Boy/Girl Scout troop, baseball team, and other clubs or associations you/your children participate in

- Grocery store bulletin board
- Your pediatrician or family doctor
- Yellow pages and newspaper advertisements
- The Internet:
  - www.babysittingcoop.com
  - www.babyonline.com
  - www.momsonline.com
  - www.redcross.org

How old should a baby sitter be?

11 **According to the American Red Cross, parents should not choose someone younger than 11 to look after their baby.** The authors of *What to Expect the First Year* are more cautious, suggesting a child isn't qualified for baby-sitting until age 14. Your judgement is critical in evaluating whether a sitter is qualified. **14**

Occasionally, Joey is cared for by a baby sitter. She plays with him, feeds him and is familiar with his bath and bedtime routine, which allows his parents to go out together alone.

Remember, some baby sitters are just kids themselves. Be clear and explicit about your instructions, and then, go have fun.

$5 15

A good baby sitter over the age of 14 should earn at least minimum wage (and more if you want her to come back on Saturday nights.)

How to help a baby sitter do her job

- Show the baby sitter around your house and yard, and let her know which areas are off-limits or dangerous to the child.
- Point out all the exits.
- Show her where the fuse boxes, first-aid kit and fire extinguisher are, and make sure she knows how to use them.
- Give her clear, written instructions about any medicines your children might need.
- Show her how to safely use any appliances she might need.
- Give her instructions about which TV show or videos the kids are allowed to watch.
- Tell her about any food issues your children may have, and show her where things are in the kitchen.

- Arrange her transportation, if necessary.
- Leave all your telephone numbers, and instruct her when it's appropriate to call you.
- Let her know when you'll be back and call her if there are any changes.
- Introduce her to a neighbor or friend whom she might call for help if she needs it.
- Call her at least once while you are gone to make sure things are going okay.
- Put all your instructions in writing.
- Make your expectations clear on things like friends visiting, phone calls, food, etc..

TIP

Treat your baby sitter with respect — this may be her first real job. She'll likely grow into a capable adult if you treat her like one.

How to tell if you should keep looking...

If a home child care is messy, disorganized or has virtually no rules, keep looking.

If your child won't get a wide range of age-appropriate activities, keep looking.

If the provider doesn't encourage drop-in visits, keep looking.

If the provider seems bored, frazzled or inexperienced, keep looking.

If someone in the provider's home smokes, keep looking.

If there are a lot of people in and out of the provider's home, keep looking.

On average, an in-home child care situation will cost about half as much as a nanny. In-home child care providers earn on average $4.69 per hour, compared to $7.18 an hour for center based workers, though these numbers may vary depending on where you live.

Source: National Women's Law Center

Joey's parents could choose in-home child care and drop him off at Natalie's house, where he would be in a home with a caring mom and older kids with whom he could learn and play.

ACTION ITEMS   Signs of good in-home child care

1 **Ground rules.** The tougher the rules about sick children, for instance, the better off everyone will be. It might make it more difficult to send your child to child care when he has a cold, but that means he won't be exposed to illness from other children as frequently, either.

2 **Structured schedules** that include plenty of time for exercise, reading sessions, group activities, free time, snacks and meals. Even outings to nearby parks or museums, as long as they are well supervised, will keep children stimulated and happy.

3 **A qualified and committed caregiver** with experience and a genuine love of children is ideal. It is also important for the caregiver to have education and training in child care, professional supervision, CPR and first aid training, as well as involvement in a professional child care network.

4 **A clean and safe environment** is crucial. Even though the child care is in someone's home, it still should be properly child-proofed, well lit and ventilated. Safe and clean toys, firm bedding and street-savvy security should be evident. Check to see that the home is a smoke-free environment; second-hand smoke can be harmful, sometimes even dangerous, especially for the youngest children. And make sure there is a working telephone.

5 **A current license.** Again, it's no guarantee, but it's a start.

There are **280,000+** regulated in-home child care facilities in the U.S.; more than three times the number of licensed child care centers.

Source: babycenter.com

In-home child care arrangements have been around forever. In-home child care appeals to parents who want to keep their child in a warm, nurturing environment but can't afford the expense of a nanny.

Pros	Cons
Smaller groups. More individualized/ personal attention.	**Communication.** It may be harder to get in touch by phone, if there are teenagers or the provider's other family members using the same line.
More like home. One consistent caregiver in a setting more like your own home might provide younger children a little more security.	**Licensing.** Not all are required to be licensed. This means you are responsible for determining whether or not your provider has CPR training, an adequate caregiver-child ratio and a safe environment.
Flexibility. If you're late picking up your child, you know your child won't be sitting in a room alone waiting. However, don't forget to offer overtime pay.	**Personality conflicts.** Not just between you and the provider, but even between parents or your child and the other children in the provider's care.
Parental Oversight. Other parents are in and out of the provider's home and are able to observe the provider when you are not.	**Back-up.** If your provider gets ill or stops providing services, it will be up to you to find alternative care for your child. Also, if she's having a bad day, there's no one there to give her a break. However, many good providers have a back-up in place.
Babies/Toddlers. In-home child care providers offer a more personal service that may be more accessible and affordable to women who are returning to work and are having difficulty finding places in quality child care centers.	
Nutritional considerations. Special dietary requests are easier for an in-home child care provider to accommodate.	**Training/Supervision.** Your provider may have limited or no education and training in caring for young children. You may also find that there is no one holding the provider accountable to maintain high standards of care.

Look for a welcoming, nurturing environment where the kids will have fun and be safe. A license is no guarantee of quality, but it's a good start.

23% of children under age six are cared for in their provider's home, either in family (home) child care (15%) or other non-relative situations (8%)

Source: US Census Bureau.

Grandparents as caregivers

About 16% of all preschoolers are cared for by grandparents while their mothers work, according to the US Census Bureau. And, the number of children who live with a grandparent grew 76 % to almost 4 million children between 1970 and 1997. However, a study published on careguide.net in 1995 suggests that child care by relatives is not always the best choice, probably because relatives are more likely to be helping out for economic reasons. Managing an employer/employee relationship with a relative is sometimes a challenge, too. But when it works, everybody benefits.

TIP
People change. What works for an infant may not work for an older child. Make sure, even with relatives, to continually evaluate your child's care.

Keys to making relative care work

1. **Develop an agreement** which includes: payment, if any; time commitments per week; drop off and pick up times; food issues like what and when your child should (and shouldn't) eat and who will provide it; schedule and activities; discipline techniques; health, safety and child-proofing; and emergency information. Revisit this agreement at regular, pre-determined times.

2. **Communicate** about how the day went. Make time for this, even when you're rushed.

3. **Be clear** about your expectations. Is it okay for the caregiver to take your child along on errands or doctor's appointments?

4. **Provide information and support**. Caring for a child is challenging and sometimes isolating work. Offer to pay for a CPR class or a child development class, find books or Web sites that offer activity suggestions, or find a story hour at a local library for them to attend together.

5. If it's working, **express your gratitude** with a lot of positive reinforcement.

Almost half (47%) of parents with children under six have used a child care program in the past year.

A majority of parents (66%) have one child under six in child care, while an additional 27% have two young children in a child care program.

According to figures based on parents' responses, a third of young children (34%) spend 40 or more hours per week in child care. Another third spend 16 to 39 hours a week in child care, and 13% are in child care for nine to 15 hours a week. Only 19% of young children spend less than eight hours a week in child care.

Source: What Grown-Ups Understand About Child Development: A National Benchmark Survey, Civitas Initiative, Zero to Three and BRIO

Will my child develop behavior problems if I send him to a child care center?

Not likely. The Study of Early Child Care and Youth Development, conducted by the **National Institute of Child Health and Human Development,** has followed over 1,200 families around the country since their baby's birth. While the study doesn't provide clear-cut answers as to what leads to behavior problems in child care settings, it does find:

Good parenting matters.
Children whose mothers were responsive, warm, and sensitive were less likely to be rated by their teachers as aggressive.

Type of care matters.
Children who spent more time in child care centers were better prepared for the academic work of school, but less likely to interact positively with their classmates.

Quality of care matters.
Children in stimulating and well-structured environments showed higher cognitive and language scores and fewer behavior problems than those in poorer quality settings.

Each day, **10 million** children under five years old are cared for by approximately three million teachers, assistants and family child care providers.

Source: U.S. Census Bureau

Demographics of the child care population

Nearly one out of three (30%) black children and one in four (24%) caucasian children are cared for in centers, compared with one in ten (10%) Hispanic children. Well over half (58%) of black infants and toddlers of employed mothers are in care full-time, compared with a little more than a third of white (36%) and Hispanic (34%) children.

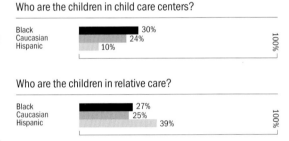

Who are the children in child care centers?

Black	30%
Caucasian	24%
Hispanic	10%

Who are the children in relative care?

Black	27%
Caucasian	25%
Hispanic	39%

Who are the children in full-time care?

Black	58%
Caucasian	36%
Hispanic	34%

Source: Urban Institute.

ACTION ITEMS   How to make drop-off time easier

1 **Be quick.** A brief hug, a kiss on the cheek and off you go. The more you linger, the worse the scene may become. If the teacher says she's fine moments after you go, and she seems happy when you pick her up, then your best bet is to not prolong the goodbye.

2 **Be understanding.** Separation is tough on a child (and on a parent) sometimes. Read about separation anxiety to understand what he is feeling, and try to be empathic.

3 **Let her bring a security object.** A stuffed animal or favorite blanky from home might be all she needs to help calm her down.

4 **Get her interested.** Find out what activities the children will do that day, and talk it up to your child. Your excitement may be contagious.

5 **Validate his feelings.** Don't belittle him or call him a baby for having difficulty separating. And don't create habits that will be hard to break later, like offering toys or treats if he stops crying.

6 **Be on time for pick-up.** Waiting for you while she sees other parents arrive for their kids might be difficult for a child experiencing separation anxiety.

A good child care center has: a well-trained, supervised and caring staff; clean facilities; a current license; rules and regulations; age-appropriate and stimulating curriculum; and good references.

A good child care center may be hard to find. Look for low staff turnover, current licenses and small group sizes.

17%

of children under age six in child care are cared for in organized centers.

Source: US Census Bureau.

A high-quality child care center would provideJoey with a lot of social opportunities, as well as a more structured environment.
His parents would also benefit from the reliability of a staff of caregivers.

TIP

Try taping a picture of you and your child together in his cubby at child care. Seeing a happy photo of you may be enough to soothe a nervous child.

Profile of the child care work force

Who are the child care teaching staff?

female 97%	
male 3%	
have children 41%	
single parents 10%	

100%

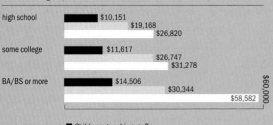

Annual wages per education level vs. all workers (1996)

high school	$10,151
	$19,168
	$26,820
some college	$11,617
	$26,747
	$31,278
BA/BS or more	$14,506
	$30,344
	$58,582

$60,000

■ Child care teaching staff
Civilian labor force, women
Civilian labor force, men

Only **18%** of child care centers offer fully paid health coverage to teaching staff.

One-third of all child care teachers leave their centers each year.

Source: Administration for Children and Families, US Department of Health and Family Services.

89

One third of white urban families and **25%** of all Americans sleep together in a family bed for all or part of the night.

More than **20%** of new mothers now share beds with their infants during the first month.

900 infant deaths a year are associated with suffocation in soft bedding.

Between 1990 and 1997, the deaths of **515** babies under the age of **2** were attributed to sleeping in adult beds. The majority of these were infants three months or younger. **121** were due to overlying of the child by an adult sleeping in the bed; **394** were due to entrapment in the bed structure (wedging of the child between the mattress and side rail, suffocation in water beds, or head entrapment in bed railings).

As many as **1/3** of babies who die from SIDS each year may have suffocated when placed on top of soft bedding, such as pillows, comforters or sheepskins.

Your child's **crib** or bed should be extra safe. The crib and her room (once she's mobile) are where she will first start to explore her environment. Make sure that her surroundings are free of traps and hazards.

When she's about **3 feet tall,** (or can climb out of her crib) your child should start sleeping in a bed.

The top of the crib rail should be at least **26 inches** from the top of the mattress. Lower the mattress as your child grows to prevent her from climbing out.

The space between the bars should be no more than **2³/₈ inches.**

This should prevent a baby's head from getting caught.

Make sure to measure the bar distance on all cribs, especially older one.

The mattress and all bedding should fit perfectly into the crib with **no gaps between it and the crib walls.** The mattress should be **very firm** and not sag under your baby.

Always make sure that **the side-rail mechanism** is locked and secured after putting your baby in the crib.

Your baby should never be left in the crib when the side-rail is down.

? Where do other babies sleep?

In Brazil, some babies sleep in hammocks with their mothers.

North American Indian babies often sleep in wicker cradle-boards lined with cedar bark and turquoise.

In New Zealand many babies sleep on sheepskins.

ACTION ITEMS Making the change from crib to bed

1 **It's time** for your child to move into a bed, once he can climb out of his crib (usually when he is 33 to 36 inches tall).

2 **Prepare her** by talking about the switch, and involve her if you can in the setting up of the new bed, preferably one that has side rails for safety. Let her help pick out bed linens and arrange her teddies or dolls.

3 **Try to pick a time** for the change when there are no other major changes going on, such as moving to a new house or adjusting to a new baby in the family.

4 **For the first few days,** have him continue to sleep in the crib, but use the bed during the day, for play or for naps.

5 **Be firm and consistent** about your child staying in the bed once the switch has been made. If your child gets out of the bed at night, gently put him back. Do not talk to him, look at him or express any emotion. Any attention, even negative attention, will only further inspire him to repeat his behavior. It can be very frustrating if your child is getting up three or four times during the night, but if you eventually give in, he'll have learned that persistence pays off.

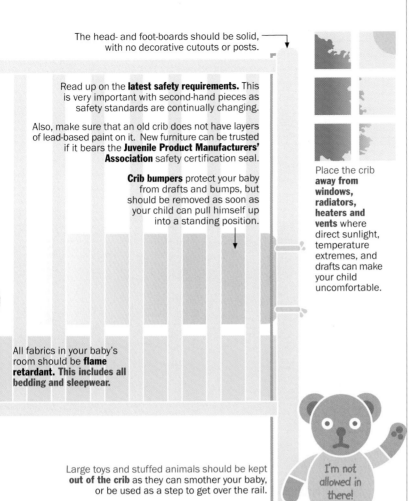

The head- and foot-boards should be solid, with no decorative cutouts or posts.

Read up on the **latest safety requirements.** This is very important with second-hand pieces as safety standards are continually changing.

Also, make sure that an old crib does not have layers of lead-based paint on it. New furniture can be trusted if it bears the **Juvenile Product Manufacturers' Association** safety certification seal.

Crib bumpers protect your baby from drafts and bumps, but should be removed as soon as your child can pull himself up into a standing position.

Place the crib **away from windows, radiators, heaters and vents** where direct sunlight, temperature extremes, and drafts can make your child uncomfortable.

All fabrics in your baby's room should be **flame retardant. This includes all bedding and sleepwear.**

Large toys and stuffed animals should be kept **out of the crib** as they can smother your baby, or be used as a step to get over the rail.

Other items such as pillows, bulky comforters, and heavy blankets should also be kept outside a crib. They, too, can smother an infant.

I'm not allowed in there!

What is a good sleep environment for my baby?

Whether your child sleeps in the same bed with you or in a crib, there are essential safety precautions you should take.

Spaces in a crib or the family bed where a child's head can get wedged and soft bedding that can suffocate a child are primary dangers, particularly for an infant.

Some Seri Indian babies in Mexico sleep in baskets filled with sand and covered with cloth.

Siberian babies often sleep under a swanskin cover in a cradle made of birch bark.

Some Fijian babies are rocked to sleep in cradles that are suspended from the ceiling.

Many Japanese babies sleep with their parents on futons.

Source: Guide to Your Child's Sleep, American Academy of Pediatrics.

---

6 **Reward your child.** The next morning, make sure to compliment and congratulate her. Offer hugs and kisses or a small treat.

7 **Keep track.** If you're having problems, record daily information— such as what time your child goes to sleep, how many times he gets out of bed, and how long he cries in protest—you can get an idea of whether the plan is working.

8 **Read about it.** Try stories like *A Big Bed for Jed* by Laurie Friedman.

9 **Be patient.** For some children this transition will not occur overnight. However, if you follow the plan faithfully each night, your child will gradually adjust to the transition and sleep comfortably in her new bed.

As children age, their nap times decrease in duration. Here is a general overview, though specific sleep times will vary greatly from child to child.

Daytime sleep: between **12** and **16** weeks, day sleep organization will develop. The reason that daytime sleeping (naps) sometimes becomes a problem is that there may be too much stimulation (light, noise or motion) and too many errands or activities which interfere with good quality sleep.

DAYTIME SLEEP

Sleep periods develop as the brain matures. This means that there are times during the day and night when your baby's brain will become drowsy and less alert. These times are the best times for your baby to be soothed to sleep, because the restorative power of sleep is greatest when it coincides with the brain being in a drowsy state.

AGE

1–6 wks Sleep is disorganized. The longest period...

7AM

6 weeks–3 months Naps are scattered throughout the day.

3–8 months   Morning nap   Second nap   Third nap may or may not occur.

8–12 months   No third nap

12–21 months   No morning nap

21–36 months   Most children are still having this nap.

Sleeping during the day improves the quality of night sleep because the better rested your baby is when it's time for sleep, the easier it is for her to fall asleep and stay asleep. If she...

ACTION ITEMS Improving your child's sleep patterns

 My 18-month-old no longer wants to take his morning nap. Do I insist on having him try two naps or should I just skip it in the morning?

Don't force it. Instead, focus on getting him to sleep for his afternoon nap, which you may want to move to an earlier time since he no longer sleeps in the morning. Also, consider making his bedtime earlier during this transition. Children tend to fall asleep easier when they go to sleep earlier, before they have a chance to become overtired, and the earlier bedtime helps them to sleep later in the morning.

 My 12-month-old is a night owl and sleeps until 10:00 a.m. How can we get him back on track?

Focus on gaining control of his morning wake-up time. Studies indicate that most one-year-olds wake up between 7:00-8:00 a.m. Therefore, wake him up at 7:00 a.m.; then, regularly adhere to a sleeping schedule appropriate for a one-year-old:

- mid-morning nap—at about 9:00 a.m.
- early afternoon nap—at about 1:00 p.m. (but starting no later than 3:00 p.m.)
- early to bed—between 6:00-8:00 p.m.

Expect your son to cry in protest at nap time and bedtime for the first few days (20-40 minutes is not uncommon), but don't let him cry more than an hour.

Nighttime sleep: Although you can't control when a baby will begin to sleep for longer periods of time, babies typically develop night sleep organization at about six weeks because: ■ we have darkness as a time cue ■ we slow down our own activities and become quieter ■ we behave as if we expect our baby to sleep.

NIGHTTIME SLEEP

...of sleep can be anytime during the day or night.

total hours of sleep

enormous variation

16
15
15
14
14

6PM

Bedtime anywhere from 6pm to 10pm. Your baby will have at least one 4- to 6-hour period of sleep during the night.

Bedtime 6pm to 8pm — **You'll still be up once or twice for feeding.**

Bedtime 6pm to 8pm

Bedtime 6pm to 8pm

Bedtime 6pm to 8pm

...becomes fatigued from nap deprivation, her body produces stimulating hormones to fight the fatigue, and this chemical stimulation interferes with night sleep and subsequent naps.

Source: Healthy Sleep Happy Child, Marc Weissbluth, MD.

? My girls, both five months old, wake up at 5:00 a.m. every morning. What can I do to get them to sleep later?

Setting an earlier bedtime is one of your best bets to help the babies sleep later into the morning. Earlier bedtimes might prevent them from becoming overtired and allow them to sleep better. On the flip side, delaying their bedtime may actually cause them to wake up earlier. Children ages four to12 months should be put to bed between 6:00-8:00 at night. Most experts agree that feeding a baby before bedtime, waking a baby for a feeding or setting a later bedtime will not be effective.

? I've been putting my child, age nine months, to sleep every night at 7:30. This worked for a while, but he has started to fight bedtime. What should I do now?

At this age he may experience a stage of attachment that makes it difficult to separate from you, or he may be simply overtired. Pay attention to his cues and consider starting your bedtime routine earlier when your son:
- misses his afternoon nap,
- has a lot of physical activity during the day,
- stops taking an afternoon nap,
- shows signs of tiredness before 7:30 p.m.,
- takes short daytime naps.

Recent studies suggest that behavioral problems in children **2-3** years of age may occur if they sleep less than **11** hours at night. Children this age should sleep up to **13** hours at night.

Lack of sleep can cause behavioral problems such as acting out, behaving aggressively and hyperactively. **Conversely, children's behavioral problems have been said to contribute to a lack of sleep in children.**

Different children need various amounts of sleep. If a child does not look well rested, he probably needs more sleep.

Waking up at night, a problem that occurs in **33**% of children **2-4** years old, can also cause behavioral problems.

Researchers believe that regular amounts of sleep deprivation may have long-term effects on brain function.

Studies on rats show that sleep is necessary for survival, demonstrating that life expectancy decreases with sleep deprivation.

Sleep is a dynamic activity.

The five stages of sleep progress in a cycle from stage 1 to **REM** sleep, then the cycle starts over.

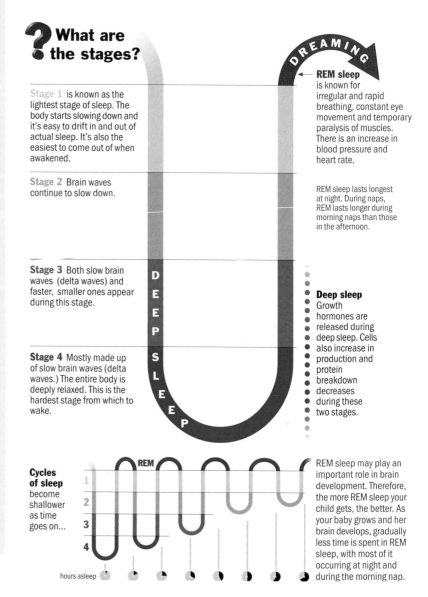

? What are the stages?

Stage 1 is known as the lightest stage of sleep. The body starts slowing down and it's easy to drift in and out of actual sleep. It's also the easiest to come out of when awakened.

Stage 2 Brain waves continue to slow down.

Stage 3 Both slow brain waves (delta waves) and faster, smaller ones appear during this stage.

Stage 4 Mostly made up of slow brain waves (delta waves.) The entire body is deeply relaxed. This is the hardest stage from which to wake.

DEEP SLEEP

DREAMING

REM sleep is known for irregular and rapid breathing, constant eye movement and temporary paralysis of muscles. There is an increase in blood pressure and heart rate.

REM sleep lasts longest at night. During naps, REM lasts longer during morning naps than those in the afternoon.

Deep sleep Growth hormones are released during deep sleep. Cells also increase in production and protein breakdown decreases during these two stages.

Cycles of sleep become shallower as time goes on...

REM

1
2
3
4

hours asleep

REM sleep may play an important role in brain development. Therefore, the more REM sleep your child gets, the better. As your baby grows and her brain develops, gradually less time is spent in REM sleep, with most of it occurring at night and during the morning nap.

ACTION ITEMS
The ABCs of catching ZZZZZs

What's the best way to help your child develop good sleep habits? There are many expert views about what role parents should play when it comes to helping their children develop good sleep habits. Ultimately, the choice is yours. If you like an approach that:

1 **is lenient** about responding to your baby when he cries during the night and emphasizes consistent bedtime routines and positive sleep associations, check out Dr. Jodi Mindell's book, *Sleeping Through the Night: How Infants, Toddlers and Their Parents Can Get a Good Night's Sleep.*

2 **advocates sticking firmly to routine** and letting your child cry at bedtime for extended intervals of time before you provide her with comfort, read Dr. Richard Ferber's book, *Solve Your Child's Sleep Problems.*

3 **focuses on training your baby to go to sleep and comfort himself** on his own by keeping nighttime feedings short, waking him if his daytime naps last more than a few hours and using your voice or a gentle pat to comfort him when he cries, try the American Academy of Pediatrics' book, *Guide to Your Child's Sleep.*

The brain is always active.

Since the 1950s, we've learned that our brains are very active during sleep. Neurotransmitters, or nerve-signaling chemicals in our brains, control whether we are asleep or awake. Neurons, which connect the brain to the spinal cord, produce other neurotransmitters which keep some parts of the brain active during sleep and while awake.

? What are dreams?

Infant **REM sleep** was first studied in 1953. However, scientists still do not fully understand the need for and purpose of dreams. **Sigmund Freud** believed that dreams are part of a human's unconscious desires.

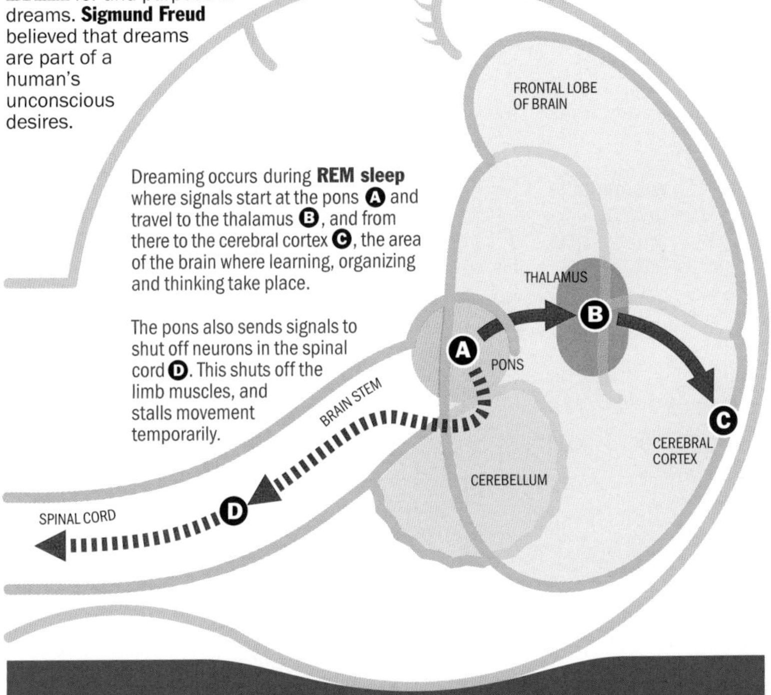

Dreaming occurs during **REM sleep** where signals start at the pons **A** and travel to the thalamus **B**, and from there to the cerebral cortex **C**, the area of the brain where learning, organizing and thinking take place.

The pons also sends signals to shut off neurons in the spinal cord **D**. This shuts off the limb muscles, and stalls movement temporarily.

FRONTAL LOBE OF BRAIN

THALAMUS

A PONS

B

C
CEREBRAL CORTEX

BRAIN STEM

CEREBELLUM

SPINAL CORD **D**

REM sleep stimulates the cerebral cortex, which helps the brain develop learning ability. Scientists believe that's why infants spend 50% of their time in **REM sleep.**

While sleeping, both adults and children pass through 4 stages and REM (Rapid Eye Movement)—in repeating cycles throughout the night.

Sources : NINDS, Brain Resources and Information Network; Healthy Sleep Habits, Happy Child, Marc Weissbluth, MD; Guide to Your Child's Sleep, American Academy of Pediatrics.

4 promotes the family bed and other ways of being there for your child to provide a comforting, relaxing sleep environment, look at Dr. William Sears' book, *Nighttime Parenting.*

5 emphasizes the prevention of sleep problems and teaches healthy sleep habits by synchronizing soothing techniques with your child's natural rhythms, read Dr. Marc Weissbluth's book, *Healthy Sleep Habits, Happy Child.*

AND REMEMBER, whichever approach you choose, be consistent.

The most important thing in establishing good sleep habits is **routine.**

If you establish a consistent bedtime routine early in your child's life, you will go a long way towards eliminating the possibility of sleep problems later.

DOING THE SAME SERIES OF ACTIVITIES EVERY NIGHT BEFORE GOING TO BED HELPS A CHILD UNDERSTAND THAT IT IS TIME...

?How do I help my child develop good sleep habits?

Make a bathtime routine
A warm water bath can be a calming experience, and is a good way to relax a young child. Also during this time, you can have him prepare for bed by brushing his teeth and putting on his pajamas.

Say goodnight
Once your child is ready for bed, have her go around the house saying goodnight to favorite people, pets or toys.

Have a chat
As you tuck your child into bed, you can talk to her about her day, your day, and things for her to look forward to in the morning.

Read bedtime stories
Reading to a child is a great pastime. Allow your child to choose a book and then read it aloud to him.

Sing a lullaby
Singing the same song to your child each night can be a wonderful way to soothe him to sleep. After this you can play a tape of familiar bedtime songs.

Exactly what you do in the routine is up to you—choose whatever activities make you and your child comfortable—but do it consistently.

Distinguish between day and night

Newborns don't pay attention to the time of day; they just sleep and eat around the clock. But you can start teaching the difference between morning and evening, naptime and bedtime, when your baby is just a few weeks old.

During the day, play with her, talk to her, and wake her for feedings. Keep daytime noises at the normal level and keep the house, including her room, sunny and bright.

At night, turn down the lights, noises and conversation when you feed and change her. Eventually she'll begin to understand that day is for play and night is to sleep tight.

ACTION ITEMS   Good bedtime practices

1 Start when your child is young. Healthy sleep is a habit, just like healthy eating habits, which are learned. The sooner you put into practice these rules, the earlier you can teach your child healthy sleeping habits and prevent many common sleeping problems.

2 Pay attention to signs that your child is growing tired. Putting your child to bed when she first shows signs of becoming tired may help her go to sleep with less fuss or crying. Learn to recognize certain behaviors, which signal that she is becoming tired, such as loss of interest in favorite games and toys and tendencies to become quiet and less active.

3 Don't neglect naps. Naps are as critical to healthy cognitive, emotional and physical development as night sleep. Naps lead to optimal daytime alertness and can help your child sleep easier at night. As much as possible, try and stick to a consistent nap schedule every day.

4 Adhere to an early bedtime. Your child may have an easier time falling asleep if she goes to sleep earlier, before she has a chance to become overtired, and she may sleep later in the morning. Often, moving up a bedtime by just 20 or 30 minutes can make a difference.

❓ How should I respond to my one-year-old's persistent crying when I put him down to sleep or when he wakes up during the night?

Here are two ways to deal with this:

Don't respond

Immediately stop going to your son at night. This approach appeals to many parents who find that it works in just days. However, it causes more prolonged periods of crying during that time, which may seem too harsh for some parents or caregivers.

The gradual approach

Respond quickly to your crying child, but each time you do, spend gradually less time with him and offer less interaction and physical contact. Rub or massage him, but **do not pick him up.** By picking him up, you make the job of teaching him to fall asleep unassisted much more difficult. This approach can take up to several weeks.

The bottom line: Pick the approach that feels comfortable to you, and be consistent about it.

Unfortunately, it's very easy to swing back and forth between firmness and permissiveness. If this happens too often, it will be hard to make any cure stick. Although the "cold turkey" approach may seem harsh, it can have the most immediate and dramatic effects and will give you the courage to keep tighter control over sleep patterns.

The routine should be the same wherever you are

When other caregivers are looking after your child, make sure that they know the routine. You may have to lay down the law for them as well as your child! If you are divorced, the routine must be the same in both homes.

On vacation, it may be difficult to keep up your routine. Try to establish actions that correspond in some way to your child's normal bedtime routine.

...TO GO TO SLEEP, HE BEGINS TO ASSOCIATE THE ROUTINE WITH THE PROCESS OF FALLING ASLEEP.

❓ How do I help my child develop good sleep habits?

Be sensitive to your child's sleep needs and establish good sleep habits from the beginning. Deciding how long you should let your child cry requires sensitivity to your child's needs, persistence and flexibility.

Sources: BabyCenter.com; Healthy Sleep Happy Child, Marc Weissbluth, MD.

5 **Start early.** Begin your bedtime routine about thirty minutes before bedtime. This will help you and your baby to relax and enjoy the winding down process.

6 **Be consistent.** Using a consistent soothing style will help your child settle down and get ready to go to sleep. You might try bathing, listening to music, reading a book, feeding, rocking, singing or massaging. Pick a style of soothing that makes you feel comfortable and stick to it. By creating consistent bedtime routines, you teach him how to soothe himself to sleep.

7 **Say good night.** After you complete your bedtime routine, say good night, close the door and walk away—even if your child cries in protest. How long you allow the protest crying to continue depends upon your own comfort level.

Approximately **20%** of all babies are colicky.

It's worth discussing colic with your pediatrician. Although the vast majority of colicky babies have no other physical problems, a few may have treatable conditions such as milk allergy or reflux.

There are no medications that cure or alleviate colic.

Colicky babies are more likely to develop poor sleep habits. Therefore, teaching them healthy sleep habits may be extra challenging.

Some research supports gastrointestinal or allergic causes for colic. Nevertheless, as a baby cries, it creates more gas and more abdominal pain, which then causes more crying.

Colic is a common problem in infants. While most infants go through phases when they are fussy, some can be extremely fussy—crying more often than others. When an otherwise healthy baby is difficult to console and has a lot of fussy, crying phases, he is **colicky.**

Some doctors describe **colic** by the rule of **3**s: A **colicky** infant fusses or cries more than **3** hours a day, more than **3** days a week for **3** weeks or more.

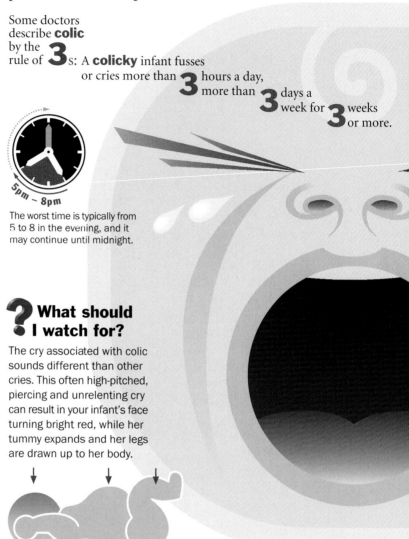

The worst time is typically from 5 to 8 in the evening, and it may continue until midnight.

? What should I watch for?

The cry associated with colic sounds different than other cries. This often high-pitched, piercing and unrelenting cry can result in your infant's face turning bright red, while her tummy expands and her legs are drawn up to her body.

ACTION ITEMS
Tips for soothing a colicky baby

1 Let your child suck on a pacifier, bottle, hand or wrist. Because sucking is a natural reflex for a baby, it is also quieting and calming.

2 Rock your baby in your arms or in a swing.

3 Take him for a drive or stroll. Repetitive motions like these tend to settle down a colicky child.

4 Sing a soft song, play a lullaby or run the washing machine or dryer. Often, a colicky baby will relax with gentle rhythmic sounds like music or even the hum of the dryer.

5 Give your baby a gentle massage, wrap him snug in a blanket, or hug him close. Your touch and close contact may help him settle down and relax

6 Turn off bright night lights and take away stimulating toys from your baby's crib. Soft, soothing environments are key to encouraging sleep and might even ease crying.

7 Alternate strategies. No one method may work every time.

When should I call a doctor about colic?

While many babies experience **colic,** frequent or high-pitched, piercing crying can also be a sign that something else is wrong.

 **Call your child's doctor if you notice any of these:**

Your baby cannot be consoled and you are worried.

Your baby has developed a fever and/or seems sick.

Your baby's crying hasn't diminished after four months.

Call immediately if:
Your baby is experiencing abnormal vomiting and/or stools.

Keep a diary

Pay close attention to your child's crying phases. Keep a diary of when he cries, noting time, location, what might have started an episode and what helped to calm him down.

Keeping a diary will help you to be specific when you talk to your child's doctor. As you make your entries, you might also note that the baby is not crying as much as you thought.

It will probably all be over by the time he is four months old.

 **What is colic?**

Crying spells unrelated to any specific problem that last three or more hours a day. Colic affects babies between the ages of **2 weeks** and **3-4 months.** Researchers believe it is related to physiological factors, such as upset sleeping rhythms and high levels of certain hormones. It is not caused by parents' actions.

Source: Colic, Yale Pediatric Guides.

Tips for relieveing your stress

1 Try to stay calm. If your baby senses that you are uptight or anxious, his crying might intensify. So take a break.

2 Try to reduce the stress in other areas of your life. Order take-out or get help with house cleaning.

3 Ask for assistance from family and friends. Or, ask your health care provider to help you find a counselor who can give you support during this stressful time.

4 And remember, no matter how frustrated you get, never shake your baby.

Beware of colic cures

Herbal remedies, which can poison your infant or make him ill.

Waterbeds and beanbag pillows, which can suffocate your infant.

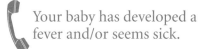

99

❓ What are the most common causes and symptoms of sleep disturbances?

Snoring

is often associated with:

- enlarged tonsils and adenoids, which block air passages
- allergies, which cause respiratory membranes, tonsils and adenoids to swell
- weight problems

Most of these problems can be treated after proper diagnosis.

Sleep talking

usually occurs in light sleep and involves mumbled words that make no sense. You may even be able to hold a conversation with your child.

Nightmares

generally occur in the second half of the night, when dreaming is the most extreme. When your child wakes up, she may be able to recount the details of her nightmare. Though she may be reassured by your presence when she wakes up, she may still be frightened and have trouble going back to sleep because of her vivid memory of the dream.

Night terrors

are less common but more severe than night-mares. You may be unable to wake your child during this time.

Symptoms include: kicking • having a glazed-over stare • trembling • screaming • being panicked or confused • crying inconsolably • sweating & rapid breathing

In addition, your child may be unable to recognize you or that you are in in his presence; he may even try to push you away when you try to comfort him.

Head banging and rolling

occurs in 5% to 10% of children in their first few years: at about eight months your child may bang or roll his head or rock himself before he falls asleep. There are no behavioral or emotional problems associated with this behavior and it will most likely last only until he is two or three. If this condition persists or begins past age three, call your pediatrician.

Teeth grinding (bruxism) at night is common for children, and may be related to stress or misalignment of muscles, but should not happen on a frequent basis. It's usually not harmful to your child's teeth, but it may cause wear and tear on her tooth enamel or headaches. If it persists after age six, consult your dentist.

ACTION ITEMS

Tips to handle sleep disturbances

1 Fear of going to sleep

- For a few nights, sit quietly with her in her room while she falls asleep.
- Turn on a night-light.
- Leave the door slightly open until she falls asleep.
- Supervise the programs she watches on TV to limit her exposure to scary images and characters.

2 Head banging

- Pad the crib by securing pillows or a bumper around the sides.
- Move the crib away from the wall.
- Set the crib on thick carpet or on rubber carpet protectors to decrease the banging noise.

3 Nightmares

- Wake up your child.
- Soothe and comfort him with hugs, kisses and words of reassurance.
- Let him talk about the bad dream or draw it. Young children can often better explain dreams through pictures.

Sleepwalking

usually occurs between the ages of five and 12, when a child is in deep sleep. It may be difficult to wake a child when he is sleep-walking, but he will most likely return to his bed, and there is no need to wake him. When he wakes up in the morning, he may have no memory of the episode. Sleepwalking may occur when your child lacks sleep or is under stress. Be sure to keep him on a regular sleep schedule.

Here are some **precautions** you can take to protect your child from harm when he sleep walks:

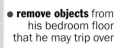

- **remove objects** from his bedroom floor that he may trip over
- put up **safety gates** to prevent him from going up and down staircases
- **lock** outside doors to prevent him from leaving the house.

Any type of interference with a healthy sleep pattern.

Half of all children under six have, at one time or another, some kind of sleep difficulty, according to the National Sleep Foundation.

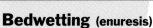

Bedwetting (enuresis)

is a problem that occurs for many children. There can be several reasons, including: ● not being able to wake up when a bladder is full ● the bladder may not yet have fully developed to make it through the night ● stress in the home caused by a move, a new sibling or divorce

4 Night terrors

- Put your child to sleep about 30 minutes earlier. For some children, night terrors are caused by lack of sleep or abnormal sleep schedules.
- Do not wake your child during the terror. Waking her during a terror is difficult and may upset her even more.
- Stay with her until the episode is over and she has calmed down.
- Comfort her with gentle touches and soft words.
- Remove potentially unsafe objects from your child's sleeping area.

5 Bedwetting

- Reward your child with a sticker on a chart for dry nights, but do not punish him for wet nights.
- Give your child lots of support and let him know that he is not at fault.
- Get him professional help if the problem persists.

SIDS claims the lives of **3,000** infants annually. **90%** of these deaths occur in babies **6** months and under.

SIDS is the leading cause of death in babies **1** year and under.

In a recent study, **41%** of parents said their infant's pediatrician had not told them to place their babies on their backs to sleep.

SIDS has decreased **40%** since the campaign to place infants on their backs or sides first began.

Between 1994 and 1998, the number of white parents who placed their infants on their stomachs significantly decreased from **44%** to **17%**. African American parents who also did so decreased as well from **53%** to **32%**.

The notion that a baby placed on his back might choke is not true.

Although **SIDS** is often called crib death, cribs do not cause crib death.

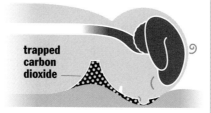

What causes SIDS?

It is not known what causes **SIDS,** but the most likely cause is an anatomical defect in the brain.

trapped carbon dioxide

This abnormality, which controls carbon dioxide sensing, has been found in some babies who have died from **SIDS.** A baby's risk of suffering from **SIDS** increases if she is placed face down in the crib, because the carbon dioxide can get caught between the air passages and the mattress. As a result of this brain defect, your baby may not be able to detect the danger and move her head.

Other theories

Low blood pressure
It is believed that a defect in some babies' brains may result in them not being able to recover from a loss in blood pressure. This would cause a decrease in blood flow to vital organs in the body, ultimately leading to breath failure and death.

Developmental delays in the defense system
Some babies are not able to become startled by blankets or pillows which threaten to impede proper breathing.

Inadvertent compression of neck arteries
can be caused by placing your baby on her stomach, where she is unable to move her head properly to avoid bedding.

Which babies are most at risk?

At highest risk are babies...

…who are placed face down on their stomachs to sleep

…whose mothers were under 20 when they became pregnant

…whose mothers did not get adequate prenatal care

…whose mothers smoked during pregnancy and later exposed them to second-hand smoke

…who were low birth weight

…who are not breast fed

…who have a sibling who died from **SIDS**

African American infants are **2.2 times** more likely to die from **SIDS** than white infants.	Native American infants are **3 times** more likely to die from **SIDS** than white infants.	Boys are more likely to die from **SIDS** than girls.

ACTION ITEMS   Tips for reducing the risk if SIDS

1 Put your baby to sleep on her back.

2 Keep toys out of your baby's crib.

3 Use firm, flat bedding.

4 Do not place your infant to sleep on soft surfaces like waterbeds, sofas, or soft mattresses or place soft materials like pillows, comforters or sheepskins under your infant.

5 Keep the temperature in your baby's room comfortable for an adult.

TIP
You can keep a new-born comfortably positioned on her back by swaddling her in a blanket with her hands near her mouth so she can comfort herself.

Bed sharing

Although bed sharing may help assure some parents that their babies are safe, there are no studies that prove that co-sleeping reduces the likelihood of **SIDS.**

Sharing a bed may actually increase the risk of **SIDS** because adult beds and mattresses are not designed with infants in mind and do not meet safety standards imposed on cribs.

A recent study* demonstrated that sharing a bed and putting infants to sleep on surfaces other than cribs increases the likelihood of **SIDS** in infants.

This study found that...

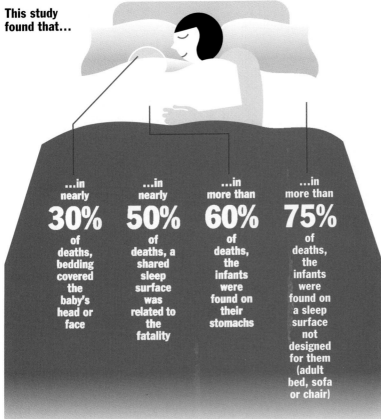

...in nearly
30%
of deaths, bedding covered the baby's head or face

...in nearly
50%
of deaths, a shared sleep surface was related to the fatality

...in more than
60%
of deaths, the infants were found on their stomachs

...in more than
75%
of deaths, the infants were found on a sleep surface not designed for them (adult bed, sofa or chair)

*Researchers from St. Louis University School of Medicine, Washington University School of Medicine in St. Louis and the offices of the Medical Examiner of the city of St. Louis and of St. Louis County reviewed the death-scene information from 119 infant deaths between 1994 and 1997. Of the deaths, the diagnosis was **SIDS** in 88, accidental suffocation in 16, and undetermined in 15.

What is SIDS?

SIDS is an acronym that stands for Sudden Infant Death Syndrome. It is also known as crib death. SIDS hasn't been identified as any one single illness or disease in infants under one year. Rather, it is a diagnosis given when an apparently healthy baby dies in his sleep without due warning and when no cause of death can be pinpointed after an in-depth investigation.

Sources: BabyCenter.com; American Academy of Pediatrics.

6 Dress your baby in as many layers of clothing as you would wear.

7 Avoid devices designed to maintain sleep position or reduce the risk of re-breathing (CO_2) since many have not been tested sufficiently for safety and none have proven to reduce the risk of **SIDS**.

8 Provide your baby with early and regular prenatal care.

9 Do not smoke during pregnancy.

10 Do not allow smoking around your baby.

Sources: National Institute of Health, American Academy of Pediatrics.

In one study with a group of middle-class, white Americans, the consistent finding was that parents viewed pretending as important to their children's development, viewed it as an enjoyable activity and thought that their role was significant in helping their children learn how to pretend.

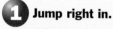

When children pretend with their caregivers, it is usually more complex, elaborate and extended than when they pretend by themselves. The children use the ideas that their parents initiate in their pretending. A child might pretend play with a toy steering wheel by simply turning the wheel and making engine noises. A parent joining in can take the child on a pretend trip, teaching along the way.

Among things that parents communicate early through pretending is their culture. Americans pretend play is most often child-centered, revolving around a toy or object; Chinese parents more often than not initiate play and use it to teach social customs or routines, like how to greet a guest or teacher.

A baby begins to play from birth. Touch him, tickle him, smile at him, sing to him. Playful loving care from a parent teaches a baby to trust and forms a strong, secure relationship between parent and child.

ACTION ITEMS
How to be a playful parent

1 Jump right in.

Babies are born ready to play. No matter what the child's age, playtime with a parent is invaluable. Whether you talk baby talk, or bounce your toddler on your knee, you are building the foundation of a strong, trusting relationship and are helping him to become a happy, caring and loving person.

2 Forget the rules.

Toys and games have possibilities beyond their intended use, and they do the most for a child's imagination, skills and development when he plays with them creatively. Explore freely and encourage him to make believe.

3 Try to think more like your child.

Add to your child's play experiences by creating imaginative games and new ways to use his toys. Pretend blocks are flying cars or zoo animals.

4 Take a break: Children benefit from playing by themselves.

Although children often learn the most when they interact with others, solitary play gives a child time to process and understand everything that he has been doing and learning. Take cues from your child. If he is happy, leave him alone. If he seems bored, help him find a new way to play.

? How can I make play more interesting for my baby?

Shake a rattle or incorporate other toys with bright colors or different shapes and textures into your play. Early exposure to simple toys will activate his imagination and help it to grow.

Let your baby shake the rattle. In a few months, she will want to hold the rattle herself. Let her try without your help.

? How can I enhance my toddler's playful activity?

Your child will get tired of many toys and household objects quickly, and will discard them. Instead of giving her several toys all at once, try to keep them hidden.

If you bring a toy out one at a time, just when a new one is needed, she'll enjoy playing with it longer.

Take advantage of a chance for your child to play with someone else his age. While he'll be interested in making friends, he'll often want it to be on his terms.

These early encounters can be rocky! Let the two of them quarrel a bit—it's good for them both to learn a little about their independence and individual rights.

Your child will get tired and need rest. When this happens, cuddle and reassure her.

Listening to soothing music or reading a book is good at this time.

Your toddler will often say "Me do it!" Let him try things by himself, even if you think they might be too difficult.

Never reply: "You can't do that, you are too little." Suggesting you do things together will preserve his self-esteem.

? Should I let my child win when we play?

Of course you are bigger, older and have more experience, but you should allow your child to win some of the time, so that her self-confidence can develop. Find creative ways to adjust the power balance between yourself and your child; give her two turns to your one, or put one hand behind your back. You might even play blindfolded!

You are your baby's first toy. Your love, smiles, warmth and affection are a playground for your baby.

You can provide opportunities and objects for play and should participate wholeheartedly in playing with your child. But remember also to give him time to play by himself. When you do play with him, follow his lead and try not to direct his play.

5 Participate enthusiastically and give the playing your full attention.

By becoming involved wholeheartedly in your child's play and going along with her games and fantasies, you encourage her imagination and ability to make believe. And, by taking her play seriously, you help her feel important about herself. Incorporate play into all your activities with your child. To help you give it your full attention, try establishing a special "playtime" tradition—a time set aside each day only for play.

6 Follow the leader: Let your child guide his play.

To make play more meaningful for your child, let him pick the activity, decide how it is played and when he is ready to move on to another. Watch him. His expressions, movements and sounds indicate if he is enjoying a game or has grown tired of it. Let his mood dictate how and what you play. Responding to his cues makes him feel comfortable in his surroundings and gives him the confidence to become a better learner.

What are the stages of play?

Noted child expert Jean Piaget divided play into three stages:

1 Infancy to the second year of life

Sensorimotor practice play

During this time your child is acquiring control over her movements and learning to coordinate gestures and her perception of their effects. Play at this stage often consists of repeating and varying motions. She takes joy in being able to cause an event to occur and recur.

2 Ages 2 to 6

Symbolic or pretend play

During this time your child is acquiring the ability to encode his experiences in symbols and images of events that can be recalled and used in pretend play.

3 At school

Games and rules

Your child has now begun to understand certain social concepts such as cooperation and competition, and she's beginning to work and think more objectively. Her play reflects this and she is drawn to games that are structured with objective rules and may involve team or group activities.

What are different types of play?

Your child's play behavior can be grouped into several types. These are generally related to the materials and tools of play and often overlap.

Quiet play	Creative play	Active play
includes looking at picture books, stringing large beads, putting together puzzles, and coloring with paints or crayons.	includes painting, drawing, collage, play dough, sand, problem solving, music and dancing.	includes the use of balls, slides, swings, push-pull toys, sand and water play, running around, riding bikes and climbing trees.
Cooperative play	**Dramatic play**	**Manipulative play**
requires more than one person. It includes ball games, tag, see-saws, playing dolls or house and hide-and-seek.	(also called pretend play) includes trying out different roles—from firefighter to astronaut—and using dress-up clothes, dolls and other props.	includes painting, cutting with scissors, using tools. Using hands and eyes develops coordination and other skills.

ACTION ITEMS

Where to find out more about play

If you need creative ideas or you're looking to learn more about play, try these recommended resources:

Internet

BabyCenter.com

This is a great web site, loaded with helpful advice, practical suggestions for caregivers of babies and toddlers, with sections devoted entirely to fun activities, toys, arts and crafts and other forms of play that help encourage learning and development.

Books

Your Child at Play (series)
Marilyn Segal

Each book in this unique series focuses on a specific age group, offering activities for all ages and stages along with easy to understand information on early childhood development. They offer wonderful perspectives and strategies for engaging babies in play.

Play is whatever a child wants it to be. There's no right or wrong way to play; what matters is that a child is given safe toys in safe places, and encouraged to experiment.

Play is one of the primary ways your child discovers her world.
Play allows her to explore and express herself, to learn on her own, control her environment, connect with other people and make sense of her surroundings.

Playtime Learning Games for Young Children
Alice S. Honig

Honig provides parents and caregivers with more than twenty games and activities for children between the ages of two and five. Activities focus on helping children learn thinking skills.

More Things to Do with Toddlers and Twos
Karen Miller

In this wonderful follow-up to her first book, *Things to Do with Toddlers and Twos,* Miller provides another fantastic resource of creative ideas for things to do with toddlers. Suggestions are fun and designed to encourage development.

Play
Catherine Garvey

An academic read about children and play. Part of the *Developing Child Series,* *Play* offers the latest findings on the relationship between various types of play and a child's social development and well being.

Opinion vs. research

A recent survey showed that what adults think about the effect of play on learning often doesn't match what researchers find to be true:

- Most parents of young children surveyed saw a connection between play and intellectual development, but 20%-30% did not.

- Play activities that researchers find less beneficial to child development, such as flash cards and computer activities, are viewed in a positive light by most parents (especially those with a high school education or less.)

- Many parents place too little emphasis on the connection between "playground play" and intellectual development.

In judging the learning benefits of play activities, adults placed reading and talking to a child at the top.

Most adults agreed that specifically playing Mozart does not have a powerful effect on the development of a child, but agree with researchers that playing music can be beneficial.

Sources: Civitas, Zero to Three, Brio.

Play stimulates curiosity and creativity.

Nothing encourages curiosity and creativity more than new and interesting environments to explore. The more a child explores and solves problems, the more she processes, and the better, more creative explorer she becomes.

Play prepares your child for school.

Many skills used in school can be learned through play. For example, singing, reading and talking introduce your child to language; while "pretend play" and problem solving help build the foundation for abstract thought.

ACTION ITEMS   Ideas for learning through play

1 Play helps children learn.

Brenda gave her six-month-old nephew, Brandon, a toy with buttons that lit up when the "on-off" switch was turned on and that played music when pushed. When Brenda pushed the buttons, Brandon listened to the music for a few seconds, but then lost interest. However, when Brenda gave him the toy to use on his own, he flicked the "on-off" switch over and over, watching the lights turn on and off as he pushed the switch. Brandon laughed as the lights went on and off. At first, Brenda encouraged him to try and push the buttons instead of the "on-off" switch, but then realized that Brandon was learning the concept of cause and effect in his own way.

2 Any situation can be an opportunity for creative play.

Kaiya, a part-time worker, often felt pangs of guilt that she could not give her two-year-old son, James, more devoted playtime. However, following a trip to the grocery store, Kaiya realized that she was giving James plenty of great opportunities for stimulation doing everyday activities. As she unpacked her groceries, she looked on the floor and found that James built a big tower out of canned soup. Kaiya made more room on the floor for James to build, and he continued happily with his construction work. Kaiya became aware of more and more chances for encouraging play in ordinary, everyday activities.

? Does play help my child become smarter?

Yes, just like other positive stimulation, play speeds cognitive development—the ability to learn—in two ways:

● **Play stimulates the brain**

The more a child plays, the more he is exposed to new things. As he absorbs these new experiences, his brain stores the new information. And healthy stimulation creates networks which are essential to understanding our world.

● **Play stimulates intellectual development**

Play is often a series of problem-solving efforts—and trial and error experiments—that help your child to learn about the world and how he can manipulate his environment.

? What type of play is best for my child's learning?

Any type of play that your child finds fun and engaging is beneficial. If your child is busy with interesting toys and games, and her interest is nurtured with encouragement and affection, then her brain will be kept busy processing information. The more information it processes, the more developed her brain's wiring becomes.

? How do I know if I am over-stimulating my baby?

Pay attention to his mood. Interesting experiences will only stimulate his brain in a positive way if he is in the mood to learn.

● If he is smiling, cooing or looking at you, he's probably interested.

● If he's pulling away or crying, he's probably had enough and will benefit more from your comfort than the stimulation.

? Why are the first three years of life important for brain development?

Most of your baby's brain cells are developed at birth, but they are not well connected. In the early years connections between cells (synapses) form rapidly. They are activated by repeated positive, nurturing experiences. To encourage the wiring process, it's important to offer your child rich opportunities to explore and discover all through his childhood starting from day one.

How does play help my child to learn?

Through play, your child's curiosity, creativity and intellectual power help him make sense of his world and learn to function successfully in it.

Stimulate your child's brain. Give her a toy and the freedom to play with it any way she wants. Play with her and follow her lead. The child who explores freely is the child who learns to imagine, invent and problem solve.

---

3 Play helps children make distinctions and recognize differences and similarities.

Two-year-old Mercedes loved her mother's hat collection. After making sure that Mercedes clearly understood that she had to be careful with the hats, her mother let her play with the collection. Sometimes Mercedes created "hat families." She sorted the hats by color and counted them. Hats allowed Mercedes to understand important concepts like counting and categorizing and to develop her creativity and imagination.

4 Play helps prepare a child's mind for school.

When three-year-old Alexa plays grocery store, she makes "pretend" lists of the items she needs on the magnetic board on the refrigerator. Then she takes her doll and pretends to walk the aisles of the store collecting the foods she needs. When she gets home from the store, she puts away her groceries in the refrigerator and checks off all the items on her list, just like her mom does. Through her pretend play, Alexa is experimenting with language in a fun and spontaneous way while also learning to recognize, recall and act out a sequence.

Opinion vs. research

Child development research shows that play is important to all aspects of a child's development, including the development of language and literacy. However, many adults do not recognize just how important it is.

In a recent survey about the importance of play in children's development, 80% of parents of children birth to six felt play was important to the development of language skills.

Of all future parents, grandparents and non-parents surveyed, only 70% thought play was important to the development of literacy.

Of parents of children ages zero to six whose income was under $30K, 70% thought it important, while 81% of parents with incomes over $50K recognized the value of play in contributing to a child's literacy.

Early vocabulary is the biggest determinant of later literacy.

Sources: Civitas, Zero to Three, BRIO.

The beginnings of literacy appear in activities such as conversations about the words on street signs or labels on favorite foods.

Crispy FLAKES

? How does my child develop literacy through play?

It is through play that your child discovers language and learns to communicate through reading and writing. **When your child sings a song, looks at pictures in a book or turns the pages in a book, she is both playing and taking important steps to literacy.** Reading, writing, talking and listening can all be encouraged through play.

Reading enhances pretend play...

Young children who are read to often introduce reading into their fantasy play. They may pretend to read books to dolls or stuffed animals, or they may incorporate written materials into their play. **Playing with story ideas can begin very early.** A two-and-a-half-year-old may act out a scene from a book or repeat a sentence.

...so does writing

From age three, children often imitate writing in their pretend play: police officers write traffic tickets, waitresses write orders. When children bring writing into their play it indicates that they recognize writing as an activity worth imitating and that **they are seeking ways to make it serve their own purposes.**

ACTION ITEMS
Avenues for enhancing literacy

1 Reading

Babies: Books are great first toys for babies. Begin with books that:
- can be propped up for a baby to look at.
- have pictures in bright contrasting colors.
- are made of cardboard or cloth to withstand a little chewing and make page turning easier.

Toddlers and pre-schoolers: Toddlers are just able to sit and listen to a complete story. Try books that:
- have repetitious text about familiar objects.
- involve activities such as counting, identifying colors, objects or letters.
- are about subjects that interest the child.
- deal with topics that relate to the child's life, such as toilet training or new siblings.
- are interactive, such as having lifting flaps.

2 Writing

Babies: Even a baby can prepare for writing. Let her:
- hold a rattle to develop grasping skills.
- play with magnetic letters.

Toddlers and pre-schoolers: To get her interested:
- give her safe writing props to incorporate into her play, like crayons, blank paper, newspaper and construction paper, thick sticks of chalk and thick magic markers.
- promote the development of her fine motor skills by letting him cut paper or trace letters.
- allow her to draw freely and creatively.

❓ How can play help my child develop literacy from the beginning?

Literacy begins with play.

It starts long before your child goes to school and masters the technical skills involved in reading and writing.

Through playful activities, such as pretend play, drawing, hearing a story and talking about its plot and characters, your child first experiments with language. **He learns what reading and writing are, and what he can do with them.** He also acquires attitudes about literacy.

For your child, every word he hears and repeats, every storybook, song and nursery rhyme become the building blocks of literacy.

Symbols used in play are bridges to literacy.

Through gestures or marks on paper, your child uses symbols to create and communicate meaning. Whether in pretend play or other activities like drawing, symbols allow her to leave her immediate environment and explore imaginary worlds.

When first experimenting with words and letters, your child may use them in the same way as symbols. Eventually she will make the connection between these play experiences and the activities of reading and writing.

Children play by pretending to read to themselves.

When he draws, pretends to read or write or invents stories, play allows your child to build his literacy skills by experimenting with pictures and symbols he has seen.

Play is a safe environment for your child to explore literacy. Because **play allows her to feel and act as if she is in control of her activity,** she can play with books and paper and pretend that she can actually read books or write stories. Therefore, through play, your child can feel like a reader or a writer before she knows how to read and write. **Such feelings can install confidence,** create positive expectations about learning to read and write and motivate a child to learn.

Give-and-take conversation and storytelling help develop literacy skills. When your child begins to learn the art of conversation and storytelling, **encourage her by asking questions, sharing stories and creating plots and characters together.**

❸ Talking

Babies:
- Talk and read with him at every opportunity.
- Sing nursery rhymes and read books that play with word sounds.

Toddlers and pre-schoolers:
- Whether at the grocery store, the park or the zoo, point out objects, signs and people.
- Engage your child in conversation and ask a lot of questions.
- Play with words by making up funny names for people and objects. Making nonsense out of language helps children appreciate the rhythm and musicality of language.
- Play rhyming games with words.

❹ Listening

Activities you can try with your child:

- A narrated version of hide-and-seek. When the child hides, the caregiver "thinks aloud" about where she could be. "Where is Laura?" a parent might say. "Maybe she's in the refrigerator—did I put her next to the milk?" Such silly discussion within earshot of the hiding child will encourage her to listen as she waits to be found.
- Singing songs. Children love to listen to songs. Try adding new words to her favorite songs to pique her interest.

Q. My child enjoys playing alone. Should I encourage her to be more social?

A. It depends. If your child prefers to play by herself, your best bet is to support and encourage her preferences. If she is shy, you may help her overcome it by having her play with other children. Keep in mind that:

- playing alone can be very healthy
- kids playing side by side seem to be playing by themselves but actually are observing and copying each other
- you can encourage her to play with others by introducing her to just one or a few additional playmates at a time

? How does play encourage the development of social skills?

By interacting with peers and playing different roles, your child learns skills such as:

- communication
- sharing
- negotiation
- cooperation
- compromise

Children do all these things when they decide on the rules of a game, or when they determine their roles in imaginary activities such as playing house or school. Involvement in social play teaches your child how to consider the feelings of others and how to be a friend.

? How does social play change over time?

Social play begins early and becomes more meaningful as your child develops. Let's use peek-a-boo as an example:

When you play peek-a-boo with a young infant, she gets a kick out of simply seeing your face. Her pleasure is in the interaction.

Several months later, the expectation of seeing your face appear and disappear is what excites your child. The pleasure is in predictable routine.

At one year old, your child will want to lead the game. The pleasure is in being in charge— the star of the show.

? When is a child too young to have playmates?

Playing with other children has benefits at any age. Even though your child probably won't start to interact directly with others until pre-school, he'll enjoy playmates at an earlier age through parallel play— watching what others do and picking up ideas.

Playing with other children is not the same as playing with adults: children relate to each other and are less predictable and controllable.

? What's the difference between a play group and a play date?

A **play group** is a group of five to ten children and parents who meet on a regular basis.

A **play date** is a good way for your toddler to develop her social play skills. There may not be much interaction at first—your child and his playmate may simply play side-by-side—and they might not meet on a regular basis. It usually works best when it's just your child and one other playmate. You should expect some frustration, but you can help by providing activities in which they can both participate, such as a sandbox or building blocks.

ACTION ITEMS

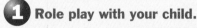
Supporting social development

1 **Role play with your child.**

When your child steps into roles, like "mom," "doctor," or "sister," she is creating scenarios that explore relationships. In addition to developing your child's imagination, role play teaches her to understand the different people in her life and lets her express care and concern for others. Therefore, if your child asks you to play a part, go along with her request—no matter how silly you feel.

2 **Encourage your child's play to evolve as she develops.**

Look for toys and games that adapt to fit and enhance your child's abilities as she develops. For example, a toddler may use the pots and pans in a kitchen play set to practice filling and emptying. As she gets older, she may take out her kitchen set at the same time her parents are preparing dinner. Also, try to "recycle" toys. Although children may lose interest quickly in a new toy, they often will "rediscover" it if you put it away for a few days.

How does play affect my child's social development?

The best way for your child to learn how to make friends and get along with others is to play with them.

Don't forget that playing alone is fine, too. If you push a child to play with other children before he's ready, you'll discourage him from interacting at all.

Through play your child learns to form meaningful relationships with other people.

Play is the vital activity that teaches a child how to communicate, share, negotiate, cooperate and compromise. Play is one of the ways your child experiences trust, friendship and love.

3 Provide your child the opportunity to play with others.

From his peers, a child gets great new ideas and learns skills for making friends and interacting with others—like communication, negotiation and compromise. Children learn to socialize and communicate by playing with their peers. From each other, they learn to share toys, take turns and cooperate. (Keep in mind that playing with other kids is not the same as playing with adults since kids relate differently to each other and are less predictable.)

4 Allow your child to play with friends and siblings of any age.

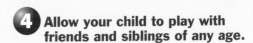

A younger child will view an older one as a role model, while the older child may use the younger to practice caretaking. While children usually do not interact directly until pre-school, they can enjoy playmates at an even earlier age. By playing side-by-side, they can watch each other and learn new ideas. Children learn essential social skills by playing together—by taking turns, deciding on rules and bargaining for roles.

113

Fantasy helps your child understand reality.

This type of play is complex intellectual activity in which children try to grasp the rules of real life through imagination and abstract thought. When your child plays "fireman," or "school," or "work," he is putting on a theatrical play in which he's the playwright, actor, director and set designer. As he steps in and out of each role and responds to the roles of others, he learns to adapt to different situations and relate to other people in his life, such as family, teachers or his friends.

? What are the stages of fantasy play?

From ages **1** to **2**	From ages **2** to **3**	As your child grows and develops, her	By age **3**
your child is making the transition from imitative play to imaginative (or fantasy, or pretend) play.	play themes expand, so that a young two-year-old's fantasy play will be mainly about routine daily activities. Your child will mostly play at eating, cooking and driving a car.	outside experiences will grow too, and you'll see this in her imaginary play style. Play themes increase as her life experiences increase. Going to more places and meeting new people allow her to find more play themes.	your child's pretend play will include more themes and more language. As she increases her verbal skills, she'll be directing the action, using dialogue and discussing details of the "play" she's creating.

? Why do children make up imaginary friends?

It's probably a sign that the child is devising a creative way to deal with being alone. These imaginary friends often have names and personalities; they can be a comfort if your child is afraid of the dark, and they might even be a substitute for the child himself in cases where he normally might not be able to express his feeling—for instance, if he was angry. You can listen to your child talking to her imaginary friends to find out what conflicts she may be having. There is no harm in playing along with your child's imagination, but don't let an imaginary friend be an excuse for bad behavior. Your child will most likely say goodbye to her imaginary friends by the time she is five or six. The only cause for worry would be if your child had difficulty making friends with other children and was relying too heavily on the imaginary friends.

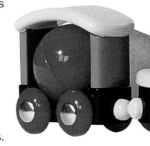

ACTION ITEMS

Play helps emotional development

1 Play helps children feel in control of their environment.

Sandra, age three, pulls her favorite yellow shirt out of the dirty clothes to wear to her friend Maya's birthday party. Her mother tells her that she can't wear it "because it's dirty." Upset by the lack of control she has over her clothes, Sandra starts to cry. Later that afternoon, as she plays with her dolls, she re-enacts the earlier scene with her mother and dresses her dolls any way she wants. Having so many decisions made for her is frustrating for Sandra, as it is for most children. Through play, Sandra can act out her frustrations, gain a sense of control over her environment and express herself.

2 Play helps children handle grief.

When Sylvie was two-and-a-half, her grandfather died. A few months later, her parents noticed that her play, whether with dolls, blocks or cars, involved dying or going to funerals. At first, they were alarmed, wondering, "Why is she acting this way?" But then they realized that Sylvie also had been asking a lot of questions about her grandfather's death. Her play was nothing more than her attempt to understand what her mom had told her about the death and to experience it in her own way.

It's important to provide the time and the space for fantasy play.

Creative thought during problem-solving activities often follows a period of dramatic play. Both teachers and parents need to give children the freedom and space to play and to make the mistakes from which they will learn. Your child's physical environment can stimulate his play; research shows that children who look around the playroom for cues are using creative problem-solving methods. So, making an environment that provides novelty and variety will increase creativity.

How does play affect my child's emotional development?

Play allows your child to express his feelings and develop empathy, to learn how to cope with difficult situations and to shape his emerging identity.

Creative play goes a long way to nurture your child's emotional health by making what he does his own, providing him with new ideas and problem solving techniques and helping him celebrate his uniqueness.

Source: Your Child at Play, Marilyn Segal.

3 Fantasy play teaches children to understand and care about others.

Three-year-old Maria spends hours playing make-believe. She uses the people and objects around her to create imaginary places and imaginary friends. Maria especially enjoys playing caretaker for a pretend baby. She rocks her, sings to her, changes her diaper and kisses her to make her "all better" when she cries. Maria's fantasy play not only helps to develop her creativity and imagination, but also lets her express care and concern for others.

4 Pretend play allows children to step into different roles.

Glenna, age two, plays mommy with her doll, Frizzie, giving her a bath by putting Frizzie in a shoebox and rubbing her body with a washcloth and warning her, "Close your eyes, Frizzie, here comes the water." After washing her hair, she tells Frizzie that it's time to get ready for bed. Glenna dries her off, and then puts on her pajamas. She reads Frizzie a story, gives her a kiss and says "Good night Frizzie, I love you." Reversing roles and doing with her doll everything her mother does with her helps Glenna understand, among other things, her mom's role in her life.

115

SUPPLIES FOR ART AND MUSIC

ART

Crayons
Markers
Water color paint
Tempera paint
Acrylic and finger paints
Sidewalk chalk
Play-Doh
Modeling clay
Ceramic clay
Glue
Safety scissors
Old magazines
Wood pieces
Craft sticks
Scraps of material
Yarn
Beads
Glitter
Construction paper
Pipe cleaners
Sewing supplies
Feathers

MUSIC

Drums
Cymbals
Rattles
Tambourines
Bells
Chimes
Flutes
Recorders
String instruments
Horns
Toy trumpets
Toy accordians
Toy kazoos
Piano (if possible)
Tape/CD player
Tapes
Compact discs

Art and music can help your child recover from a traumatic experience.

How can art help your child heal?

- **By helping your child express hidden feelings and thoughts.**
Art therapy is a recognized field within psychology. Visual arts often reveal emotional issues that are too difficult for a child to put into words.

- **By helping professionals diagnose and assess childhood problems.**
Most therapists recognize that a child's drawings can be revealing, and will often ask him to draw himself or his family doing something together. A child who has been traumatized will often show some kind of impairment in the drawing.

- **By helping your child relax while she is addressing stressful situations.**
Your child might have an easier time discussing a difficult situation if she creates art while talking. She can channel some of her nervousness about the subject into the physical activity of the art and avoid some of the distress of dealing directly with the problem.

- **By being a useful form of communication for children with developmental delays or disabilities.**
Children with developmental delays or with ADHD often focus better on pictures than words. The visual arts provide another means for them to communicate through symbols as well as speech or writing. Some children will easily draw a picture of a concept or feeling they are trying to express. Others, who are less able or too inhibited to draw, may still prefer to talk about a picture of a sad face that you have drawn than answer a direct question about being sad.

- **By helping your child develop expressive new skills using a variety of art mediums.**
The healing uses of artistic creation are endless since children are generally curious, naturally creative and unrestricted by the self-criticism that often hinders adults. Sculpting, doll- and jewelry-making, collages and body art encourage self-expression especially in a child who is overly constricted.

- **By helping your child develop trusting and cooperative relationships.**
Visual art projects can serve to build confidence and faith in relationships, especially if you use the artwork to broaden communication with your child. Art is not only a healing tool for stressed children, it also provides a good way for all children to explore, create and learn by creating the art together.

ACTION ITEMS

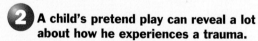

Help your child heal through play

1 **Play can help build attachments and trust** between a child and a caregiver. Look for games that encourage children to take increased risks toward depending on others or games that give children a chance to depend on you in ways that they could not depend on previous caretakers. For example, you can toss a sponge ball back and forth while talking, color the same picture together or do a painting where both you and the child have paints and brushes and the child directs the creation of the painting.

2 **A child's pretend play can reveal a lot about how he experiences a trauma.** Pay close attention to the scenarios a child acts out with stuffed animals or dolls. If they include troublesome themes, are repetitive or never get resolved they may indicate trauma.

3 **When a child engages in constructive play,** which involves building or fitting pieces together, it helps her to restore a sense of order and control about her world. Constructive play increases confidence in her cognitive and motor skills, and the healing power of this type of play is greatly enhanced when a caring adult participates.

? How can music help your child heal?

- **By transforming moods and calming or stimulating impulses.**
Children are greatly attracted to and emotionally affected by music. Your baby can be positively affected by music even while still in the womb.

- **By helping your child express hidden feelings and thoughts.**
Because music engages the intuitive and sensory, rather than the analytical, it reaches beyond cognitive reasoning and stimulates emotion. A child's choice of music might therefore help a parent to understand how her child is feeling. As with art, your child is naturally less self-conscious at this time, and should be encouraged to create her own melodies and sounds.

- **By enhancing self-confidence and trust.**
Music has a powerful effect on groups as well as individuals. A musical creation shared with others can enhance its healing quality by helping to build relationships. Any non-judgmental person who loves music can be a positive musical companion to a child.

- **By releasing pent-up energy.**
Encouraging children to bang on drums, blow on horns, strum on minature guitars, shake rattles and make up songs is a constructive and creative outlet for stored energy that might otherwise be expressed through aggression or destruction. Music also stimulates movement to channel the jitters children get when sitting still in a classroom or assembly. Some music, with movement, allows for release and free expression, while other music encourages a child to sit down and focus.

- **By helping a traumatized child find emotion and voice.**
Sometimes traumatic events can numb a child. Music can provide a safe forum for the trapped emotions. Singing can allow a frightened child to regain his voice and express the despair—even rage—he felt when he was traumatized, but was unable to do anything about it at the time.

The music of nature is healing to children.

With the modern technology of music, we often forget to expose our children to the sounds of nature. The earth, the seas—and all the creatures in them—provide lovely music that teaches and heals children. The gurgle of a brook or the chirping of a bird can soothe and focus a child.

Finally, introduce your child to the peaceful sound of stillness.

How does play help in healing?

Play helps a child work on developmental issues, counter the loneliness of trauma, deal with strong emotions and regain a sense of order and control.

Play helps a child build trust and regain confidence and self-esteem. It can also provide a way for adults to understand a child's feelings and needs.

Source: Laura Sanders, University of Michigan School of Social Work.

---

4 **If managed properly, aggressive play can provide a healthy outlet for angry emotions.** By creatively channeling a child's aggression with play, you allow him to express his feelings as well as learn new, more suitable communication skills. An aggressive child should also be encouraged to explore gentle, orderly play such as puzzles or board games. You can help an aggressive child by giving him toys that give him an outlet for aggressive energy like a kick ball or a punching bag. Pretend play, such as acting like angry, roaring lions, is another good outlet for aggression.

5 **Play can help a child learn to contain, as well as express, emotion.** Certain toys and games, like action figures and martial arts, are ideal for helping children experience and release emotions. Others are suited for teaching a child to control emotion. For example, a simple game of checkers will move him away from strong emotion and into the present. This type of game, which involves a child's growing intellectual capacities, encourages him to focus on an appropriate developmental task.

The power of peers: A boy named Jeremy led a revolution at childcare. At the ripe old age of two, he declared himself ready for big-boy pants. The motivation? The large, brightly colored Superman insignia on the seat of said pants. Within the week, big-girl and big-boy pants were all the rage in the toddler room at Joy McCormack's All-Day Nursery in Manhattan. Following Jeremy's lead, these ten pint-size kids came to the collective conclusion that wearing diapers was nothing short of humiliating, while using the potty was a sign of emerging maturity—the ultimate hipness. Every one of them had occasional accidents, but most were fully toilet trained within the month, a feat that awed parents and teachers alike.

Scientific research shows that generally, a 15 month old child is too young to be expected to share his toys. In a recent survey, however, 50%-60% of adults believe that a 15 month old should be expected to share. In terms of sharing, it seems that many parents and grandparents expect too much of young children.

A play date among two-year-olds might resemble a barroom brawl, but their squabbling is actually a lesson in human relations. Between 18 and 24 months most children enjoy company and have started to experiment with language. However, there may not be much togetherness in playing together at this age.

A typical play date at this age is apt to include some interaction, some parallel play (both children entertaining themselves separately), and probably some frustration.

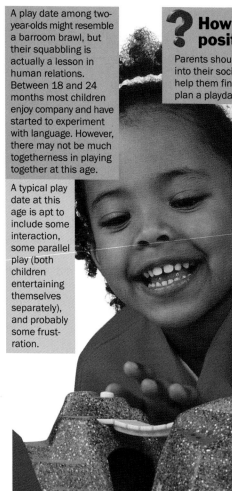

? How can I create a positive play date?

Parents should be patient while children ease into their social circle. Frequent playdates can help them fine-tune their social skills. When you plan a playdate, consider these points:

Keep it simple. Toddlers do best when playing one-on-one.

Find a good match. A shy child may be easily overwhelmed by a boisterous playmate.

Consider inviting an older child from time to time. A three- or four-year-old may be able to accommodate a younger one's outbursts and demands without himself lashing out. A preschooler can also set a constructive example.

Get the timing right. Plan your playdates for first thing in the morning, or after a nap.

Encourage sharing. To ensure fewer fights, set out large items (perhaps a sandbox), identical or ample quantities of toys (several balls, or sandbox buckets and shovels), or multipart sets.

Know when to stop. Be flexible about how much time you expect the children to play together. When your child or her guest shows signs of social wear, it's probably time to stop.

? Why is it so hard for a 1-year-old to share?

Because it's your child's territory that the new toddler is invading. Your child must share his toys, his home, and you. But don't get angry at his behavior or pressure him. This will make him more upset because his feelings are upsetting you. Structure the situation so that he continues to feel special to you, while you can still meet the other child's needs.

ACTION ITEMS

Tips for teaching sharing

1 **Read books about sharing to the group.** Children learn a lot about how to behave from characters in a story, and they often like to mimic the characters' actions.

2 **Offer praise and positive reinforcement to children when they share a toy with another child.** Let them know that their willingness to share made another person happy. Recognize all the different forms of sharing, including letting another child use a toy, giving another child a piece of candy or a cookie or inviting another child to participate in play.

3 **Make sharing seem fun.** Since children learn from example, make a point to share with the children and other adults. Bring objects of your own from home to pass around to the group. Talk about sharing with a positive, enthusiastic attitude.

? Do children learn from their peers?

Yes, and so much so that some nursery schools have a formal peer-learning approach in which children are put into groups to help each other learn. The idea is that one child can explain things to another in a language that is more effective and direct than that of an adult.

? How do I know if my child is ready to share?

Children will not start sharing unless they feel a need to do so. Your son may not want to share a beloved toy, but when he wants to play with anothers', he will quickly learn the virtues of parting temporarily with his favorite things.

Some rules to play by.

Which toys? Let your child decide which toys she is willing to let others play with. Put the rest away.

Take turns. At three, your child knows that when he shares a toy, he'll get it back. Until then, taking turns with toys will help him to understand this. Keep the turn-taking to a minute.

Suggest the guest brings a toy of his own. Your child may be more willing to share his precious toy if his guest does so, too.

Take a break. If things don't go well, ask each child to pick out a book for you to read aloud, or try fixing a snack together.

When it's over, talk about it. If your child would not share something, ask how he would feel if his guest had behaved like that. Then discuss how it might be better next time.

How can I help my child learn to play with his peers?

Introduce the concept of playing with other children early on and consistently reinforce it. It is integral to living successfully with other people.

A very young child learns a lot just by being around other children. As he gets older, play dates and play groups can help him learn social skills and ways to get along with other kids.

4 Encourage children to work together and cooperate. Have children pair up and paint or draw a picture together or build a tower together out of blocks. When they are finished, ask them to share whatever it is that they have made together.

5 Provide play opportunities to share. Have children bring a favorite toy from home and take turns with each toy, so everyone gets a chance to play with each one. Or, have play activities that involve a limited number of toys so that the children have to wait their turn to use them. Make sure that the children take turns going first so that everybody gets a chance at it.

6 Don't force children to share or reprimand them if they have not done so. If young children are forced to share, they will be less likely to do so voluntarily. Therefore, give children the opportunity to share or give to another child, but do not demand it.

For more on play groups:

www.onlineplaygroup.com

www.playdateconnection.com

What about computers?

While many parents think computers are valuable to young children, experts agree that early computer use, especially when paired with regular TV watching, may undermine the development of skills children need to succeed.

THE DOWNSIDE

Early use may

- stifle creativity and imagination,
- shorten attention spans,
- curb perseverance,
- distance and distract from social interaction, and
- decrease motivation.

Two-dimension play is not as good as three-dimension.

Poor quality software may do more harm than good.

THE UPSIDE

In a nine-month study, 4-5 year old children exposed to high-quality developmental software showed significant gains in intelligence, nonverbal communication skills, long-term memory, and self esteem.

Computers have helped children in low-income families, geographically isolated children and children with learning disabilities to find alternative forms of learning letters, writing, and organizing their work.

Remember that there is no "right way" to play.

When a child plays, he is exploring, experimenting, practicing and learning. Every child will play differently, based on his own changing developmental needs.

? What toys will hold a child's interest over the years?

Simple open-ended toys have the longest life. A set of wooden blocks is a toy that keeps a growing child's interest in different ways. It can also survive wear and tear.

Infants will touch the blocks, bang them to make noise, and put them in their mouths.

Toddlers often line up blocks by shape or color.

3-year olds can incorporate them into make believe play. Simply ask them to build you a castle, a schoolhouse or a zoo!

? How are toys labeled by age?

Toymakers follow the age grading guidelines of the Consumer Product Safety Commission, which has four main criteria:

- the ability of a child to physically manipulate and play with the features of a toy
- the ability of a child to understand how to use a toy
- the child's play needs and interest at different developmental levels
- the safety aspects of the toy itself

Don't be tempted to buy a toy labeled for an older child. Remember that the age label has been thoughtfully assigned based on many factors, including safety. If you give a child a toy that is too simple or too advanced, she may be frustrated and/or exposed to a safety hazard. **Remember: the purpose of toys is to have fun.**

? What toys are best for a child in a wheelchair?

(Of course, this will depend on preferences and personality, as well as a child's particular disability.)

those that are:

- adaptable and flexible in how you can set them up, so she can reach and control the toy
- multi-sensory, such as stuffed animals, since certain senses may be less responsive than others
- suitable to his muscle tone and strength so that he is able to use and manipulate the toy on his own

To make a wheelchair feel less restrictive, look for toys that will be fun to play with on a tray and will allow other children to play with her.

ACTION ITEMS
Tips for choosing quality toys

1 Safety first

Toys should be age appropriate to match a child's developmental level and should not contain unsafe, toxic or flammable materials, sharp corners, or small detachable parts. They should also be easy to clean.

2 Durability

What is the toy made of? In order to survive the wear and tear of a child's repeated handling, it must be made of sturdy, reliable materials.

3 Easy to use

A child must be able to operate the toy by himself in order for him to enjoy it. Therefore, pick out toys that fit and enhance a child's level of development and ability. When selecting toys for a child with physical disabilities, make sure they require only simple motions to activate and can be played with while in a number of positions (sitting, side-lying). Also, as a general rule, simpler toys are more likely to do what they are supposed to do.

physical and emotional development. Experts point to a variety of interactions that form the basis of early relationships; they include feeding, playing, talking and bedtime routines. **Through the progression of attachment shown here,** you and your child will form a trusting relationship, and your child will be allowed to move from dependence to self-assertion, confidence and the abililty to function independently in her world.

6 months → 12-15 months	12-15 months → 36 months
● sitting up and crawling—she can move away from and towards you.	● learning to walk. He is curious and actively explores his world.
● developing object permanence— she can find a hidden toy and knows that you exist even when she can't see you.	● capable of symbolic thought or pretend play.
● showing growing attachment to her primary caregiver with dis-pleasure when she leaves, and relief and pleasure when she returns.	
● providing a safe and loving environment that she can explore.	● emotionally available to your child.
● comforting her when she is stressed.	● setting limits and allowing your child to explore his world, his autonomy and his emotions.
● A meaningful relationship has formed between you and your child. Your child knows what to expect from you based on prior experiences. She also begins to become aware of her own behaviors and abilities.	● Although excited by his exploration and autonomy, your toddler will also become overwhelmed and scared and will need to rely on you for comfort— he will often move away but then come back to the safety of being with you.
● Your child often looks to her primary caregiver, usually her mother, for a sense of safety and security. She uses this person as a secure base, a trusted figure who provides comfort and love.	● Tantrums and power struggles may ensue as your toddler learns to use his own will.
● Armed with trust and the confidence of a secure base, your child can explore her world and risk the bumps she encounters along the way.	● As you set limits and demonstrate that you will continue to love and care for your child, he will learn self-control and understand that he can "fall apart" and still survive and be loved.

Building a healthy relationship through sensitive and responsive care— with an emotional investment— allows your child to feel safe and secure, provides him with a solid base for exploration and allows him to communicate his feelings.

Source: Fran Stott, PhD.

6 Take things slowly. When you are getting ready to go back to work after being with your child at home, it is a good idea to have a transition time with the new caregiver, your child and yourself. This gives everyone an opportunity to get acquainted and become comfortable with the new situation.

7 Arrange same-time departures. To make saying goodbye easier, try having your child exit first. When you drop her off at the nursery, have the caregiver take her outside to play. Be sure to wave bye-bye to her as she is leaving you.

8 Employ favorite pastimes. You might also like to have your child care provider involve your child in a favorite pastime. He may get upset when she sees you are leaving; however, it will be much easier for him to get re-involved in something he is already working on.

9 Help her learn to deal with separation. Eventually your child will learn how to cope and understand that she must be separated from you sometimes. This may take some time, but she must learn this important developmental task. She will use it for the rest of her life.

? Why is she scared of water, or dogs?

Sometimes children develop fears of tangible things such as the water or dogs. Your child may not have had a bad experience with either of these, but it won't help if you try to make her overcome her fear by forcing her to confront them, or the tangible objects of any fears she may have. There is a good chance that insisting she come into the pool with you, or making her move towards a dog will have bad results. She will probably outgrow her fears by herself in time.

? Why does my baby fear the dark?

Fear of the dark is one of the most common childhood fears. It's also a fear that adults can easily understand and identify with: most of us are not as confident in the dark. Not being able to see clearly acts on the imagination and leads many people to imagine that they are being followed. If your little boy is scared of the dark, leave his bedroom door open or leave a nightlight on. Keeping him well-occupied with games and other activities during the day will stop him from brooding over any fears. Eventually, he will realize that there is nothing to fear.

? How can I help my child get over her fear of the mall?

Your daughter's meltdown in the mall is her way of telling you that she's being overwhelmed by the crowds, the noise, the bright lights and even the smell of the place. In time she'll be able to tell you that she needs to leave. Until then, be aware that visiting the mall is no fun for her. You however, need to go shopping, so **try building up to the visits gradually.** Take her when it is quiet and less intimidating. Start with a ten-minute trip. Let your child's reactions be your guide. If loud music from the music store worries her, avoid that part of the mall. Remember, even the calmest adult can be put off by the flashier aspects of some malls. And **go after your daughter's nap,** so she is well-rested.

? Why has the once-beloved family dog become an enemy?

Remember that **your child's early fearlessness stems from the fact that ignorance is bliss**—what she does not know cannot hurt her. That's why she used to put her hand into your dog's mouth, but now runs screaming when he comes near. As your child grows, she learns that dogs can bite. Her **curiosity and imagination** are developing together, and she can make connections between her actions and their possible consequences.

ACTION ITEMS
Helping your child deal with fears

1. **Don't push too hard.** Follow your child's lead when he is ready to branch out and explore things on his own. If you push him too soon, for example, pressuring him to go down the slide at the playground when he's afraid to do so, he will not only feel badly about himself, but it can cause him to be afraid of you, as well.

2. **Acknowledge her fears.** Your child needs to know that you understand that she is fearful and that you will be there to protect her. For instance, say "I am not leaving you, Sara, I am just going in the other room for a minute, and I will be right back."

3. **Discuss them.** It is very important to talk about your child's fear when he is calm. This enhances his ability to be less afraid when a similar situation comes up again.

4. **Provide comfort objects.** You could always allow a favorite toy or blanket to be carried along for reassurance for your child when facing a fearful situation.

5. **Give pep talks.** It is a good idea to prep your child when she is about to be put in a situation that could potentially scare her. Discuss what is going to happen. For example: If you are taking your child to a new class, tell her that she will get to see many of her old friends and get to meet new ones.

? How can I help him get over his fear of bugs?

Resist the temptation to lecture your son about the wonderful world of insects. Acknowledge his fear, and remember that a two-year-old is too young to be told to "face it"—it's perfectly natural for him to be scared of many things at this age. You don't want to turn his fear into a lifelong aversion. Eventually, most children get over this fear and become fascinated by creepy crawly things.

? Are movies too scary?

Until the age of seven, most children find it difficult to separate fiction and reality because of their overactive imaginations. So when the wicked witch sends your child into floods of tears, take her home. Better yet, don't bring her to a scary movie until she is ready.

Never ridicule your child's fear, for it is very real to her. Encourage her to talk about it. Give her the confidence that nothing bad is going to happen to her and that you are right there beside her.

But do not overdo the sympathy; she may get the message that her fears are justified.

? What about fear of death?

Don't be surprised if a child can't understand what happens when a pet or a person dies. Try to be casual about it, while reassuring her that she will be around for years and years to come. The first thing to do is tell the truth. If your child knows the person who died, seeing your sadness will help her cope in the long run.

? What do young children fear most?

The things most small children are afraid of are:

  animals
  insects
  the dark
  water
  imaginary monsters
  school
  doctors and
  strangers.

The good news is that all of these anxieties are completely normal for toddlers and will almost certainly fade as they mature and gain more control over their feelings.

Sources: BabyCenter.com, indiaparenting.com.

6 **Go step by step.** Don't expect your child to naturally accept changes without an adjustment stage. Transitions are not easy for children and need to be taken one step at a time.

7 **Offer praise.** Let your child know that you are happy with his accomplishments. Do not ever tease or make fun of your child's fears.

8 **Tell or read stories.** Tall tales seem to take the fear out of certain situations. Try telling a story about an imaginary fairy protecting her from bad dreams or reading books like *Where the Wild Things Are.*

9 **Be an example.** Do not allow your child to see you jump at every little "boo." Your child can pick up on your fear very easily. Also, do not say, "You are safe now, I am here." This only reinforces his fear by confirming there was something to fear.

10 **Ease bedtime fears.** If your toddler worries that monsters are hiding under the bed, assure her that you'll keep those nighttime nasties away. Make his room as cozy and comfortable as possible. Get a cheerful nightlight. Post a sign on the closet door that says "No monsters allowed!" and don't expose her to scary TV shows or movies.

127

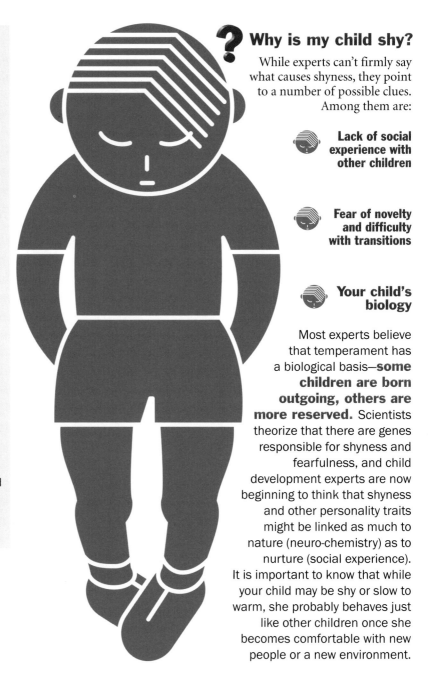

❓ Why is my child shy?

While experts can't firmly say what causes shyness, they point to a number of possible clues. Among them are:

Lack of social experience with other children

Fear of novelty and difficulty with transitions

Your child's biology

Most experts believe that temperament has a biological basis—**some children are born outgoing, others are more reserved.** Scientists theorize that there are genes responsible for shyness and fearfulness, and child development experts are now beginning to think that shyness and other personality traits might be linked as much to nature (neuro-chemistry) as to nurture (social experience). It is important to know that while your child may be shy or slow to warm, she probably behaves just like other children once she becomes comfortable with new people or a new environment.

ACTION ITEMS — Supporting a shy child

Things to do

1 Be sympathetic. Your child needs reassurance from you to let him know that you understand what he is feeling. Say something like "It's not easy to speak when the other kids are being so loud, is it?"

2 Give frequent encouragement. Be sure to let your child know that you are pleased when she offers the slightest indication of willingness to get to know others. For example, say "I think Grandpa is so happy that you said 'hi' to him."

3 Get involved in small group activities. Small group activities will not overwhelm your child as much as large gatherings. Eventually you will be able to introduce him to activities that provide opportunities to meet more children.

4 Respect her feelings. When she is adamantly refusing to interact, respect that.

What are some different types of shyness?

 Slow-to-warm toddlers take their time and watch carefully before venturing out. They tend to adapt slowly to change and withdraw under stress.

 Fearful toddlers are naturally shy. Sometimes this shyness can transform into a pervasive fear of new situations and unfamiliar people.

Shyness can turn into aggression under circumstances such as enduring physical or emotional abuse, witnessing violence or being overwhelmed by stimulation, including parental demands that are difficult to meet.

How can parents help a child cope with shyness?

Parents need to strike a careful balance between protecting their child from overwhelming stimulation and becoming overprotective.

 Perhaps the most useful formula in helping a shy toddler tackle new situations is to take one step at a time.

 For the slow-to-warm child, you should encourage and remind him that he usually enjoys himself after he gets used to a new situation.

 When your child shows excessive withdrawal or too many fears, you should look for specific sources of stress in his life.

What can I do to help my child in new situations?

Do not send her to a new situation alone. Go with her and draw her in. Stay near until her mood changes from caution to enjoyment.

If she calls you, modulate your response to match the intensity of her needs. A simple wave lets her know you are available.

Start a conversation with a child who seems like a compatible partner for her.

What makes some children shy?

Shyness involves anxiety and behavioral inhibition in social situations, usually novel ones or instances where the child feels conspicuous or that he is being judged. Shyness may be partly genetic or caused by the absence of a solid parental bond, poor acquisition of social skills or teasing and criticizing. Shyness, or being slow to warm, may also mean that your child is more thoughtful and sensitive.

Sources: BabyCenter.com; The Emotional Life of a Toddler, Alicia Lieberman, PhD.

5 **Help interpret your child's shyness.** If your child appears shy when she meets someone new, say "She'll be shy at first, but soon she'll warm up and be your friend."

6 **Stay away from labels.** Labeling a child as "shy" can stick. Instead, think about your child liking to take her time when entering a new situation.

7 **Avoid criticism.** Negative comments undermine a child's self-esteem and can cause him to retreat and isolate himself from social situations.

8 **Don't pressure.** You can make suggestions without making your child feel pressured to do something she is not ready to do. Be patient.

What are the causes of anger and aggression?

A child's special needs

If your child has hearing, visual, neurological or intellectual problems that she cannot explain to you, she may become frustrated at your lack of understanding and become angry and aggressive.

Parents who take sides

When one parent takes a child's side against the other parent, it gives the child more power. Parents must work together as a team, ensuring consistent rules of behavior, otherwise the child may become aggressive.

Playing too roughly

Seemingly innocent rough play and teasing can become an invitation for your child to imitate such behavior when he's not playing. For him, hitting and touching could become the automatic way to interact with other people, because he does not understand that he is being aggressive. If you think this is happening, make your rough-housing less aggressive.

Exposure

Children's TV programs and video games sometimes involve just as much aggression as adult ones. Research shows that children often model what they see.

Being a victim

Children who have been treated aggressively may imitate that behavior. However, it's wrong to think that every aggressive child has been abused.

Hidden inner anger

A child might have inner anger because she does not understand something that went wrong in her life. A child who was neglected as an infant, who was involved in divorce arguments, or whose parents have serious medical problems, might be acting out an unconscious inner frustration.

Poor attachments

Children who have had poor attachments early in life, such as chronically unresponsive care, tend to show aggression.

It's natural for new parents to want their child to be comfortable with her feelings and to be able to express those feelings appropriately. But the violent expression of anger is not acceptable. **Understanding the many causes of anger and aggression will help you and your child deal with aggression.**

ACTION ITEMS Tips for controlling aggression

1 **Be reasonable.** If your child is playing a game with other children, and starts throwing the pieces at the others, take him out of the game. Take this opportunity to explain why you removed him, and explain that he may rejoin the group when he can play without throwing things. Expressing your anger in a similar manner will only encourage outbursts in the future.

2 **Be consistent in discipline.** It is very important to stick to the same discipline for each episode. This way, patterns will be established and your child will begin to understand what behavior is and is not acceptable.

3 **Set boundaries.** Responding immediately and consistently when aggression is shown will teach your child that she has done something wrong. For example, you might simply take her out of the action for a few minutes to allow her to realize that when she has done something wrong, she will be penalized for it.

4 **Provide options.** Once your child has settled down, talk with him about what happened. Explain that it is okay to have angry feelings but they must be expressed in a non violent way, such as kicking a ball or talking to an adult. Also, be sure to emphasize the need for apologies.

❓ Why all this hair-pulling, biting, pinching, hitting, kicking...?

Hair-pulling and other aggressive behavior is a way for your child to express himself, and to feel that he's in control of his environment.

According to Mark W. Roberts, a professor of clinical psychology at Idaho State University, there are three reasons for this behavior:

1 **To get a reaction.**
A toddler, aged 12–18 months, quickly learns that pulling hair causes screams. For him, this attention and reaction is fun.

2 **To stop a bad thing from happening.**
When a friend takes a toy away from a toddler, she knows that grabbing, hitting or pulling hair will stop the action.

3 **To exert control.**
If a boy and girl toddler are playing together and he takes a toy that she wants, she may display aggressive behavior as a way to correct what happened.

What makes children angry and aggressive?

Anger is the most difficult emotion for young children to handle; they cannot distinguish feelings from actions, so when they are upset, they bite, hit, kick, throw things or scream. Aggressive behavior is a normal part of your toddler's development. Emerging language skills, a desire to become independent and undeveloped impulse control make toddlers prime candidates for getting physical.

Sources: BabyCenter.com, indiaparenting.com.

5 **Offer praise.** When your child is visibly controlling his temper in front of others, acknowledge it. For example: She asks for a turn playing with a truck and patiently waits for the other child to give it to her. Tell her, "That was so wonderful of you to wait your turn!"

6 **Monitor television shows.** Many TV shows and cartoons have violent and aggressive content. Be aware of what your child is watching and limit these types of shows. If you do allow him to watch a more aggressive show, discuss with him your views and tell him why you do not agree with that type of behavior.

7 **Provide sufficient playtime.** Your child needs time to burn off all of the energy that has been building or she will constantly be getting into trouble at home. Scheduling some time for physical activity will work wonders.

8 **Talk about it.** Even if your child does not have many verbal skills, it's important to show him that talking is a better way to solve problems than hitting or pulling hair.

This is the time of the terrible twos (and threes). It's when your child is gaining independence and is trying to become his own person. There'll be lots of tantrums and refusals—those endless

NOs.

And there will be other characteristics you can expect to encounter in your child's search for herself. They include:

Impatience
She wants what she wants NOW.

Hitting, biting, kicking
Physically lashing out is a means of communicating for your child at this age when he is frustrated or angry.

Mood swings
Your child is developing emotional balance at this age. Sharp mood swings are inevitable and predictable.

A need for routine
Routine is a kind of security for a toddler who's going through emotional development. Her need for daily routine helps her to know what to expect. There will be some days when this isn't possible, so expect difficulties with your child on those days. If you take her grocery shopping during her naptime, you are setting up the possibility of a tantrum.

the terrible twos

? Why does he have so many tantrums?

A temper tantrum is the emotional equivalent of a summer storm— sudden and sometimes fierce. One minute you and your child are in a restaurant enjoying dinner, the next he's a whining monster screaming to go home. **Some of the problem may be attributed to developing language skills.** "Toddlers are beginning to understand a lot more of the words they hear, yet their ability to produce language is so limited," says Claire B. Kopp, a professor of applied development psychology. As a result, **frustration builds when your child can't express how he feels.**

ACTION ITEMS
Tips for taming tantrums

When your child throws a tantrum

1 Don't lose your temper. When your child has a tantrum or fit, it is important for you to control your temper. If you start shouting back at him, you will only add fuel to the fire. It is also important that you do not leave the room angry because this will lead to feelings of abandonment. Instead, try to just sit and wait it out.

2 Remember you are the one in control. Never forget that! You are the adult so do not give into unreasonable demands, even if you are in public. If you do, your child will come to realize that if she wants something, you will give in if she has a tantrum.

3 Discuss the issue. Once your child has calmed down, it may help to discuss why the outburst occurred and what he was feeling. Remember to give him a big hug to let him know that you love him no matter what.

4 Circumvent problem-causing situations. If you see a problem on the horizon, try to get around it before your child gets upset. So, if your child throws a fit when she gets hungry, remember to carry snacks with you.

5 Leave him alone. Make sure he is in a safe place and back away. Giving him space may help calm him. Then, you can go back and give him some comfort.

132

? Why does she whine?

Children are pragmatists. By the time they reach two, most realize that increasingly higher-pitched demands for cookies while you're at the checkout will force you to open the new box. At this age, **most children get frustrated.** They are not intentionally trying to be annoying, they **are just doing what they know brings results.** It is crucial to help them learn different ways to express themselves, because the more you respond to whines, the more they'll think that it's an effective way to rule their world.

TIP Before you label it, **make sure that your child understands what you mean by whining.** Point it out to him when you hear it and ask him to use a different tone of voice. Some experts suggest recording both the whine and normal conversation, so a child can hear the difference himself.

? Why does he say "no" all the time?

The simple answer is that a child says "no" **because he can.** It has to do with the **will,** suggests Susanne Denham, a professor of developmental psychology, "[Children] have just found out that they have a will, and they want to exercise it." The "no" phase can appear suddenly, leaving you perplexed about your child's show of defiance. While this phase will run its course eventually, it may make you want to go running out of the house screaming "no" yourself.

But safety concerns are not the only reason to be firm. "A toddler has a will, but he can't always be exerting it all over the place," says Professor Denham, "It's just too messy." Sometimes you should pull rank on your rebellious child and say, "You cannot do that because I'm the mommy, that's why."

? What are tantrums and refusals?

Tantrums among toddlers are most often meltdowns in response to frustration. They are not usually deliberately manipulative.

Refusals reflect your child's fascination with the word "no," the discovery that she can say it and her first efforts to become an independent little person.

Both are normal, age-appropriate behaviors for toddlers.

Source: BabyCenter.com.

Watch for signs of stress ...

Although daily tantrums are a perfectly normal part of mid-toddler years, you do need to keep an open mind about possible problems brewing. Has there been an upheaval in the family? An extremely busy period? Tension between mom and dad? Any of these can provoke tantrums.

you may need to try this

If your child is older than 30 months and is still having major tantrums every day, talk to your pediatrician. If he is younger than that but has three or four tantrums a day and isn't cooperating with any routines such as getting dressed or picking up toys, you may also want to seek help.

Tips for dealing with refusals

When he just keeps saying, "no"

1 Offer options. Believe it or not, this is the best way to avoid an immediate no from your child. Ask, "Do you want water or juice?", "Do you want to wear your blue shirt or your green shirt?", etc.

2 Teach alternatives. Turn the response of "no" into a learning experience or set up a situation where the answer is something other than "no." Example: "What would the cat say if you said, 'Miss Kitty, would you like some milk?'" When she answers with a "yes," then say, "And what would you say if I asked you if you wanted some milk too?"

3 Stand firm. When all of your attempts to distract from and avoid the "no's" have failed, and a showdown ensues, you must be firm. Be aware of the fine line between talking it out and talking too much, and eventually he will come around. Or, if your child refuses to put his shoes on so he can go outside, don't let him go outside until he puts them on.

Recommended reading:

The Emotional Life of the Toddler
Alicia F. Lieberman

How do I know that that my child is spirited?

Look for these signs, or some combination of them:

Emotionally intense
Everything is black or white, happy or sad—there's no middle ground in his choices, opinions, or life in general. As a baby, he cries more than others. He's always loud and forceful whether miserable, happy or angry.

Demanding
She feeds voraciously, especially as a baby. She needs your attention constantly, draining your energy. She has very strong preferences in most matters.

Extra sensitive
A low threshold for all five physical senses means that he is quickly and easily overstimulated by what's going on around him. Since touch overstimulates him, he hates to be confined.

Easily distracted
Since she is highly aware of her environment, she notices everything going on around her all the time, and this leads to trouble with concentration and paying attention.

Needs less sleep
He wakes up often at night and needs less sleep than usual in the daytime. He does not keep to a regular schedule for sleeping.

Intelligent
She's bright, even gifted, with a high IQ. She's creative and a keen observer. She "locks in" to important ideas, and loves to debate.

Should I get help?

You can't keep an eye on your high-energy child every moment. There will certainly be times when help is essential. When you go shopping, take a friend with you so you can find what you need without worrying where your toddler is.

ACTION ITEMS
Tips for handling a "spirited" child

1 Keep him informed. When you explain to your child what he should expect, it defuses his anxiety about what is coming. For example, on the way to a doctor's visit, tell your child that the doctor only wants to listen to his heart and make sure he is okay.

2 Be consistent. High-spirited children need a secure set of rules established. Once you set the rules, stick to them. So, if you have established a normal eight o'clock bedtime for your child, and her favorite cartoon is having a special on television, tell her that you will record it and she can finish it the next evening. If you let her stay up to finish it, she will want to stay up for the rest of the week.

3 Provide quality time. Though your child may be gaining some independence, you need to maintain a day-to-day special time with him. This establishes a trust that you will always be there. Try making bath time a fun time! Ask if he wants to play ducks and boats. This is a perfect time to play with him and do a necessary task at the same time.

4 Let her help. When your child wants to start doing things for herself, let her. It may take a few extra minutes or become a little messy, but it will probably save you from tantrums and battles. When you are preparing a cake in the kitchen, give her a bowl with some flour and water in it and let her stir! Or, don't put on her shoes for her; let her do it.

Likes to perform

She is charming, and among her peers she's a charismatic leader. But she is always hungry for attention, feeding on external stimulation. This leads to a tendency to base her worth on feedback from others.

Insatiable

He demands immediate responses from you, but whatever you do, it never seems to satisfy him.

Controlling

She's highly verbal and has a strong need to control others. This often means that she does not get along well with them. She fails to recognize social clues which are non-verbal.

High energy level

He's physically active, always exploring things, and is unable to slow himself down without help. He's restless, fidgety, constantly on the move. He has no sense of what is appropriate behavior and won't follow rules.

Bad at adapting

Fearful of new situations, she clings to you. She's unable to make transitions to new routines or activities. She'll probably be shy and reserved when meeting new people.

Moody

He has extreme, unpredictable swings in mood. He's stubborn, may have long tantrums, but is basically a serious child who may be cranky.

What is a spirited child?

All toddlers are busy, but the spirited child is much busier. As a parent, you'll have more on your hands. While the high-energy child is normal, he's more intense, persistent and emphatic than most others.

Sources: BabyCenter.com; Raising Your Spirited Child, Mary Sheedy Kurcinka; The Fussy Baby Book, Dr. William and Martha Sears; Living with the Active Alert Child, Linda S. Budd; The Difficult Child, Stanley Turecki, MD.

5 **Anticipate.** If your high-spirited child acts up in certain places, make other arrangements. Don't go to a noisy restaurant that will cause a problem. Instead, try a picnic at the beach or the park.

6 **Offer praise.** Positive reinforcement offers encouragement and raises your child's self-esteem. When your child sits through a dinner without playing with her food, let her know that you are pleased with her progress.

7 **Avoid labels.** Be careful how you describe your child. Labels have a tendency to stick. Use positive labels instead of negative ones. Instead of saying, "Jeffrey is so stubborn and mischievous," try "Jeffrey is so confident and energetic!"

8 **Soothe her senses.** If your child usually reacts negatively to her environment, try to soothe her senses. So, if it is very hot outside, get the water hose out and let her run through the sprinkler. Or, give your child some finger paints to keep her occupied when you are cleaning the house.

9 **Recognize his feelings.** When he starts to blow his top, let him know that sometimes you feel like doing that too. For example, if you have been driving for a while and your child starts to lose his cool, pull over to the side of the road and explain that sometimes you get tired of riding in the car too.

? At what age should I start to discipline my child?

When thinking about discipline and punishment, always take your child's age into account. Here are some guidelines:

Infants under six months	Six months to walking age	Toddlers, age one to two	Two years and up
DON'T DISCIPLINE HER YET	**GIVE HIM THE SPACE HE NEEDS**	**REDIRECT HER ACTIVITY**	**SET RULES AND ACT ON THEM**

Infants under six months

DON'T DISCIPLINE HER YET

Discipline is inappropriate for a child of this age.

Give your child the attention she needs. you can't spoil an infant. Your caring responses will help you create a strong bond.

Respect her as an individual and respond to her needs. When she cries, try to determine why. Is she hungry, wet, tired? Does she need to burp? Is it just her fussy time of day?

Keep her safe. Make sure that dangerous objects are out of reach.

Six months to walking age

GIVE HIM THE SPACE HE NEEDS

Focus on safety and exploration. At this age your child still doesn't understand discipline.

Give your child a safe place to explore. Your child will want to touch everything he can—this is how he learns about his world. Make his play space safe.

Encourage him to explore. Tummy time is important for learning to crawl. Play on the floor with your child as much as possible.

Get ready to set limits. Once you notice that your baby "looks around" to see if you are watching him, he is showing you his awareness of the "forbidden." At this time it is appropriate to begin to set limits.

Toddlers, age one to two

REDIRECT HER ACTIVITY

At this age your child is beginning to understand discipline. Focus on teaching through positive reinforcement.

Safety is still a high priority. Make sure your house is well child-proofed. Keep a close eye on him at all times.

Be positive. Encourage good behavior and redirect undesirable behavior. Give your child plenty of activities. If he becomes distracted with something unsafe, redirect him to a new activity.

Use "No" primarily for safety issues. Your child will begin to understand that electric outlets are "no-no's" if you are firm and consistent.

Two years and up

SET RULES AND ACT ON THEM

At this age your child is starting to understand expectations and consequences. Use discipline to teach values and set limits.

Be clear and consistent. Explain expectations up front. Your child should know the boundaries you expect.

Create natural consequences to reinforce desired behavior. If a child hits a friend, remove him until he is ready to play nicely.

Act swiftly and in the moment. Don't threaten or negotiate and don't leave the consequences until later—your child may not understand what you are trying to teach him.

ACTION ITEMS Discipline Dos

1. Be a good role model.
2. Set clear expectations and explain them to your child.
3. Be consistent.
4. Provide natural consequences for bad behavior. Consequences should reinforce the behavior you are looking for.
5. Ignore small, unimportant incidents for young children.
6. Give "time-outs" for cooling off.
7. Use non-verbal communication, such as a stern look, for small misdeeds.
8. Provide a warning or distraction and a chance to amend behavior before disciplining.
9. Give praise for good behavior.
10. Be patient.

What's a time-out?

A time-out is one of a number of strategies caregivers can use to promote appropriate behavior. It's an opportunity to teach your child and you how to deal with her frustrations. It's not a punishment. When you impose a time-out, your child should be on her own, and you should not pay attention to her—if you do she'll take it as a positive reinforcement of the behavior that caused the time-out. The good thing about time-outs is that they defuse situations in an un-emotional way.

Don't impose a time-out until your child is ready. Trying to get your young toddler to sit still could turn into what she thinks is a game, as she runs away and you chase after her.

You might introduce the idea of time-outs by taking one together at first. Just sit quietly and read a book or listen to music.

Leaving your child to sit quietly alone for a few moments allows her to calm down, and allows you to leave the scene rather than getting involved in that moment's problem.

The time to start time-outs is after age two, when she is beginning to understand what rules are.

Don't suddenly impose time-outs: warn your child that her behavior is going to result in one if she continues.

Results won't appear overnight. **Be patient, and consistent.** Remember, that what you see as bad behavior is often your child testing your reactions to make sure she really understands her world.

The word discipline means "to teach." When you are disciplining your child, you are teaching him how he needs to behave in that particular situation.

How long?

When your child is very young, the point is to plant the idea of a parentally mandated break from some undesirable action. You don't have to force her to sit in a particular place for a predetermined length of time. You might get her to sit still where she is. **30 seconds to a minute is enough of a cooling-off period for a toddler.** Don't implement the one-minute-per-year rule until she is three.

Is it OK to spank my child?

Parents and child development experts differ as to whether spanking is ever permissable. **61% of parents of young children** think it's appropriate to spank their children according to a recent study by Civitas and Zero to Three. However, other studies show that physical punishment contributes to a lack of self-control and increases aggressiveness in children. **If you spank your child for running into the street, you are certainly punishing the act but you're not teaching anything about what was wrong.** Spanking will teach your child that adults get their way by the use of physical force.

Sources: BabyCenter.com; amazingbaby.com; Touchpoints, T. Berry Brazelton.

Discipline Don'ts

1. Don't threaten, warn, cajole or negotiate with your child.

2. Don't punish your child for normal behavior, such as occasional bedwetting.

3. Don't punish for accidental mishaps such as spilled milk. Instead, remind her to be careful next time and give her a cloth to help clean up.

4. Don't give unrelated consequences.

5. Don't use physical punishment. Remember, you are trying to teach, not create fear.

6. Don't make punishment too severe or prolonged.

137

Bad language

Your child's first swear word is usually the result of direct mimicry.

TIP: Try not to react.
If it's you she's heard, admit that you should not have said the word and distract her with a song or a story. In any case, the first time she swears resist the urge to laugh out loud; this will encourage her to do it again.

TIP: Set guidelines and be consistent.
If your child continues to repeat a serious profanity, don't get angry. In a disinterested voice, say, "That's not a word you may use in this house or around other people." If he persists, stay calm but respond with a swift consequence such as a time-out.

TIP: Set an example.
Be careful with your own language, and remember that your child is a sponge—he soaks up what he hears and is eager to share what he learns.

Nose picking

He's probably only doing it because it's there, and may not even realize what he's doing. If he has allergies, he may sense there is something inside his nose that's hard to leave alone.

TIP: Try a humidifier.
Your heating or air conditioning may be drying out the house.

TIP: Avoid punishing.
Punishing won't help. Since he may not know he's doing it, gentle reminders when you notice it are better.

TIP: Keep his hands busy.
While watching TV or in the car, give him a rubber ball to squeeze or finger puppets to play with.

Masturbation is a lot like nosepicking. Children do it because it's there. For toddlers it's not sexual and is a completely normal thing to do.

TIP: React carefully.
If you tell your child that what she's doing is dirty or naughty, she may grow up associating sexual feelings with shame and guilt.

Interrupting

Your 2-year-old thinks the world and everything in it, including you, exists for his benefit. Also his short-term memory is not developed, and this means that he wants to say things right now, before he forgets. Therefore, **the concept of interrupting makes no sense to him.** And, whatever directs your attention away from him (a phone call, for example) is by nature threatening.

Meow. Oops, sorry, I meant "excuse me."

The best strategy is to **limit the situations in which your child can interrupt your conversations,** and to divert his attention whenever he does.

TIP: Schedule calls
Try to make and return calls or plan conversations when your child is napping. You might also redirect her attention by keeping a drawer with special toys and art materials that are used only during these times. Try giving him a toy phone so he can talk to an imaginary friend.

TIP: Choose the right location
Minimize your frustration by going to a quieter room for your conversation or by making plans to meet friends in places, such as a park with a sandbox, where your child can play and you can chat.

TIP: Set a good example
Children copy what they see and hear, so take advantage of this. If you and your partner tend to cut each other off in conversation, end that habit. And do not interrupt your child while she is talking to you. (if you do, stop and say, "Sorry, I interrupted you. Go on.")

REMEMBER
Show her how to be polite to others. **Basic social graces don't appear overnight.**

ACTION ITEMS
Tips for teaching manners

1 Set an example. Children are always watching what their parents and other adults do. Model good manners and your child will start to pick them up. For example: You are cleaning up the kitchen and your child brings her glass from the table. Respond by saying, "Thank you so much for helping me."

2 Don't over-react. By blowing up, you are showing your child that he can get your attention whenever he wants by performing an act that embarrasses or angers you. Remember to be patient while he is learning what does and does not please you.

3 Read your child books. Stories that offer lessons on how to have good manners are excellent teaching tools. Examples:

Just Say Please
Gina and Mercer Mayer

The Berenstain Bears Forget Their Manners
Stan and Jan Berenstain

Elmo's Good Manners Game (Sesame Street)
Catherine Samuel, et al

Mind Your Manners
Peggy Parish and Marylin Hafner

Playing with food

At one time or another, your child with play with his food, throw his cup and silverware on the floor and refuse to eat what you serve him. Here are some ideas for teaching table manners:

TIP: Don't create a mealtime battleground Be clear and consistent, but avoid arguing over what he's doing. If he starts to build forts with his potatoes, remove his plate saying that you can see he's finished eating. Remind him that food is for eating, not playing.

TIP: Set an example. When you sit down for a meal, concentrate on and enjoy your food, and assume he will too. If he doesn't, remember that he won't starve. Active two-year-olds will eat when they are hungry. They need an endless supply to fuel their growing bodies and minds.

TIP: Eat what you are serving. Operate on the assumption that everyone is eating what's on the menu, and your child will soon learn to eat what you make.

Saying thank you

To expect a toddler to incorporate manners flawlessly into her daily routine is asking too much. Saying please and thank you is still a new skill for your child and one that will take time to learn. **TIP: Set the example.** Thank her when she does things for you, and say please when asking for assistance. Your child is listening to your words when you least expect it. **TIP: Provide praise.** Rather than scolding her for a lack of manners, pour on the praise when she gets it right. **TIP: Don't over-react.** Try not to make a fuss when she forgets. Blowing up about it could cause her to resist your efforts to teach her considerate behavior.

Sitting still

Toddlers have a limit to how long they can sit still. It's unrealistic to think that a young child will remain in her seat for an entire church service or while you are at a meeting, for example.

TIP: Keep her busy. Bring along a bag of books, crayons and paper. let her work quietly while you listen to the service or meeting.

TIP: Have an escape plan. Sit near the end of a row so that you are away from the center of activity. Be prepared to take her outside if she gets antsy.

The best way to encourage a toddler to behave nicely is to model good manners.

Starting early with **please** and **thank you** and offering praise for your child's good manners when he demonstrates them will go a lot further than punishment for his failures.

4 **Give praise.** When your child exhibits good manners, let her know that you are glad she did by saying, "I am so happy that you let your sister play with your toys."

5 **Be patient and consistent.** Remember that very young children aren't yet capable of controlling much of their behavior. But, they do watch and listen to you very closely. Don't get discouraged when your child continues to throw her sippy cup on the floor or grabs toys from other children. Keep reinforcing positive manner behaviors and, over time, you'll see that the lessons you've taught your child have actually been applied.

6 **Be your child's coach.** Be proactive about using real-life opportunities to teach your child what you expect in terms of manners. For example, when someone offers your child something he wants, remind him "What do you say to Aunt Ashley?" Reinforce the message by also thanking that person yourself.

7 **Use your child's favorite characters to help make the point.** Children love to be like the characters and people they love most. If your child is in a Barney stage, for example, ask her "What would Barney say if he wanted me to get him a glass of water?" Reinforce good manners by reminding her, "I'm happy to get you what you want when you say please."

? Do the costs of raising a child vary depending on your family's income?

A family with a before-tax income of less than $38,000 (average: $24,000)

$8,970	$9,120	$9,480	$12,390	$17,550	$23,820

A family with a before-tax income of between $38,000 and $64,000 (average: $50,500)

$11,640	$10,680	$16,560	$18,510	$24,420	$28,650

A family with a before-tax income of more than $64,000 (average: $96,000)

$13,380	$13,770	$26,520	$30,090

what's in the categories

Health care
expenses include:
medical and dental services not covered by insurance; prescription drugs and medical supplies not covered by insurance; health insurance premiums not paid by employer or other organization.

Clothing
expenses include:
children's apparel such as diapers, shirts, pants, dresses, suits; footwear; clothing services such as cleaning, alterations and repair.

Child care & education
expenses include:
child care tuition and supplies; baby-sitting; elementary and high school tuition, books and supplies.

Miscellaneous expenses include:
personal care items; entertainment; reading materials.

Based on the Consumer Price Index (CPI), the $10 weekly allowance you received in 1976 is the same as giving your child $31.49 in today's money.

? What's a family?

Any combination of two or more persons who are bound together over time by ties of mutual consent, birth and/or adoption or placement and who, together, assume responsibilities which can include:

— physical maintenance and care of group members
— addition of new members through birth or adoption
— socialization of children
— social control of members
— love and nurturance

ACTION ITEMS Four ways to help you get started

1 **Update insurance coverages.** Make sure you have sufficient life, disability and health insurance in place. Term life insurance is an affordable way to provide for a growing family in the event of your death. Disability coverage is also very important since studies show that one out of every four workers will become disabled during his or her lifetime.

2 **Make full use of additional employee benefits.** If your employer offers a flexible-spending account, use it to your advantage. For example, you may be able to reduce your taxable income by paying for non-reimbursable medical expenses (orthodontia, eyeglasses, etc.) with pretax dollars. And, don't neglect saving for your own retirement. Contribute as much as you can to your employer's 401(k) retirement plan (if available) or an IRA.

How much does it cost to raise a child?

$39,900

TOTAL
$121,230
per child from birth to 18 years

$55,170

TOTAL
$165,630
per child from birth to 18 years

$32,760 $35,760 $89,580

TOTAL
$241,770
per child from birth to 18 years

It's important to weigh the value of family time over wealth and achieve a satisfactory balance.

Transportation
expenses include:
net outlay on purchase of new and used vehicles; vehicle finance charges; gas and motor oil; maintenance and repairs; insurance; public transportation.

Food
expenses include:
food and beverages purchased at grocery, convenience and specialty stores (including purchases with food stamps), dining at restaurants and household expenditures on school meals.

Housing **expenses include:**
shelter (mortgage interest, property taxes, or rent; maintenance and repairs; insurance); utilities (gas, electricity, fuel, telephone, water); house furnishings and equipment (furniture, floor coverings, major appliances, small appliances).

For homeowners, housing expenses **do not** include mortgage principal payments, which are considered in the Consumer Expenditure Survey to be a part of savings. So total dollars allocated to housing by homeowners are underestimated in this report.

3 **Adapt long-term investment strategies.** Consider investing regularly in equity mutual funds for your child's college years and your own retirement. And although past performance is no guarantee of future results, historically, equities have outperformed other types of investments. The longer your time frame is until you need the money, the more risk you can afford to take—potentially earning greater rewards.

4 **Establish an emergency fund.** Consider keeping a minimum three to six months' worth of living expenses in a money market account. You could also open a home equity line of credit for use as an emergency reserve fund.

America's elite colleges and universities are the best in the world. They are also the most expensive, with tuition rising faster than the rate of inflation over the past thirty years and no indication that this trend will abate.

Source: Tuition Rising; President and Fellows of Harvard College

Nationally, the cost of tuition at a **private** college has risen four times faster than inflation since 1960, and reached $16,500 per semester in 1997. The cost of tuition at **public** four-year colleges went up at triple the inflation rate during the same period, and reached $3,500 per semester.

Over 70% of college students attend four-year colleges where tuition is less than $8,000 per year.

At four-year **public** colleges and universities, more than 60% of full-time students receive some type of financial aid. At four-year **private** colleges and universities, more than 75% of students receive some form of financial aid.

Saving for your child's college...

The amount you need to save each month to pay for the tuition and other costs* of a four-year college career depends on when you start saving, and whether you are saving for a public or private college ...

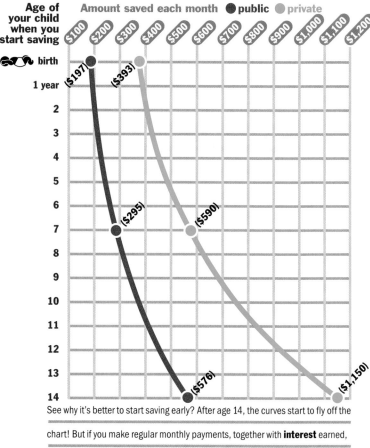

See why it's better to start saving early? After age 14, the curves start to fly off the chart! But if you make regular monthly payments, together with **interest** earned, you'll be able to meet these projected college costs: (each 🏦 = $1,000)

ACTION ITEMS
Strategies for Funding College

1 **Growth Stocks and Mutual Funds.** Sound investments in the stock market have the potential to provide better returns than insured, fixed-rate investments (such as savings accounts and CDs). Keep in mind that these investments can be risky, however, especially as college age approaches.

2 **U.S. Savings Bonds (Series EE).** You can buy Series EE U.S. Government Savings Bonds at your local bank. Their face value ranges from $50 to $10,000. If these are used to pay qualified higher education expenses, and all requirements are met, no federal income tax is due on the interest.

3 **Life Insurance.** Talk to your insurance representative about the advantages of life insurance when planning your child's college education.

4 **Savings Plan Trusts.** Certain states offer these special college savings accounts, which allow the contributor to save on behalf of a designated beneficiary's qualified education expenses. These trusts may guarantee a minimum rate of return and generally provide favorable tax treatment.

5 **Prepaid Tuition Plans.** Some states offer prepaid tuition plans. Residents of these states can buy a contract or bonds at a fixed price, based on current tuition rates. Payments can be made in lump sums or monthly installments. The state, in turn, invests the money to earn the difference between the amount you are paying and the projected cost of tuition at the time your child reaches college age. Those who sign up are fully protected, as the state assumes all investment risk.

142

...start the process early and harness the power of interest

Saving any amount of money can make a big difference in what you can afford to pay for college. The earlier you start the better, but don't pass altogether because you think it's too little or too late. Harness the power of interest; for every dollar you save, you earn money through interest.

For example...

If you save **$50 a month** from the time your daughter is born, you'll amass more than **$16,000 in savings** by the time she graduates from high school. Almost **$6,000 of this is interest** earnings.

BUT, if you start saving when your daughter is seven years old, you'd need to save about **$100 a month** to end up with the same amount at high school graduation.

While the cost can vary a great deal, sending your child to college will be one of your largest single expenses. The key is to start saving for it when your child is very young—ideally at birth.

What happens if I can't save enough?

You do not have to be the only source of funding for your child's college education. Think of **financial aid** in the broadest of terms. If your child gets a gift of money, put it into a college fund. When grandparents ask what to give their grandchild as a birthday present, suggest a contribution to this fund. And don't forget these sources of financial aid:

- scholarships
- grants
- work-study programs
- government loans

Your child's school record, what he chooses to study, his athletic ability, and choice of college are some of the factors affecting the availability of these options.

*Annual costs include tuition, room and board, transportation, books and other expenses and assume a 6% annual increase.

$24,000: freshman year, public college
freshman year, private college: $54,000

$25,000: sophomore year
sophomore year: $57,000

$27,000: junior year
junior year: $61,000

$29,000: senior year
senior year: $64,000

Sources: kiplinger.com; future.newsday.com; collegeboard.com; National Center for Financial Education; Department of the Treasury.

6 **Educational IRAs**. You are now able to set up IRAs to pay for college expenses. Contributions are allowed until your child reaches 18 and are made with after-tax dollars. There is no tax deduction, but earnings grow tax-deferred and there is no penalty for qualified withdrawals made for the purpose of paying college expenses.

7 **529 Plans**. These investment plans are qualified state tuition plans that help families save for future college costs. The advantages: owner-controlled accounts, substantial contribution allowances, tax planning advantages for contributors and no federal income tax on growth or on qualified withdraws. And, with virtually no income limitations or age restrictions, 529s provide anyone a very easy, hands-off way to save for college.

8 **Roth IRAs.** Although they come with limited contribution allowances, a Roth is owner-controlled and offers tax-deferred growth and no federal income tax on qualified withdrawals.

9 **Custodial Accounts.** Under the Uniform Transfers to Minors Act (UTMA), accounts set up in a minor's name can offer you substantial tax breaks. Use caution though. These accounts can pose tax consequences for the minor, and the monies in them become his or her sole property at the minor's legal age of majority in that state.

10 **CDs and Bank Accounts.** Although these are generally FDIC insured, they usually offer a lower return potential than other investment vehicles and are most appropriate for those with short-term goals.

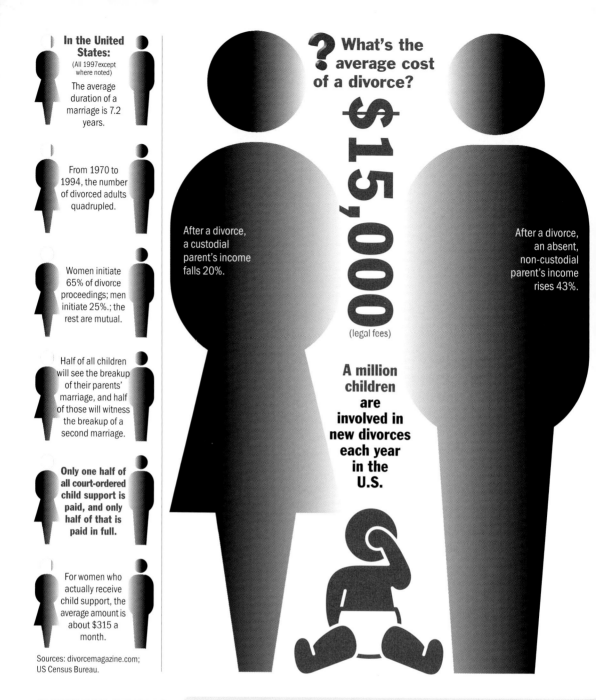

In the United States:

(All 1997 except where noted)

The average duration of a marriage is 7.2 years.

From 1970 to 1994, the number of divorced adults quadrupled.

Women initiate 65% of divorce proceedings; men initiate 25%.; the rest are mutual.

Half of all children will see the breakup of their parents' marriage, and half of those will witness the breakup of a second marriage.

Only one half of all court-ordered child support is paid, and only half of that is paid in full.

For women who actually receive child support, the average amount is about $315 a month.

Sources: divorcemagazine.com; US Census Bureau.

? What's the average cost of a divorce?

$15,000

(legal fees)

After a divorce, a custodial parent's income falls 20%.

After a divorce, an absent, non-custodial parent's income rises 43%.

A million children are involved in new divorces each year in the U.S.

ACTION ITEMS — Steps for collecting child support

If you don't already have a child support order:

1 Locate your state or local Child Support Enforcement (CSE) office.

The Child Support Enforcement Program is a federal/state/local effort to locate parents, their employers, and/or their assets; establish paternity if necessary; and establish and enforce child support orders.

Apply.

2 Call your CSE office to learn how to apply for enforcement services and what documents (birth certificates, financial statements, etc.) you should provide. Then, follow through.

3 Establish paternity.

The first step, if a child was born out of wedlock, is to establish paternity—or make a legal determination of who fathered the child. Either parent can request a blood test in contested paternity cases, and while many men will voluntarily acknowledge paternity, your caseworker will help you to establish it.

4 Determine the amount due.

Your CSE office will be able to tell you how support award amounts are set in your state and can also request medical support for your child.

Child support is a payment by one parent to the other parent for the support of their common child.

(This is often the parent who is not looking after the child day-to-day.)

It is in the best interest of a child for both parents to be obligated to pay for the support of their child. **A Child Support Order,** which is a document issued by a court, considers the income of both parents so that their combined incomes are available to use for the support of their child. The document states **when, how often, and how much** a parent is to pay for child support.

What is child support used for?

It covers everything a child needs during his growth and formative years. But it is more than the bare necessities: if one parent is wealthy, the child is entitled to share that wealth. Child support may therefore improve the standard of living of the custodial parent even though that parent has a lower income than that of the non-custodial parent who is paying the support.

How is the amount determined?

Federal law requires states to set child support guidelines in order to remain eligible for collection subsidies. As a result, most states have established a **formula** to determine how much one parent pays the other. The formula is based on the gross incomes of both parents, and can be overridden at the discretion of the judge in cases where the parties'income is especially high. In addition, **the factors below** are considered in the formula:

For how long must it be paid?

It depends on state law. All states require both parents to be financially responsible for their child during the child's minority, which is generally through high school years. A few states have extended the time for payment beyond this for full-time students, but not past age 22. Child support can be terminated if the child goes on active duty in the armed forces, or if he becomes self-supporting.

If divorce becomes necessary, the primary concern of both parents should be the welfare of the children.

The number of children in common between the parents. Certain fixed expenses do not rise with the number of children for whom support must be provided, so the amount per child is lower given the greater number of children in common.

Special circumstances such as extraordinary medical expenses, special educational needs, travel expenses for child visitation, uninsured catastrophic loss, and the basic cost-of-living expenses for children from another relationship can affect the formula.

Time spent with the child is considered, since the parent who raises a child (the custodial parent) will spend more of his income than the other parent.

Best advice: get a lawyer.

Sources: family-law.freeadvice.com; National Data Resources.

If you already have a child support order:

 Find the non-paying parent.

When a parent has disappeared, it is usually possible for your local child support enforcement office to find him or her and his or her employer with the help of state agencies, such as the Dept. of Motor Vehicles, or the Federal Parent Locator Service. Your caseworker can tell you what information is needed.

 Collect.

With the exception of deducting child support from a federal or state tax refund, the enforcement of child support payments must be done through the local court system where the support-obliged parent resides.

States have laws that allow them to use liens on real and personal property, orders to withhold and deliver property or seizure and sale of property with the proceeds applied to the support debt. Many states routinely report child support debts to credit bureaus and smart parents are bringing their payments current so that their credit won't be affected. In addition, the local court would have the authority to hold the non-paying parent in contempt, which could include incarceration until the support arrearage has been paid.

Source: www.acf.dhhs.gov.

A will is perhaps the most important legal document the average American will ever sign.

But, over

70%

of adults in America do not have a will.

Key words

Probate is the process of legally passing ownership of property from a dead person to his heirs or beneficiaries. Probate courts administer the process.

Beneficiaries are family members, friends or charitable organizations who will receive your assets as your will directs. Your will includes specific gifts (such as jewelry or a specified amount of money) to named beneficiaries.

The executor is a person or institution named in your will and appointed by the probate court, who collects and manages your assets, pays your debts and expenses and any taxes that might be due, and then distributes your assests to the beneficiaries.

What makes a will legal?

In all states except Louisiana, these are the requirements for a will to be legal:

● **The testator** (that is, the person whose will is being made) **must be an adult.**

● The testator **must be of sound mind.**

● The will must specifically **state that it is your will.**

● The will must do what wills are supposed to do, such as: **appoint beneficiaries of your "worldly goods;" appoint a guardian for your minor children; appoint an executor.**

● The will must be **signed and dated by the testator, in front of the required number of witnesses.**

Can my will be contested?

Usually a challenge to have a will invalidated comes from people who believe that they are potential heirs or beneficiaries, but to whom you left nothing. Their objections might be:

● **The will was not properly drawn up, signed or witnessed, according to the requirements of the particular state.**

● **You lacked mental capacity when the will was made.**

● **There was fraud, force or undue influence on you when you made the will.**

● **The will is a forgery.**

If the will is held to be invalid, the probate court may invalidate all provisions or just the ones that are challenged. If the entire will is invalidated, the proceeds are usually distributed as though you had died intestate (with no will). The distribution is according to the laws of the state that has the probate court.

How do I find a lawyer to write a will for me?

The best way is to get a referral from someone whose judgement you trust—friends, associates or your employer. In addition, your local bar association maintains a list of State Bar-certified lawyer referral services in your area.

ACTION ITEMS

You should review your will:

1 every five years.

2 if you have lost the one you had.

3 when you get married.

4 when you have your first child.

5 if you decide to change the provisions of your will.

6 if you move to another state.

7 if your executor(s), guardian(s) and trustee(s) move to another state. Keep in touch with them. You should think about making a new will when they move.

How can my will provide for my minor children?

Children who are minors (under 18 in most states) cannot legally own anything except for small amounts—under $5,000, in most states. However there are three ways to leave property to your minor children:

● **Appoint a property guardian** to manage your child's inheritance. The role is different from that of the **personal guardian** whom you will be naming in other parts of your will. (The personal guardian raises the child, if necessary, and may or may not be the same person as the property guardian.)

● **Create a custodian account.** This is usually better than appointing a property guardian. Your will states that you are making a bequest to the Uniform Transfer to Minors Act. This act permits your named custodian to manage the property as she sees fit for the benefit of your child, without having a court review her actions annually, as is the case with property guardians.

● **Establish a trust for your child.** Unlike your will, which is public, the content of a trust is private. There are no limits to the length of time that a trust is in effect, although most trusts distribute money until the recipient is about 35. A trust can be made before you die or as part of your will. **A trust is generally considered to be the best way to provide for minors.**

What is not included in a will?

Life insurance
Because cash proceeds from an insurance policy on your life are paid to the person you named as the beneficiary of the policy, it is very important to keep this information current. Monies to deceased beneficiaries will be left to your estate if you die.

Retirement plans
Assets held in retirement plans (401(k), or an IRA) are transferred to the person you named as beneficiaries in the plan documents.

Jointly owned assets
Real estate, cars, bank accounts and other property jointly held passes to the joint tenant on your death, not in accordance with any directions in your will.

Laws vary from state to state, and you should check with your State Bar (the Estate Planning, Trust and Probate Law Section) about what laws are currently on the books.

What happens if I die without making a will?

Without a will, the state, and not you, will decide who is entitled to your personal items. A court will appoint a guardian for your child if she is under 18. Most likely, the court will appoint your spouse as the guardian, but a bond may have to be posted. The court will also, among other regulations, require an annual accounting of income and expenses, and any investment of the money from your estate by the guardian may be limited.

Do I need to have a will?

Yes. Having a will allows you—and not the state—to determine how your estate will be distributed and how your children will be protected.

If you die without a will and have minor children, the court will have to appoint a guardian to manage your child's share of your estate. This can cause major problems and expense.

Sources: pcwills.com; legalzoom.com; New York State Bar Association; State Bar of California.

8 if you get divorced.

9 if you've had a significant increase in wealth.

10 if there has been a change in estate tax laws.

For more information:

National Association of Financial Estate Planning

www.natep.com

TIP
If the value of your estate is around the $700,000 mark or higher, you need to find a good estate planner (unless you like the idea of having a large chunk of your estate go to Uncle Sam).

Stay-at-Home

A new but growing segment of the American culture, stay-at-home fathers now number **2 million**. A relief to working moms, research shows that children in these families form strong relationships with both parents.

Furstenberg and Nord found that 76% of children report positive relationships with their non-resident father.

A study by Johnson, Stein and Dadds in The Journal of Pediatric Psychology indicated that children who lived with their mother and her boyfriend were more poorly adjusted psychologically and had more behavior problems than children who lived with both biological parents.

Young

Only **30%** of children born to teen mothers were fathered by adolescent males.

Married with Children

Although once the norm, today only **24%** of American households include married couples with children.

1/2 of all male prisoners in the US are fathers of children under 18.

Jailed

ACTION ITEMS — Tips for new stepfathers

1 Start early.
Begin the process of getting to know your partner's children well before you say "I do." The success of your new marriage will have a lot to do with how well you get along with her kids, so take the time to get to know them.

2 Take it slow.
Do not expect to become an instant family. Connecting with children takes time, so don't be upset if the kids don't like you right away. Don't push them—just be yourself and good relationships will form.

3 Honor her father.
Your role as a stepfather is not the same as a father's role, so don't expect your stepchildren to treat you like their biological father or insist that they call you "dad." Try not to compete with their biological father. If anything, work to develop a relationship with him and encourage the children in their relationship with the father by supporting him and allowing them to spend time with him. You are there to support them, and even discipline them if necessary, but not to take the place of their dad.

Grand

Step

6% of US children live in grandparent-headed households. Although an older male caregiver may spend less time in physically active play, he will likely spend more time in imaginative play.

Custodial

Father-only families account for **4%** of all US children. These fathers spend signifi-cantly more time with their children than fathers in two-parent households.

There are **23 million** stepfathers in America. Those who show both warmth and control have an easier time adjusting.

Based on self-report-ing, there are **2 to 3 million** gay fathers in North America. Evidence shows they do as well as hetero-sexual dads in raising children.

Approximately **120,000** children are adopted in the US each year. Adoptive fathers often do a better job at child rearing because they are usually older, more financially stable and ready for fatherhood.

Unwed

4 out of every **10** cohabiting couples have children. Only **4** in **10** of these will see their parents marry.

Adoptive

Forming families is serious business.

—Marian Wright Edelman

Sources: The National Fatherhood Initiative; Gay Fathers of Rhode Island; www.parentsplace.com; Fatherneed, Kyle Pruett, MD; Civitas; www.slowlane.com; The Fatherhood Alliance; University of Washington; US Bureau of Justice; US Census Bureau.

4 Be consistent, committed and loyal.
When you say you are going to do some-thing, do it. Children rely upon consistency and predictability. It provides them with security and a strong base for your future relationship.

5 Participate in your stepchild's life.
Learn about her favorite activities. Take time to play with her and participate in her daily care. Pick her up from child care or get involved in her bedtime routines. Once you've developed a more comfortable rela-tionship, you may want to create special tra-ditions of your own.

6 Stand united.
It's important for you to support each other when making parenting decisions. You may not have the ability to take an effective disciplinary role until you have developed a secure relationship with your stepchildren. Until then, give quiet support to your partner.

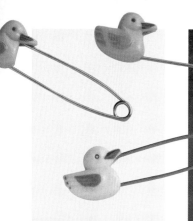

Some research shows that fathers are likely to be more involved with:

- Their firstborn
- Prematurely-born infants
- Infants with difficult temperments
- Their younger children if they have a large family

A father's employment may affect the amount of time he spends with his children. On average, fathers with lower-level white-collar and pro-fessional jobs have the highest level of involvement with their children. Fathers with blue-collar or middle-to high-management jobs and fathers who are self-employed have the lowest level of involvement with their children.

Source: Paternal Involvement, Joseph H. Pleck.

In general, a man's behavior becomes more nurturing once he becomes a father.

ACTION ITEMS
Want to be involved?

1 Define your own role.
Don't get discouraged that a breastfeeding baby has more time to connect with her mother. Infancy allows for plenty of oppor-tunities for hands-on dads. Be a diaper changer, bather and soother. Play, touch and talk to her as much as you can.

2 Create your own rituals.
Turn everyday activities like running week-end errands into regular routines for you and your child. Although they may seem mun-dane, simply having consistent one-on-one time will make them special to you and your child.

3 Take on your own responsibilities.
Pick your child up from child care and get his daily report. Get him dressed in the morning. Prepare his meals. Take him to the doctor. Directly caring for your child goes a long way in earning trust and appreciation from him and his mother or caretaker. And, it will make you feel good about yourself and your fathering skills.

4 Try to balance work and family.
While being involved is critical, be careful not to overdo. Wearing yourself down does no favors to you or your child. Ask for some time to yourself so that you can refuel and have something to offer your child.

Although fathers have become more involved in their children's lives in recent decades, they are still less involved than mothers.

Fathers are **engaged 2/5** as much as mothers

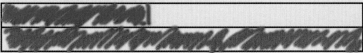

Fathers are **accessible 2/3** as much as mothers

Engagement: Time spent physically and actively involved with a child (including feeding, bathing and playing).

Accessibility: Time when the parent is available to the child.

85% Men who report that they share equally with their partner in homemaking and child care.

30% Women who report that they share equally with their partner in homemaking and child care.

Four factors influence the level of paternal involvement: motivation, skills and self-confidence, social supports and institutional practices.

—Joseph Pleck
The Role of the Father

Sources: Connecticut Commission on Children; Rubenstein; The Role of the Father, Joseph Pleck.

Of all one-on-one time, **fathers** spend *45%* **playing**, while **mothers** only spend *15-20%* **playing** .

A study of 27 preschoolers found that popular children are more likely to have fathers who are physically playful, affectionate and socially engaging and mothers who are highly verbal.

Source: Bridging the Gap: Parent-Child Play Interaction and Peer Interactive Competence, Mac Donald and Parke

ACTION ITEMS Questions of equality

 When it comes to connecting with an infant, does a mother have an advantage over a father because the baby has heard her voice for nine months?

Surprisingly, mothers do not have this type of advantage, however many men report feeling like strangers to their children at the very beginning. Fathers should not give up hope—the connection will form if they spend time with their child and play a role in her life. After all, parenting is something that both men and women learn through practice and persistence.

 Women tend to play with their kids in a more structured manner than men do. Is one style better than the other?

One of the truths in life is that men and women are different, and that means moms and dads too. A child has just as much fun playing with a father, even if it is not planned out or structured—and the child is learning. By simply allowing a child to be a part of whatever task a father is involved in gives him the chance to explore, learn and bond. Structured time together can be beneficial because kids like routines, but they enjoy spontaneity, too.

Mom   *Dad*

Communication

Mom	Dad
Indirect	**Direct**
asks questions	gives imperatives
Do you want the ball?	*Go get the ball.*

Discipline

Mom	Dad
Less Successful	**More Successful**
boys are less compliant	boys are more compliant
girls show no difference	

Stimulation

Mom	Dad
Soothing	**Active**
rhythmic	physical
one-on-one	social

Responsiveness

Mom	Dad
Tender	**Assuring**
to social cues	to gross motor cues
with soothing sounds	with rhythmic pats

Time

Mom	Dad
Structured	**Impromptu**
caregiving activities	play-oriented activities
educational play	less directed play

Props

Mom	Dad
Things	**Self**
uses toys	uses body
more cognitive	more physical

Help

Mom	Dad
Direct	**Indirect**
assists child	guides child
points him to answers	lets him find answers on own

Your child's recognition of the differences between mother and father care actually enhances his development.

—Kyle Pruett, MD
Fatherneed

Sources: Compliance and Self-Assertion, Power, McGrath, Hughes and Manire; Fatherneed, Pruett; Infant Mental Health Journal; Paternal and Maternal Behavior with Premature Infants, Marton and Minde; And Daddy Makes Three: The Father's Impact on Mother and Young Child, K. Alison Clarke-Stewart; Developmental Course of Parental Stimulation and Its Relationship to Mastery Motivation During Infancy, Yarrow, MacTurk, Vietze, McCarthy, Klein and McQuiston.

Men, more so than women, tend to encourage persistence when it comes to learning new things. Is it detrimental to be more demanding?

Research shows that fathers, more than moms, tend to challenge their children and encourage them to be persistent when facing a difficult task, and that such lessons translate into social and academic confidence later in their lives. Although letting a child get too frustrated while trying to accomplish a task can be detrimental to learning, if an adult can figure out just how far to push and when to give in, he will help her understand the benefits of pushing through a hard task and build self-esteem.

Hispanic

MYTH:
The Hispanic father is a macho-man who leaves childrearing to the woman.

Although Hispanic men from many cultures have had to suffer the "macho" steroetype, evidence shows that many play a very active role in the home. The macho man is becoming the nurturing man. This is particularly true the more time he spends with his children. His commitment to his family increases and he's likely to be less authoritarian than if he didn't spend time with them. Evidence also shows that father involvement is typically high, whether or not the parents were ever married.

Compared to white fathers, research shows that black fathers who live with their children:

- Are more likely to share housework
- Practice more severe discipline
- Expect earlier autonomy from their children
- Place more emphasis on obedience than autonomy

A survey of black men revealed that those who experienced a positive relationship with a father who cared and sacrificed for them were more likely to be responsible fathers themselves.

Sources: Journal of Marriage and the Family; The Role of Race and Poverty, Mosley and Thomson.

Asian

MYTH:
The Asian father is a workaholic with no time for his children.

Asian fathers come from many cultures including those of Japan, China, Vietnam, Korea and the Philippines. In recent years, there have been marked social and demographic changes that have resulted in Asian fathers changing from workaholic dads to more nurturing dads. Interestingly, although Japanese boys spend only half as much time with their fathers as American boys do with theirs, they tend to spend more time with their daughters than American men do. And, where dinnertime is often "dad time" in America, Japanese fathers spend time with their children at breakfast.

ACTION ITEMS
Resources for all kinds of fathers

Fatherneed
Kyle Pruett, MD

With advice to fathers ranging from how to speak to toddlers so that they listen to how to avoid the common tendency to reinforce gender stereotypes in young children, Fatherneed is the perfect resource for all dads—including divorced fathers, fathers of adopted children, stepfathers, and fathers of special-needs children—as well as moms who want kids who are meaningfully connected to their fathers.

The Role of the Father in Child Development
Michael E. Lamb, PhD

Lamb, the head of the Section on Social and Emotional Development at the National Institute of Child Health and Human Development in Bethesda, Maryland, and other leading experts, discuss major perspectives on the role of the father in child development. The book also covers nonconventional relationships, such as those experienced by divorced fathers, stepfathers, gay fathers and adolescents. A terrific source for exploring the research topic of fathers involved in developmental psychology or child custody issues.

Black

MYTH:

Black fathers are invisible and uninvolved with their children.

Black fathers have had to battle several stereotypes, but research has emphasized some very positive points about their fathering skills. Evidence shows they are typically very nurturing to both their sons and their daughters and that they participate equally with their wives in child-rearing decisions. They feel strongly about the kin and friend network that is present in their community, often seeking advice from others. They tend to be involved in the household work and childcare and demonstrate better communication with the family if they were involved with the care of their children from infancy.

White

MYTH:

The breadwinning white father steps in at day's end for dinner and a hug.

IN SUMMARY: American mainstream culture has often relied on negative stereotypes to describe the fathers of different cultures. These unfortunate but enduring stereotypes mask the ways American men of different cultural groups successfully raise their children. And, they keep us from recognizing the positive beliefs and behaviors that fathers share across cultural, racial and class boundaries.

Do fathers differ across cultures?

One theme holds true for all: Fathers who are involved make a difference.

—Kyle Pruett, MD
Fatherneed

Sources: Civitas; The Role of Race and Poverty, Mosley and Thomson; Journal of Marriage and the Family; Aisha Ray, PhD; Kyle Pruett, MD.

The New Father:
A Dad's Guide to the First Year
Armin A. Brott

Brott breaks each month of a child's first year into chapters to create a thorough reference book for fathers. Written by a father with levity and tales of his own experiences, this unique book talks about parenting issues from a father's perspective. Touching on a range of issues, including the emotions that surface with the birth of the child, the changes in the relationship between parents, breastfeeding and financial planning, the book is an informative guide for fathers and mothers alike.

A Families and Work Institute survey indicates that men with the strongest aspirations to advance are fathers of children in the primary child-rearing years. Of dads with children under 18 years, 64% want more responsibility, while only 55% of men without children want more.

Fathers.com reports that more companies are starting to recognize that their employees link family satisfaction with productivity at work. In fact, a DuPont Corp. survey of 18,000 employees concluded that their most remarkable finding was the positive impact their work life program had on business results.

A national survey by Kinder Care at Work found that working fathers whose children were enrolled in corporate-sponsored, work-site childcare centers reported increased job productivity.

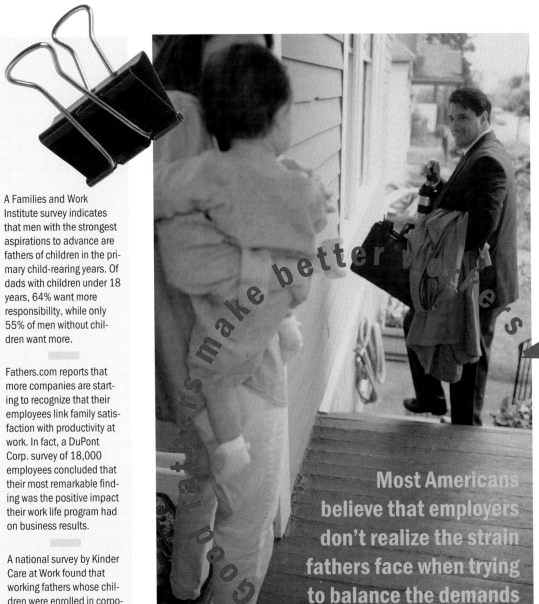

Good fathers make better ***

Most Americans believe that employers don't realize the strain fathers face when trying to balance the demands of family and work.

ACTION ITEMS Working father's travel checklist

Worried about staying close to your child while you're on the road?

Ask yourself:
- is the trip necessary?
- if so, can you make it shorter?

Ask your wife or partner:
- how does she feel about the trip?
- is it an acceptable time to go away?
- will she need help while you are away?

Talk to your child before your trip:
- tell her where you are going and why
- explain in simple terms why you are going
- mark a calendar together with your return date

Phone home:
- ask questions that require something more than yes or no answers
- call at a specified time each day
- make surprise calls every now and then

Women call **involvement**
the **#1** quality of a good father.
Financial support is **#2**.

Survey says...

Fathers and mothers should be equally responsible for:

Infant care and feeding

76%

Bedtime routine

94%

but...

Financially supporting the family

58%

Good workplaces make better fathers!

Bringing home the paycheck is no longer seen as sufficient to fulfill the fathering role.

—www.fathers.com

Sources: National Center for Fathering; Child Magazine; Working Fathers, James Levine, EdD.

Family and Medical Leave Act: President Clinton signed this Act in 1993. It allows parents who worked at least 1,250 hours during the year prior in establishments with 50 or more employees to take up to six weeks of unpaid leave to care for a newborn or newly adopted child.

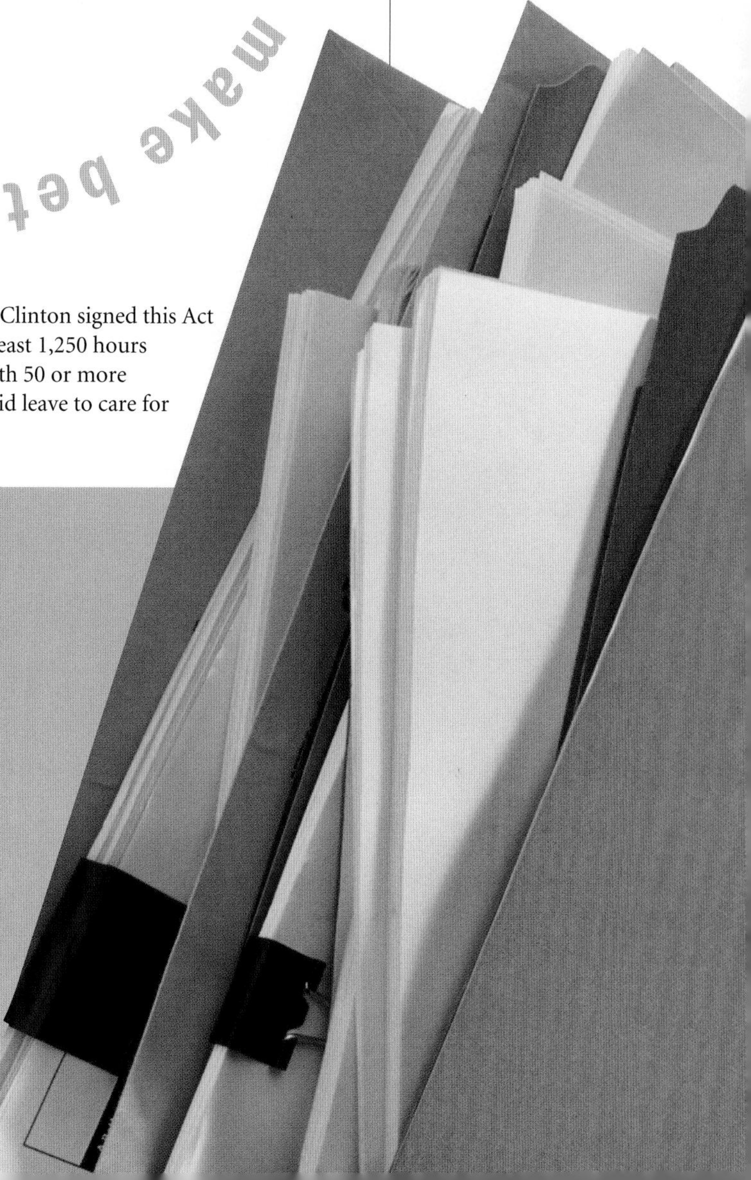

Use faxes to stay in touch:
- send pictures
- look at homework

Get creative with:
- email
- postcards
- digital photos
- videotapes
- cassettes

Source: Fatherneed, Kyle Pruett, MD.

The good and bad news about divorced and non-resident fathers…

The National Center for Health Statistics says 38% of white children and 75% of black children will experience at least one parental divorce.

The results of a 2000 Time/CNN poll show:
• 62% say that parents should not stay together for the children's sake
• 23% feel that children are better off with unhappily married parents
• 42% think that children are almost always harmed by divorce

 25% of fathers see their child at least once a week

 33% of fathers see their children only a few times a year or less

 90% of fathers with joint custody pay their child support on time

 25% of non-custodial fathers pay no child support at all

Source: The Role of the Father in Child Development, Michael Lamb, PhD; Fatherneed, Kyle Pruett, MD.

ACTION ITEMS Tips for easing the pain of divorce

 Tell your child together.
Assure your child that although his parents may be separating, you both will still be there for him and that you are still a family. Keep the explanation age-appropriate and never place blame on each other or your children.

 Don't try to be superdad.
Parenting is tough, and single parenting is even tougher, so don't feel guilty if you have to ask for help. In an attempt to compensate for a failed relationship or less time with the kids, many fathers go overboard with gifts or leniency. What matters to your child is the opportunity to spend time with Dad.

 Make plans ahead of time.
By setting a date for the next time you will see a child and honoring that commitment, you help a child realize that she will be a part of your life even if you physically aren't in her home. Also, kids need consistency, and more than anything, they need a parent's time. Their trust in people they care for has already been challenged; don't reinforce the negative by canceling dates or not making them in the first place.

1 in **10** **children**
will go through
2 **divorces**
of their resident parent
before **age** **16**

 Who gets the kids?

10.3% Father
15.7% Both
72.5% Mother

Source: The National Fatherhood Initiative

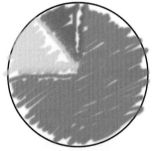

A warm relationship with an authoritative, non-resident father has been associated with higher self-esteem, better social and cognitive competencies and fewer behavioral problems.

—Hetherington

Fathers who use mediation report higher satisfaction with joint custody arrangements

4 **Create familiar space for your child.**
To help ease your child's transition and preserve your role as father, make him feel at home no matter what the parenting (custody) arrangement. This also means helping sustain his normal routines. Keeping some of his things only at your house will help give him a sense of home and ease the challenge of readjusting with each visit.

5 **Don't turn divorce into a war.**
How you deal with the divorce or separation process greatly affects your child. His world already has been turned upside down, and bad-mouthing his mother or dragging out painful custody battles hurts your child much more than your ex-spouse.

6 **Financially support your child.**
Financial support translates to love and concern for a child, so making support payments is a critical factor in helping a child deal with divorce or separation. Paying on time, and consistently, helps a child feel secure that you still care about her and are involved in her life. When fathers become delinquent in child support, for whatever reason, they are not only breaking the law, but are sending a message to the child that she is not important or has been forgotten. (See pages 144 and 145 for more information on child support.)

gone Fishin

25 million children are affected by **fatherlessness.** Emotional fatherlessness affects millions more.

The most common paths to

Children from fatherless homes are more likely to:
- Be poor
- Be involved in alcohol and drug abuse
- Suffer from health problems
- Drop out of school
- Have emotional and behavioral problems
- Smoke cigarettes
- Have lower grade point averages

Boys from fatherless homes are more likely to:
- Be involved in crime

Girls from fatherless homes are more likely to:
- Become preganant as teens

Sources: US Department of Health and Human Services; Stanton, Tian and Silva; Hong and White-Means; McLanahan and Sandefur; The Charles Kettering Foundation.

ACTION ITEMS Tips for getting back to fathering

 It's never too late.
Of course, the earlier you're involved with a child, the better. But, no matter when you join in, your regular and reliable participation in your child's life will play a unique and critical role in his development. Consistent involvement may also help you feel more responsible and better about yourself.

 Re-establish a relationship with the mother.
Before you can reach your estranged child, you must first reach out to your child's mother or other primary caregiver in order to show a genuine interest, intentions and a willingness to help and communicate.

 Make an effort to be part of the child's life.
Generally, with consistent love and attention, you can regain a role in your child's life. And, although it might take time, your child's mother will probably appreciate your efforts. Go out of your way to share meaningful time and show your affection—ask to babysit, arrange to spend an evening, a day or a weekend with the child.

 Behave consistently with the child.
Consistent behavior is key in helping your child understand and trust that he can count on you to play a permanent role in his life. So be reliable about spending time and never break dates.

The two leading causes of fatherlessness are divorce and out-of-wedlock births.

People who say fatherlessness is the most significant social problem facing Americans

72%

Children who live absent of their father

36%

One in **five** children living in female-headed households have not seen their father in **five** years.

These are the best of times and the worst of times for America's children.

Although fathers are emerging as vital contributors in their homes and communities, there are more father-deprived children than ever.

—National Center for Fathering

Source: www.fathers.com.

5 **If you're far away, be creative.**
Send him family photo albums, record his favorite story on cassette for bedtime listening, play a game of tic-tac-toe through the mail and as often as possible, schedule visits with the child. To help your child get to know you, use your imagination. Fathers who live far away can use the phone to teach a child to recognize his voice, the fax machine to exchange drawings, the mail or email to exchange letters, pictures, postcards and surprises.

6 **Pay child support.**
If you've lost touch with your child following a divorce, making child support payments on time and regularly is a critical factor in helping your child feel secure that you still care about him and are involved in his life. When fathers become delinquent in support, they not only commit a felony, but they send a message to their children that they are not important or have been forgotten.

74%

of households now have a dual income.

Spanking

has never been proven to be effective

Violence has never been proven to work better than any other form of discipline and it is likely to teach your child to be aggressive. Today, time-outs are a widely used method of getting kids to think about what they have done wrong.

Whiskey was commonly rubbed on a baby's gums to sooth teething. Now we know alcohol can be harmful.

TEETHING REMEDY

Before the chicken pox vaccination was discovered, parents thought that if one kid had the infection you should expose them all to "get it all over with."

18%

18% of all children in the USA are now born outside of marriage.

1,150,000

There were 1,150,000 divorces recently recorded in in the USA.

ACTION ITEMS

Get up-to-date

There are many myths that are spread to new parents by family members, friends and sometimes even their pediatrician. Many are just 'old wives tales', and while they may not be harmful, they can be confusing to new parents who are trying to learn to do the right thing for their children.

1 **Myth: Television stimulates a child's development in the same way face-to-face talking does.**
The "talking" from a television does not offer your child the same benefits as the sound of your voice because the TV cannot respond to his attempts to interact. Whether you talk, sing or read, it is the sound of your voice — not just any voice — that will help your grandchildren connect with you and feel the love and affection that he needs to grow and develop.

56% of kids under 13 are now in child care, and both parents share the responsibilities of caregiving.

1.9 was the average number of kids per family in 1999.

3.6 was the average number of kids per family in 1899.

"Be seen and not heard," was what parents used to tell their children. Now experts say that listening to your child and validating his feelings is important to his self-esteem.

Clean your plate

Forcing your child to eat may cause feeding problems in the future. Provide your child with healthy choices and allow experimentation.

Methods of parenting have changed as society has evolved. For instance, new parents now put infants on their backs to sleep. Babies who sleep on their stomachs are more prone to SIDS (or crib death). Before this was discovered, parents were told that if a baby slept on his back he could spit up and choke to death. Research now proves this is not true. Even babies who don't have full control of their neck are safe on their backs and at no risk of choking.

Sources: BabyCenter.com, BabyZone.com.

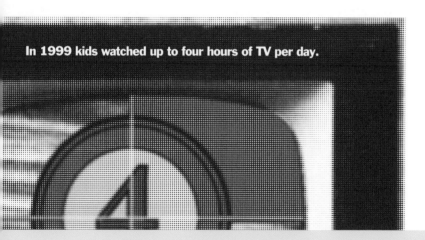

In 1999 kids watched up to four hours of TV per day.

2 Myth: You can help infants sleep through the night by feeding them infant cereal. It is true that infants will, on occasion, wake during the night because they are hungry. However, sleeping through the night has more to do with their development and having a good bedtime routine. In fact, parents are cautioned against giving babies solid foods earlier than four to six months since their digestive systems may not be fully developed. Also, they may not be able to swallow solids, which can cause choking.

3 Myth: Mobile infant walkers help children learn to walk better. Contrary to former belief, mobile infant walkers do not help your child learn to walk faster. Actually, they can be dangerous because they can make a child overly mobile. Therefore, stationary walkers are a safer way to go. If your child does use a mobile walkers, keep them away from stairs and in a child-proofed area, and make sure that they are supervised at all times.

Send pictures and small treats

Letters will never go out of style and a saved letter will become meaningful over time. Get your parents to be creative by writing in colored ink, sending treats, and perhaps enclosing a self-addressed envelope so it is easier for your child to send a drawing in return.

It's your call

Help your parents keep in regular contact with their grandchildren by phone

85% of grandparents call once a month.

90% are encouraged to call.

It's helpful if you tell them the best times to call.

Remind the grandparents to ask open-ended questions.

Advise your parents to listen patiently and ask questions.

Stay

33%
of grandparents live near enough to see their grandkids a few times a week

7%
sent an email this week

15%
wrote a letter this week

53%
of grandparents have sent a greeting card to their grandchild sometime in the last month

ACTION ITEMS

Tips for staying close

Unquestionably, maintaining closeness with grandchildren is more challenging for long distance grandparents than for those who live around the corner. Both daily and one-on-one contact are very valuable in establishing a strong bond—no matter where they live.

1 Go the extra mile. Grandparents can have tight connections with grandchildren who live across the country if they make an effort to communicate frequently and meaningfully. They must get creative about finding ways to get to know their grandkids, stay up-to-date with their interests and play a part in their lives. By doing so, their presence in spirit makes up for their physical absence.

ing in touch

How can my child stay close to long-distance grandparents?

Overcome the effects of distance by keeping your children and their granparents connected.

The majority of families do this through visits or phone calls. Although these may be the more obvious ways to stay close, don't forget that there are other methods, such as writing emails or letters.

Help your parents stay on top of what toys, games and videos interest their grandchildren

Source: AARP.

2 Take advantage of technology. Phones… faxes… videotapes… email… the many new and traditional methods of communications are terrific tools for distant grandparents since they promote immediate and constant correspondence—the key to close relationships.

3 Plan visits when you can. Set aside time and money so that your kids can be with your parents as much as possible. Send your children to stay with your parents for a long weekend, or ask them to stay with your children while you're away. Also, make an effort to spend holidays and other special occasions with the family since such events are often a great chance for you and your children to participate in cultural or religious rituals.

4 Communicate creatively. There are plenty of unique ways to share experiences without the benefit of physical proximity. Grandparents can arrange to watch a grandchild's favorite television show at the same time, or see a movie over the same weekend, and discuss it over the phone or email. Grandparents could also send a scrapbook of family photos or books about topics of interest to help establish common interests. Of course, letters and cards are fun to receive, personal to read and long lasting.

D*i*ve**rsi**ty!

Proud kids

Evidence from studies shows that when cultural differences are respected, kids learn to accept and be proud of both cultures. They could develop into healthy, strong individuals, with a strong sense of personal identity.

Good homes

"No studies have found that the kids of gay or lesbian parents are disadvantaged in any significant respect relative to kids of heterosexual parents," says a recent American Psychological Association report. "Home environments provided by gay and lesbian parents are as likely as those provided by heterosexual parents to support and enable kids' psychosocial growth."

Lone parents	**Interracial kids**	Split parents	**Clever stepgrands**	**Single moms**
30% of households in the USA consist of single adults with children	There are 700,000 interracial couples and about 5 million multicultural kids	50% of children will experience divorce before they are 18 years old	67% of children said they could learn a lot from their step-grandparent	80% of all single parent families are headed by women

---

ACTION ITEMS   Tips for dealing with diversity

1 **How to handle grandparents' advice:**
When your parents voice unwanted advice or criticism about your situation, try to address the issue rather than eliminate your parents from your children's lives. Explain how and why you choose to parent, and offer your parents reading material so they can learn about the recommended parenting techniques of today.

2 **How to handle religious differences:**
Talk to your parents about your feelings about religion, and ask them to respect your decisions regarding religion. Allow them to educate your children about their religion by sharing traditions and time, but encourage them to ask you first.

3 **How to handle divorce:**
Remind grandparents that divorce does not have to mean the breakup of family connections. Encourage them to focus their attention on the grandchildren rather than the parents. Let grandparents know how important their role is during this tough period of time, when grandchildren need loyal listeners, emotional support and opportunities for care-free fun.

166

How can I help my family to embrace our diversity?

Five million

is the estimated number of interracial or multicultural kids, although statistics on multicultural families are difficult to obtain because there is no official US Census category for people of mixed parentage

Good parenting is influenced most profoundly by a parent's ability to create a loving home which does not depend on sexual orientation race nor family structure

Give it time

Adjusting to new members of the family and learning new family dynamics can be emotional and complicated. But over time, step-grandparents can become close to their kids. Certain factors, such as the child's age when the family structure changed, will impact the ease of this relationship.

50% of kids said that having a personal relationship with their step-grandparent was very important

The best thing you can advise your family to do if they do not agree with a family situation is to preserve their relationship with your child. Because of society's bias, being part of a non-traditional family is challenging. For the best interests of the child, grand-parents should not add to the difficulty but put their preju-dices aside. Step-grandparents should take things slowly, and be sensitive and tactful to the new family's needs.

Divorced twice	**Cross cultures**	**Stepkids**	**Gay or lesbian**
40% of all second marriages in the USA will end in divorce	Interracial marriages more than doubled between 1980 and 1995	10% of all children in the USA are part of a step-family	Between 8 and 10 million children are raised in gay and lesbian households

4 **How to handle step-grandparents:**
Let step-grandparents play an important role in your child's life without being competitive with the biological grandparents. Suggest that they slowly build a friendship with your child and that they make themselves available without asking for anything in return.

5 **How to handle non-traditional families:**
Let your parents know that even if they are not comfortable with the situation, the child is the pri-ority and needs plenty of emotional support. Teach your parents about your diveristy, so they can bet-ter understand and support you.

6 **How to handle conflict:**
To avoid misunderstandings and frustrations, clarify what each one expects of the other. Hold a family session to iron out issues and avoid poten-tial problems. Talk about your concerns and together offer suggestions for a smoother-run-ning relationship.

Life's gifts

Of the most important ethics or values that grand-parents would like to pass on to their grandchildren:
42% said morals and integrity
21% said success or ambition
20% mentioned religion
14% said consideration
10% said to be reasonable

60 million grandparents

The number of grandparents in the US has increased dramatically as the population gets older and people live longer

 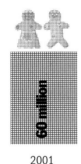 

58 million
60 million
76 million predicted

1993   2001   2005

Source: American Demographics; AARP

Sweet little ones

A typical grandparent in the US has five grandchildren

29%

of those interviewd say they pass on stories about the old days

Elder
Showing how to age with dignity

Mentor
Fostering the child's ambition

30%

of grandparents earn at at least $50,000 a year

Nurturer
Being closely involved in their life and providing help when needed

Roles of

ACTION ITEMS

What role will your parents play?

Parents and grandparents should talk about the role the grandparents will play. And, while it is important for the grandparents to respect the parent's wishes, parents need to allow the grandparents to create their own identity. The two most important gifts they can give are love and time. How they do it is their decision.

 What are the different roles your parents play when interacting with your child?

☐ Companion/friend

☐ Advisor

☐ Teacher

☐ Family historian

☐ Confidant

☐ Playmate

☐ Nurturer

☐ Travel companion

Role Model
Imparting a strong work ethic

Counselor
A wealth of family wisdom

35%
of those interviewed say they often give their grandchild advice

Confidant
Someone to trust and talk to

33%
of those interviewed say they tell their grandchildren the family history

Friend
An imaginative counterpoint to a child's day

Playmate
Fun-seeking and informal

Spiritual Guide
Helping find the meaning of life

Teacher
An example of good manners and morals

49%
of grandparents interviewed describe themselves as a friend to their grandchild

grandparents

There are many different roles your parents might play. An effective grandparent might be altruistic, nurturing and put the needs of family members ahead of their own. They may be full of vitality, bring a sense of wonder to their grandchild's life, be warm, be easy to talk to, or be patient and careful listeners. If they value a close family, they will make an effort to make themselves available and be a support to their children and grandchildren.

Source: AARP,
Arthur Kornhaber, MD.

? What values or ethics would you like your parents to pass on to your children?
- ☐ High morals and integrity
- ☐ Success or ambition
- ☐ Religion
- ☐ Consideration of others
- ☐ Family importance

? What gifts do your kids get from your parents?
- ☐ Clothes
- ☐ Books
- ☐ Toys and other play items
- ☐ Financial investments

? How often do your kids see their grandparents?
- ☐ Child care on an everyday or regular basis
- ☐ Babysitting on occasion
- ☐ Live in the same household as grandchildren
- ☐ See grandparents every week
- ☐ See grandparents at least once a month
- ☐ Both see and speak by phone to each week
- ☐ Have little contact

Going for a visit

When you take your children to visit your parents, you should be as prepared as you can. Help them to give your children the best stay and have the most fun by letting them know how to look after them in the way you do.

Favorites
Let your parents know your child's favorite activities

Being flexible
Ensure your visit isn't too short or too long.

In touch
31% of grandparents speak on the phone to their grandchild each week

Good timing
Explain about your child's routines like eating and sleep times

Rules of the game
Explain the house rules to your toddler before they visit

1. *Play quietly when other people are resting*

2. *Always remember to say "please" and "thank you"*

3. *Don't play with your food at the table*

4. *No arguing, hitting, or kicking*

5. *No jumping on furniture and no screaming*

6. *Ask before you take things— some things are off limits*

7. *Always put things away when you have finished with them*

Safety first
Make sure your parents have only safe household items and toys within reach

Giving gifts
72% of grandparents will have bought a gift for their grandchild in the past month

Priceless
Grandparents spent $489 a year on things for their grandchildren

---

ACTION ITEMS — Preparing for a visit

When you visit them:

1. **Find out what you can do to help.** A lot can be done by way of bringing things or preparing for the trip. Talk to your parents about planning for the visit and ask them which activities they'd enjoy and how much time they'd like to spend with their grandchildren. If you are dropping off your child for a weekend, make it easier by sending your child with the right clothes and favorite toys or security blanket. Review your child's schedule and habits including your child's napping and bedtime routines and your approach to discipline. Don't forget to ask if there is anything you can do to help make the visit go smoothly.

2. **Ask them to childproof their house.** A healthy, safe environment for your children requires "childproofing." Suggest that when they inspect their home, they focus less on removing objects that their grandchild may harm and more on removing those that may harm your child like household cleaners, medicines and choking hazards. They should keep handy a first-aid kit, children's pain reliever and your pediatrician's phone number. (See pages 38 and 39 for more information on childproofing.)

Play time
43% of grandparents say it is easy to come up with potential activities for a child

Fleeting visit
12% of grandparents have little contact with a grandchild, talking on the phone every few months or less

Staying close
44% of grandparents see their grandchild every week

It takes careful planning to make taking your child visiting a success. A similar thing applies when people visit your home.

Try to communicate with your parents or others that you are visiting in advance, agreeing on the fore-seeable aspects of the visit. This way, everyone knows what to expect and no one is disappointed. It is also very helpful to provide the tools they might need to entertain, look after and keep your child safe.

Source: AARP.

Having fun

The activities that grandparents did the most with their grandchild in the past month were:
Staying over night
Engaging in exercise or sport
Watching a TV comedy
Shopping for clothes
Having dinner

A bite to eat
72% of grandparents will have shared a meal with their grandchild in the past month

Compromise

Sometimes you find that the older generations don't agree with watching too much TV. One way to deal with this before it becomes an issue is to suggest that your child spends one hour "reading" books or drawing pictures for every hour he spends watching TV.

Plan B
Don't ever expect a visit to go as planned

3 **Plan for favorite meals and activities.** Let your parents know your kids' special interests and needs ahead of time. If your child has any special dietary needs, tell your parents in advance and give them written instructions. If your child is a picky eater, explain what he will and won't eat and bring portable favorites if possible.

When they visit you:

1 **Be flexible.** Ask them to offer you several dates and decide together which is most convenient. Holidays are a good time as people often have time off work. Remind your parents that a three- or four-day stay is a good length.

2 **Remind them not to expect the visit to go as planned.** Even the best laid plans can change when they involve children. This does not mean that you can't plan in advance. Let your parents schedule activities that your child will enjoy, but prepare them to be flexible.

SEARCH

Websites can help you discover family history

www.nara.gov/genealogy

Gives access the National Archives with guides to help you request records from them.

www.myhistory.org

Also has a venue for exchanging family stories and guidelines for preserving family treasures.

lcweb.log.gov/rr/genealogy

Has an extensive collection of US and foreign genealogical and local historical publications.

www.genealogy.com

An online course, database and guides.

www.ellisisland.org

Lets you search passenger record archives to learn about relatives who came to the US via Ellis Island.

Home truths

Like a family photo or an old letter, your home is evidence of your history, especially if it has remained in the family for a few generations. You could take your kids to visit homes and towns where previous generations have lived. Houses are an expression of the people who lived in them. They also reveal trends in architecture and construction. Fixtures and landscaping are tied up with tastes and technologies. And an addition to a home might offer clues about births, jobs, and the local economy.

Picture perfect

Help grandchildren to identify with the family history by gathering and preserving photos and old records. Ask relatives for originals they might have that you can have copied. Find out from them who is in the pictures and if they know any interesting stories about them. Arrange all your collected memorabilia in a scrapbook, using materials that will protect them from damage.

AARP suggests getting the grandchildren to help, "so they can learn, and start to connect the past and present." Perhaps you can make photocopies of pictures for younger children, so they don't get dirty. In the scrapbook write down the details of the picture and how it connects to other information you have about your family, such as diaries, letters, and interviews.

ACTION ITEMS

How can I involve my family?

Go the extra mile and capture your family story on video:

1 **Describe where their family lived.** What did they like best about it? How did it look? What was the color of their room? Who did they share it with?

2 **Discuss ethnic heritage and customs.** Talk about religion—discuss what traditions and practices are most important to them.

3 **Describe past historical events.** This could be wars, past presidents, etc.

4 **Where did they go to school?** Take a trip to the building, if possible. Talk about best friends and teachers, favorite classes, sports played and other activities and highlights of these years.

5 **Did they go to college, serve in the military or go to technical school?** What did they study? What were the highlights of these years?

Hand-me-downs

If one of your parents had written a journal, wouldn't you want to read it? Keep a journal and write what you think and feel, see, read, and hear about—weddings, jobs, scandals, news, politics, parades. Relax. Start small. Keep it fun. Years from now you will have a document that will fascinate your descendants.

Clothing, silver, furniture, and works of art make the journey from one generation to the next. But the stories that help give meaning to these treasures often don't survive the trip. Ask family members about their possessions from the past, the original owner, and special stories or memories about each item.

A child will learn about history when it is told in the most lively and relevant way, and if they can connect to it visually. Grandparents are often uniquely qualified to teach family history. They have first-hand experience of recent history and may know older family legends and rituals by heart. They may be able to give more detail than anyone else, and usually have a collection of interesting memorabilia, such as the family records, photos and recipes.

Source: AARP.

Talk about it

Pass on stories of your family's past by emphasizing the funny, adventurous or uplifting, and highlighting similarities or differences to your child's experience. Gather these stories by interviewing your relatives and writing down their answers, or recording them on tape. They will probably interpret your request for an interview as an honor. Your time and effort prove that you take their memories seriously. Conduct the interviews with a little care, and you'll end up with a coherent oral history rather than random reminiscences. The tapes will also preserve something fragile and precious—your narrators' voices, how they express themselves, a sense of who they are.

Road trip
Take your family on a vacation to the sites that are significant in your family history. This will bring it to life for your children

Welcome to **Brinkley**

---

6 **Share pictures from their childhood.** Describe or visit their old house and neighborhood. Talk about neighbors and places they used to visit.

7 **What kinds of friends have they had in their life?** Discuss what qualities made these people special. Arrange to meet them, if possible.

8 **Tell the tale of their relationship with their spouse.** Where did they meet? When did they get married? Where? What was the wedding like? Why do they love their partner?

9 **Talk about work — the jobs they've had over the years.** Talk about the challenges they have faced, the rewards they've received. If possible, visit a place of current or past employment.

10 **Pass on life lessons.** Share hopes, philosophies and disappointments and advice.

Who are they? 33%

Hispanic
17.6% are hispanic

Children who are cared for by their grandparents are from many different backgrounds and have various ethnicities, although the majority are white.

of kids in grandparent-maintained homes have no health insurance, which is often part of an employment package. 13% cared for by their parents have no insurance.

Black
34.5% are black

White
43.8% are white

6,000

Where do they live?

16.9%
in the Midwest

18.7%
in the Northeast

21.1%
in the West

43.3%
in the South

Cities & suburbs
41% of children brought up in families where grandparents are the main caregivers live in the suburbs. 38.9% live in cities. 19.8% live in non-metropolitain areas.

ACTION ITEMS — Tips for grandparents as parents

1 **Be prepared to deal with the adult child.** Grandparents who are caring for their grandchild are probably doing so because the adult child is not willing or able to do it. First, come to terms with the child's circumstance—let go of guilt and don't blame yourself. Also, although you love your adult child, protect yourself and your family by setting firm rules on issues such as whether she can move into your home and how often she can see your grandchild. Be consistent to avoid being manipulated, and if necessary learn to let go.

2 **Brace yourself for changes in your lifestyle and family.** Caring for a grandchild usually forces grandparents to put the Golden Years on hold— suspend travel plans, restrict spending, rearrange work and social routines and redirect already limited energies. How you handle these changes is critical for everyone. Start by keeping life as simple as possible and the lines of communication open. Make time for yourself, ask for help, and focus on the good you are providing.

3 **Don't try to take it on alone.** The changes in lifestyle often provoke a complex array of emotions. Support is the key to easing the burdens and sorting out feelings. Turn to relatives, friends or a support group (our country boasts more than 850). See www.aarp.org /grandparents to find one near you.

Half

of kids cared for by their grandparents are under 6

50.8% of these kids are under six years old. And 28.8% are between six and 11 years old.

,000

children under the age of 18

are being raised in households maintained by a grandparent or other relative.

65.2%

of grandparents looking after kids are between 45 and 65 years of age

1 in 4

kids live in grand-parent-maintained homes in poverty.

1 in 5 kids live with their parents in poverty.

The children being raised by their grandparents are from all different backgrounds. Many of them are not very well off, because often the grandparents are no longer working. And, because most of the children in these families are young, the grandparents are relatively young themselves.

Source: Generations United, US Census Bureau, AARP.

4 Take advantage of financial assistance. This can be limited. However, if a grandchild's parents are not willing or able to provide the support, she may be entitled to Temporary Assistance for Needy Families (TANF), Social Security Survivor's Benefits or Medicaid. Contact your local government, grandparent's support group, or an attorney to help you figure out what benefits are available. Don't let your pride or the frustrations of government bureaucracy deter you.

5 Brush up on parenting. You are begining a new role with your grandchild. Try to learn all you can about his developmental and emotional needs. Read recent parenting books, attend parenting classes and talk to your grandchild's teachers. Educate yourself on your grandchild: When was your grandchild's last medical exam? Where should you enroll him in school? Recognize that you may have the added challenge of helping your grandchild heal emotionally, as he probably has endured tragic life experiences at a very young age.

6 Know your rights. See pages 202-203 for more information on the legal rights of grandparent guardians.

Cry baby

Babies whose parents respond promptly to their cries actually cry less than other babies. Comforting a crying baby isn't spoiling. Meeting their needs is not spoiling. In fact, prompt attention to their needs gives babies confidence that their world is safe and predictable, and this builds a good foundation for the capable, caring people they will become.

Give love

Try to avoid doing things for your children that they can do for themselves. Even so, no matter how skillful babies become at doing things for themselves, only others can satisfy a child's need for love, attention and affection.

Too young to spoil?

% who **wrongly** believe that the act described below will spoil a child	All adults	Future parents	Non-parents	Parents of children age 0 to 3	All grand-parents	Grand-parents who take care of their grand-children
Always answering the needs of a baby under 6 months old	62	62	62	56	64	62
Allowing a 2-year-old to get down early from the dinner table	44	48	43	48	45	43
Letting a 6-year-old child choose what to wear to school every day	38	39	36	29	46	47

Sources: Civitas, Zero to Three; BRIO.

Many people are wrong about what kind of treatment will spoil a child, as the chart on the left shows. Groups of adults were asked which types of reactions to a child's behaviour, at various ages, they considered spoiling. The figures shown are the percentages who were **wrong** in their answers. The reality is, that you can not spoil a child younger than six months old. Neither is allowing a two-year-old down from the table early or letting a six-year-old choose what they wear to school every day spoiling him.

ACTION ITEMS
How to prevent spoiled behavior

It's all about encouraging positive behavior and setting limits.

1 **Don't worry, neither you nor your parents can spoil a baby who is less than six months old.** Babies this age are unable to control how their behavior affects other people. Therefore, there is no need to set limits with a crying or fussing baby—go to her when she cries. Research shows that by meeting an infant's needs, she will be more self-reliant and calm when she grows older.

2 **Update yourself and your parents on age appropriate behaviors to determine if a child is acting spoiled or just acting his age.** For example, a two-year-old's tantrums often seem to be obnoxious behavior. However, tantrums are really just an attempt to communicate. A parent should focus on setting limits and more acceptable ways of communicating, rather than worrying about a spoiled child.

3 **Suggest ways to curb spoiled behavior with more positive attention.** Children who lack sufficient positive attention and affection from a parent may act out in negative ways—such as tantrums, whining and clinging—in order to gain attention. By consistently offering warmth and positive attention, a parent can reduce a child's need to act in such unacceptable ways.

176

Act your age

Bad behavior may simply be normal for a child of a certain age. And, normal children still need limits. It is not unusual for a two-year-old to throw a tantrum if he or she can't have something he badly wants. Kids do things that are irritating, like ordering people around and testing limits. Time, patience and guidance will teach them more acceptable ways of communicating and getting their wants and needs met.

Free time

Allowing your baby to spend time alone each day will teach him independence and self-esteem, and will encourage him to provide some of his own pleasures from life.

Never leave your baby alone for for an extended length of time, even when you can. Remember, if a baby is quiet for a very long time he could be enjoying something dangerous or messy.

Before you consider giving your baby this time, first ensure you meet his physical needs – hunger, thirst, soiled diapers, overstimulation, and general fatigue.

Offer a small selection of toys to be alone with. Too many at once is confusing: babies prefer familiar items and repetition.

Change your baby's location and view. Or change the wall hangings in his room from time-to-time to stimulate the learning process.

Demanding

Give plenty of time and encouragement to children as they benefit from hearing your good feelings and positive attitudes. This will also encourage them to respond positively to your guidance. Kids who don't get enough positive attention may try to get it in ways that irritate their parents...

Clinging! Whining! Tantrums!

No amount of affection and love can spoil a child when it is given in the right way. When a baby is younger than six months old it's not possible to spoil that child and give him or her too much attention. As your children grow up it is important that you and your family encourage them to be independent while knowing the rules and limits. And if you show your children attention for the right behavior, they should not resort to other ways to get noticed.

---

4 **Allow your child to be more independent to reduce spoiled behavior.** Often children exhibit spoiled behavior when a parent or grandparent does too much for the child. Such children learn to believe that they deserve to be catered to and do not appreciate a parent's efforts. Therefore, a parent should set clear expectations and allow a child to do for himself those tasks that he is physically able to do.

5 **Stick to consistent rules and limits.** Setting and enforcing strict limits can help limit spoiled behavior. To feel secure, children need a firm structure with regularly enforced rules. By setting and following firm limits, parents teach children to be respectful and responsible. When parents don't enforce rules—either because it is difficult or they don't want to upset their children—they teach their children that the rules don't apply to them, which encourages disrespectful, spoiled behavior.

Diversity

Diversity Statistics

In 1998, the nearly 16,000 children adopted in the U.S. from abroad were:

Male 36%   Female 64%

< 1 year old	46%
1–4 years old	43%
5–9 years old	8%
>9 years old	3%

In 1998, an estimated 15% of 36,000 adoptions of foster children were transracial or transcultural.

33% of children adopted from foster care find homes with a single parent.

Source: National Adoption Information Clearinghouse.

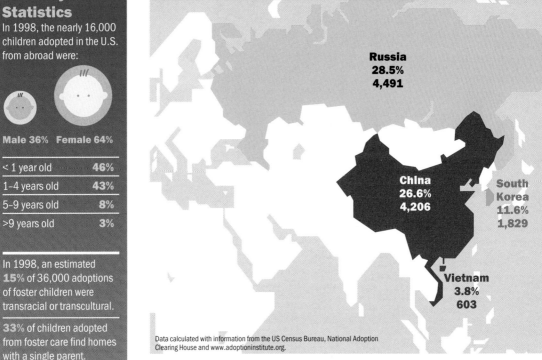

Russia
28.5%
4,491

China
26.6%
4,206

South Korea
11.6%
1,829

Vietnam
3.8%
603

Data calculated with information from the US Census Bureau, National Adoption Clearing House and www.adoptioninstitute.org.

Why is there a rise in adoption of female Chinese babies?

International adoption—adopting orphaned or available children from other countries— began in the late '50s with Korean adoptions, became more common in the late 1990s and continues today. In the United States and Europe, children are being adopted from all over the world.

The surge in the adoption of Chinese female infants is due to Chinese laws restricting families to one or two children per family. Male children are considered more likely to provide for the family and carry on its name. Daughters, however, belong to their husband's family once married. Therefore, families are more likely to surrender female babies for adoption.

ACTION ITEMS   Embracing diversity

1 Acknowledge and accept differences. Acknowledging differences in appearance, family structure and culture between your adopted child and the rest of the family is a natural, healthy step in making everyone comfortable. Keep an eye out for signs that he is becoming aware of differences. Make sure he knows he is a cherished member of your family with a rich and valued cultural heritage.

2 Seek supportive surroundings. Embracing diversity will be easier if you surround your family with other families dealing with similar issues. Seek out people who are sensitive to your issues through support groups, adoption agencies or social service agencies.

3 Celebrate your child's culture. Educate your family about her ethnic heritage and discuss her minority or cultural experience. Try to incorporate her heritage into her everyday world through relationships with people of the same background and exposure to art, books, music and cultural celebrations that portray people of all types in positive and productive roles.

4 Do not tolerate negative slurs. Whether in the home or out, racially- or ethnically-biased remarks should never be tolerated in the presence of your adopted child. If confronted with insensitive language, you should gently correct it. You can do this through education, honesty, discussion or humor.

States with the highest per capita adoption rates

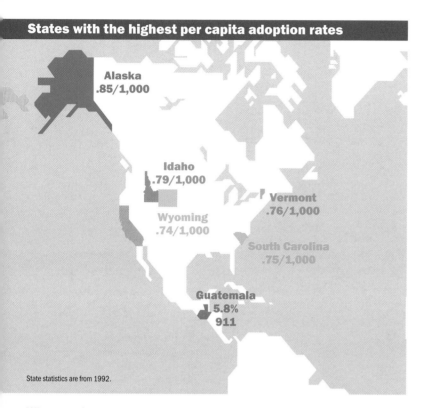

Alaska
.85/1,000

Idaho
.79/1,000

Vermont
.76/1,000

Wyoming
.74/1,000

South Carolina
.75/1,000

Guatemala
5.8%
911

State statistics are from 1992.

Issues related to diversity between a child and his adoptive parents may stretch beyond differences in appearance to cultural and language barriers. Diversity may also be created by mixed-race or same-sex couples who adopt. Dealing with these differences presents not only challenges but great opportunity for growth.

Why have international and transracial adoptions increased?

In the past, adoptions were arranged through public and private agencies that took great effort to match children to families based on physical characteristics. Today, transracial adoption is common, and matching characteristics between adoptees and adoptive families is not a primary concern. Families with young, adopted children are coping with diversity. Even if a family has a matched-race adoption, the child and the adoptive family have differing genetic backgrounds and are unlikely to be exactly alike physically, intellectually or emotionally. Attachment may be strengthened by the understanding that family togetherness and caring—not matching—are most important.

Source: Laura Sanders, LCSW.

5 **Learn and educate.** Adoptive parents often must respond to societal attitudes, concerns and questions regarding adoption. While respecting your child's privacy, parents should respond by educating both strangers and people who impact the adopted child's daily life with answers that are honest, sensitive and appropriate.

6 **Handle sexuality issues with understanding.** Parents in gay and lesbian families should bring up the subject of sexuality with their children the same way any family should—with love, respect, commitment, understanding and honesty. Stress the importance of these values and explain that there are many different cultures, communities and families around the world.

Recommended books:

The Best Face of All
Wilesse Commissiong

All The Colors We Are
Kate Kissinger

This Is Our House
Micheal J. Rosen

Just Like Me
Harriet Rhomer

Sources: adoption.about.com, adoption.com.

Types of Adoption

How long?
Waiting time for adoption varies on the type of adoption and any unforeseeable circumstances that may arise.

Estimates

Infant	1-7 years
International	6-18 months
Foster care	4-18 months

Are there subsidies?
The most common level of employer coverage for adoption is

$2,000

74% cover legal fees

50% cover birth mother medical costs

47% cover agency and placement fees

Are there tax credits?
There are federal adoption tax credits for domestic or international adoptions of

$10,000 per child.

Can I get reimbursed?
Reimbursement through the public child welfare system cannot exceed **$2,000** per special needs child.

Source: National Adoption Information Clearinghouse.

Private agencies are funded by private money and must be licensed or approved by the state in which they operate.

Public agencies are the local branches of a state's social service agency. Public agencies generally handle only special-needs adoptions—those children who were abused, neglected, or abandoned by their birth parents.

Open adoption means that both sides know each other, choose adoption and agree to an arrangement that provides some ongoing connection. It can be anything from an occasional photo or letter to regular contact between birth parents and adoptive parents and child.

Closed adoption is when all records are sealed by the courts. Although confidentiality is not guaranteed, neither side has direct access to that information.

Average cost by country

Romania
$12,000 to $22,000

Haiti
$7,000 to $12,000

Guatemala
$11,000 to $24,000

Columbia
$8,000 to $20,000

Ethopia
$6,000 to $8,000

Source: www.iccadopt.org.

ACTION ITEMS
Are you ready to start the process?

Before starting down the road to adoption, you and your partner should ask yourselves these questions:

1 Would you like to adopt an older or younger child?

2 Would you be willing to adopt a child with clear disabilities?

3 Do you prefer adopting a child of the same race?

4 Are you interested in domestic or international adoption?

5 Would you be willing to adjust your lifestyle for the best interests of the child?

6 What are your views on how and when to tell a child he is adopted?

7 What are your views on helping a child locate or learn about his birth family?

8 Why do you want to be a parent?

Source: adoption.com.

Semi-open adoptions are different from open adoptions in that full names and addresses are not used, an intermediary is responsible for exchanging information and no long-term connection is agreed upon.

Independent adoptions are directly arranged between a pregnant woman and pre-adoptive family, with the help of an attorney. Legal in all but a few states, the parties involved need to be aware of significant variations nationwide.

Russia
$10,000 to $21,000

China
$10,000 to $21,000

Korea
$10,000 to $20,000

Vietnam
$9,000 to 20,000

How expensive is the adoption process?

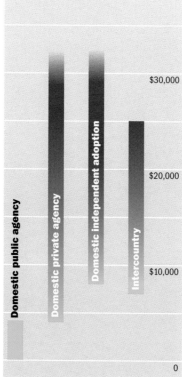

Domestic public agency
Domestic private agency
Domestic independent adoption
Intercountry

$30,000

$20,000

$10,000

0

Costs may include agency fees (application, homestudy and preparation services, post-placement supervision, physicals, and psychiatric evaluations), attorney fees (document preparation, petition and court representation), birth parent expenses (medical, living, legal representation and counseling) travel, genetic testing, homestudy and developmental assessments.

Sources: adoption.about.com, adoptioninstitute.org.

Basic Steps for Adoption

- Educate yourself about adoption.
- Identify the type of adoption (intercountry or domestic, open or closed) you would like to pursue.
- Understand the expenses associated with adoption and determine how you will cover them.
- Choose an adoption agency or hire an attorney who specializes in adoption.
- Submit an adoption application.
- Participate in a home-study and enroll in pre-adoption classes.
- File a petition to adopt and upon being matched with a child, ready yourself for the child's arrival.
- Finalize the adoption.

Sources: adoption.about.com; The Family of Adoption, Joyce Pavao.

What will the adoption agency want to know?

The agency will conduct a "homestudy:"

- A minimum number of visits, usually three.
- Some of the visits are required to be in the home.
- Individual discussions with each member in the household.
- Preparation of a family financial history.
- Initiation of a criminal background check.
- Documentation of physical health history and current health status.
- Request for references.

During the "homestudy" the agency will ask:

- Do you wish to adopt?
- Are you prepared for adoption?
- Are you able to support a child, physically, mentally, and financially?

The following topics are usually discussed:

- Each parent's family of origin.
- Parenting practices and beliefs.
- Marital and other relationships.
- Infertility issues, if applicable.
- Types of children being considered.

Source: adoption.about.com.

Discussing Adoption

The chart below is intended to be used as a general guide to help you better prepare for discussing and handling issues related to your child's adoption.

What are the risks of waiting to tell your child about his adoption?

Shame
Your efforts to keep the information private may set a prohibitive tone regarding the issue. An adopted child may translate these perceptions as shame.

Secrets
You may not be able to keep your child's adoption a secret. There is a high risk of your child finding out about his adoption from other relatives who may mention the subject.

Confusion
Not giving your child a clear explanation may not provide your child with the confidence or language to handle questions about their adoption.

Emotional issues
Your child may have trouble adjusting emotionally if their adoption is not discussed openly and early on in their childhood.

For these reasons, and because young children tend to have a very positive view of adoption, many experts suggest introducing the topic of adoption right from the beginning.

Baby-parent connection	Attachment-separation cycle begins	Identity, feelings, and fears characteristic of preschool years	
1	2	3	4

During their first months, children have an inborn capacity to connect to ensure their survival. The most important and valuable thing you can do is to show, through attention and affection, that you love your child, so she learns trust and feels content. This is true for all children, adopted or not.

Toddler behavior is characterized by alternating attachment and separation phases, including aggressive behavior toward both parents and peers. These actions ordinarily have nothing to do with adoption or with negative genetic traits inherited from birth parents, but rather are normal for the age.

Ages 2–4 is a good time to introduce the word "adoption" and tell your child she is adopted, especially if she was adopted after 2 years of age and is of a different race. It is important for adopted children to acknowledge their memories of the past.

At ages 4-5, continue to talk to your child about adoption. It may be helpful at this time to use context of things he can relate to like books or movies.

From 2-4, children are trying to understand and make sense of relationships in the family.

From 2-5, all children fear getting lost, being abandoned, or no longer being loved by their parents.

From 2-6 there will be opportunities and pressure to begin explaining adoption, as children hear adult conversations.

Be prepared for any struggle to connect with your child. It may be difficult at times, but remember: Don't take it personally.

Older babies and children may either seem to cling too much or not care at all. Parents may need to work harder to assure them that they are loved and will not be abandoned.

Children who are adopted when they are older usually follow the same attachment and separation paths as other children, but often in a different time sequence.

Children who have been traumatized or abused may be fearful, uncertain about showing affection, or show symptoms associated with sexual abuse. See *Action Items* below for references to this problem.

Source: adoptiveparents.com.

ACTION ITEMS
Talking to your child about adoption

1 **Always answer a child's questions about adoption.** If you don't have time to give a good answer when he asks a question, make clear to him that you will talk about it later…and do so!

2 **Looking at family photo albums or videos** provides an excellent opportunity to discuss adoption. However, take your cues from your child. If she sends signals that she does not want to talk about the subject, then let it go.

3 **Make a lifebook with the child.** A lifebook is a scrapbook that records all the people and places that have played an important role in the child's life. Working on a lifebook together generally presents many natural chances to discuss adoption.

4 **Join an adoptive families group** so that the child can meet other adopted children. A child can come to understand much about adoption simply by interacting with other adopted children.

Honesty is the best policy. Adoption is no longer a secret. Society has become more tolerant of adoption, so discussing adoption is easier. Also, in transracial and international adoptions, the physical differences between the adopted child and other family members make adoption obvious. Questions raised about differences and birth heritage require conscious and sensitive responses. Therefore, the real issue is not whether to answer questions about adoption, but how to answer the questions sensitively, with consideration for timing, the child's development, and the community's need for education on the issues.

Opinion differs on the ideal age to begin discussing adoption with your child, and at what age the child is really able to grasp the concepts of where babies come from, how they are born, and how families are formed.

In any case, it is likely to take years of periodic returns to the subject before your child fully grasps what it means to be adopted. Studies suggest that adopted adolescents are better adjusted if they come from families where all emotional issues, including adoption, are discussed openly among family members as soon as possible.

Loss is a feeling that runs through the lives of adopted children. It is difficult for parents to know how much information about the adoption to share and whether the child is wanting or dreading to hear it; parents should probably bring up the subject if the child doesn't. An older child needs to deal with the fact that her birth parent relinquished her for adoption; she also needs to understand that her adoptive parents will not be angry with her for wanting to find out more about her birth parents.

Children able to understand where babies come from	During the elementary school years children further develop their psychological identity as individuals, their confidence, and their self-esteem						
5	6	7	8	9	10	11	12
		From 6–11 children have the need to consolidate their identification with their parents and cement their sense of belonging to a family.					
		From 7–12, children will be feeling the emotional impact of the sense of loss.					

Many young children believe that they were either adopted or born. They need to know that they were born first, that all children are conceived and born the same way, and that some are adopted while others are not.

Telling your adopted child about her adoption may awaken painful memories for you if, for example, you chose adoption due to infertility.

Do not wait until adolescence to reveal your child's adoption to her: it could be devastating to her self-esteem and to her faith in her adoptive parents.

5 **Be aware of bad times to talk about adoption,** such as when the family is going through a crisis or stressful situation; you are angry with the child or otherwise upset; the information about the adoption could be interpreted by the child as an attack, such as during an argument with the child.

6 **Have a positive attitude about adoption and discussing adoption.** Your child will pick up on your attitude. Therefore, when you talk to others about adoption or discuss adoption around the house, act in an open and positive manner rather than a defensive one. Also, keep an eye out for other means, such as television shows, that present adoption in a positive light.

Recommended books include:

A Forever Family: A Child's Adoptive Story
Roslyn Banis

How I was Adopted
Joanna Cole

The Day We Met You
Pheobe Koehler

Source: National Adoption Information Clearinghouse.

Foster Care

Most adoptions from foster care are by the foster parents.

How long does it take?

After termination of parental right, how long do children wait before being adopted?

3%
wait less than one month;

18%
wait 1-5 months;

30%
wait 6-11 months;

19%
wait 12-17 months;

11%
wait 18-23 months;

6%
wait 24-29 months;

4%
wait 30-36 months;

6%
wait 3-4 years;

2%
wait five years or longer.

Source: AFCARS.

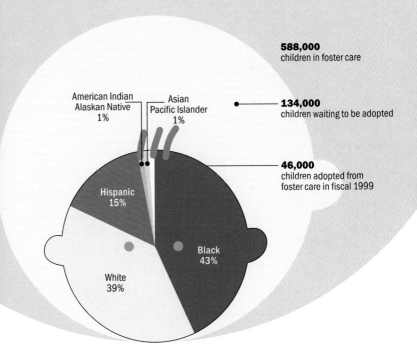

588,000 children in foster care

134,000 children waiting to be adopted

46,000 children adopted from foster care in fiscal 1999

American Indian Alaskan Native 1%

Asian Pacific Islander 1%

Hispanic 15%

Black 43%

White 39%

Who adopts children from foster care

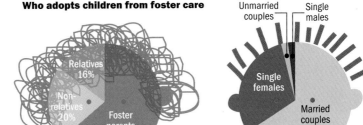

Relatives 16%

Non-relatives 20%

Foster parents 64%

Unmarried couples

Single males

Single females

Married couples

Source: AFCARS.

ACTION ITEMS

How do I become a foster parent?

1 **Contact your local Department of Social Services** (DSS) office or certified private placement agency and request information on foster parenting.

2 **Attend an information meeting.** Get an opportunity for a more comprehensive look at the scope of foster parenting as well as ask any questions or express any concerns.

3 **Make sure you qualify.** Mandatory requirements include: minimum applicant age of 21; an agreement on your part to share information regarding your background and lifestyle; successful completion of a criminal background check and staff-led homestudy of all household members and a completed application.

4 **Participate in a foster parenting preparation and training program.** This generally includes upgradeable training and orientation of approximately 30 hours and may include several home visits.

5 **Pass the final assessment.** This will be done to ensure that you are in compliance with all licensing requirements. If so, you are issued a family foster care license. Congratulations!

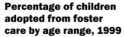
Can children be adopted from foster care?

After a decade of stagnant numbers of adoptions from foster care in the '80s, adoptions from foster care in the '90s have risen dramatically.

Almost half of children adopted from foster care are adopted before the age of five, after which chances for adoption lower dramatically.

The percentage of disrupted adoptions rises dramatically for children adopted from foster care at an older age.

Number of children adopted from foster care, 1990–1999

Percentage of children adopted from foster care by age range, 1999

Percentage of adoption disruption by age range, 1998

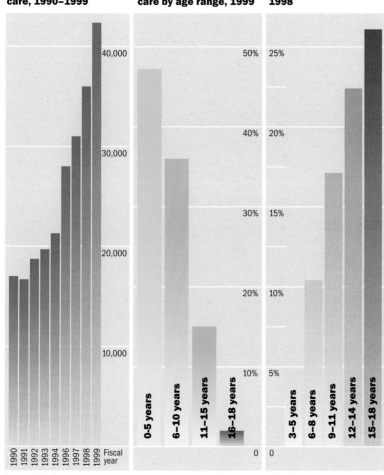

Source: adoptioninstitute.org.

Foster parent adoption is becoming increasingly popular. When a child becomes free for adoption, their foster family is often the preferred placement especially when close relationships have resulted. Although the change from foster care to adoption is usually easy as far as the family's daily routine goes, the adoptive family and adopted child may experience significant changes in other areas. The family will now have sole responsibility for making decisions about the child's well being. The child may take the family's last name and will have the same legal rights as a birth child. Even with few adjustments, adoption from foster care is a major life event that should be celebrated.

How can we make the transition?

1 **Celebrate.** Even if no physical move occurs, you and your child should understand the significance of the change and celebrate this joyous event accordingly. Have a party, plant a tree, take a family portrait or create a lifebook (a personalized account of your child's birth and placement history).

2 **Incorporate.** Include the child in decision-making whenever possible. Let him feel like he truly is part of the family and that his input is not only welcomed but encouraged.

3 **Educate.** Learn how incidents of abuse and neglect from your child's past can affect him in later stages of development. Make yourself aware that what happened to your child before he came into your life might create challenges later on.

4 **Mediate.** Consider when and how your child will maintain contact with birth or former foster family members.

5 **Reiterate.** More than ever, your child needs to know that you love him and that he's part of the family. He may even feel guilty about "joining" a new family and leaving his "real" one. Reassure him that while those feelings are natural, he's not lessening his feelings for his biological parents, he's merely strength-ening his bond with his primary caretakers.

Birth Parent Search

Research has revealed that there is a high degree of support among adoptees, birth parents and adoptive parents for the adopted child

Number of people touched by adoption

Average number of births in the U.S. each year

5,000,000

118,000
are adoptions, equalling

2.36%
new adoptees each year.

4.7% of the U.S. population are adoptive parents.

2.3% of the U.S. population are women who have placed children for adoption.

11% of the population are part of the adoption triangle, not counting aunts, uncles and grandparents to adoptive families and birth families.

Whenever you are in a room of strangers

1 in 10
is a member of the triangle.

Source: Bill Betzen, LMSW, ACSW.

Adoptees as adolescents

72% want to know why they were adopted.

65% want to meet their birth parents.

94% want to know which birth parent they look like.

Adoptees and birth parents

95% of adoptees want to be found by their birth parents.

81.1% of adoptees support access by adult adoptees to identifying information about their birth parents.

100% of birth parents surveyed wanted to be found by the child they had put up for adoption.

85.5% of birth mothers support access by adult adoptees to identifying information about their birth parents.

Adoptive parents

98% of adoptive parents support reunions between their adopted child and members of the child's birth family.

84% of adoptive mothers and **73%** of adoptive fathers support access by adult adoptees to identifying information about their birth parents.

10%	20%	30%	40%

Source: National Adoption Information Clearinghouse.

ACTION ITEMS — Adoption Dos and Dont's

Talking with the adopted child

Do

Emphasize how much she is loved and wanted by her new family.

Explain that her birth parents planned a better future for her than they would have been able to provide.

Help her deal with the sadness that she did not actually grow in her mother's tummy.

Don't

Use adoption-insensitive language such as "real" mother or father; use "birth mother" and "birth father."

Talking about the new family

Do

Explain how the entire family is better off because of her adoption.

Be sure she knows that her needs—physical and emotional—will be addressed exactly as if she were your biological child.

Help her feel as much like her siblings as possible.

Don't

Tell her she was adopted because she was "special." She may feel burdened by having to live up to that description.

Paint your family as saviors for adopting your child.

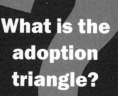

to have access to identifying information about his birth parents and to meet them if he desires.

Among adolescents there is a very high desire to know why they were adopted and more about their birth parents.

A **triangle** is the connection between the child, birth parents, and adoptive parents. In every adoption, all have a role. This is true whether an adoption is **open** (the adoptive family and adopted child have much information or contact with birth parents) or **closed** (they have virtually no information or contact at all).

There is a very high degree of interest among adoptees in getting information on their birth parents and a correspondingly high degree of support among birth parents for access to information about adoptees.

Adoption today recognizes that each party plays a vital role in the health and well-being of the adopted child, since the understanding of birth history and heritage is critical to the formation of the adopted child's identity and sense of self.

A signifcant majority of adoptive parents in different studies support reunions and adoptees' access to identifying information about their birth parents.

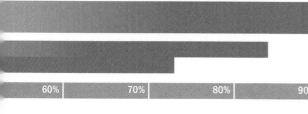

| 60% | 70% | 80% | 90% | 100% |

Talking about birth parents

Do

Present her birth parents as real people who weren't able to care for their child.

Assure her that her birth parents are probably alive and well and reassure her that her birth parents won't come and take her away.

Show her a picture of her birth parents if you have one.

Don't

Depict the child's birth parents as bad people or she may feel that if her parents are bad she may be bad, too.

Reveal negative information about her parents (for example, that one or both are in prison) or her conception (for example, as the result of rape) before she is ready to understand.

Quality of care matters for all children. It can even have a long-term effect on school achievement. Yet it is the combination of the home environment, the relationship between mother and child and the quality of care that a child receives that seems to have the biggest impact on a young child's outcome in school.
Source: National Association of Child Advocates.

Children who participate in high-quality care programs at early ages benefit in many ways. Once in school, they are more likely to advance from grade to grade and less likely to be placed in special education programs. Their language, math and social skills also tend to be more advanced. Although all children benefit from high-quality care, studies suggest that disadvantaged children gain the most from it. Unfortunately, these are the children who, more often than not, receive poor care and for longer hours.
Source: The Urban Institute.

Early Head Start

Started in 1995, it offers quality child and family development services to pregnant woman and infants and toddlers, from birth to age three.

What Is the Impact of Early Head Start?

Early Head Start parents are more supportive of learning and reading at home, more regular at setting bedtimes, less likely to spank their children, more likely to show praise and affection to their children, more informed about child development and more likely to participate in job-training programs.
Source: US Department of Health and Human Services.

ACTION ITEMS — How to access federal assistance

Child and Dependent Care Tax Credit

CDCTC is the largest tax-based subsidy a family can receive for child care. It allows a credit of up to 30% of the initial $2,400 of the cost of caring for a child under the age of 13 or an incapacitated dependent or spouse.
www.irs.ustreas.gov or call 800.829.3676

Dependents Care Assistance Plan

If an employer participates in DCAP, an employee can apply up to $5,000 in pretax earnings for child care, thereby reducing the employee's taxable income. This benefit does not phase out as taxable income increases.

Employer Tax Credit

Fourteen states offer this program. Generally, the program allows employers to claim a corporate tax credit of up to 50% of the cost of an employee's child care benefits.
ftp.fedworld.gov/pub/irs-pdf/f8812.pdf
www.irs.ustreas.gov or call 800.829.3676

Head Start

Head Start is a federally funded program for low-income families with three- and four-year-old children. The programs include child development, early education, social health, and nutrition.
www.nhsa.org

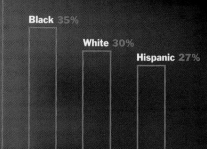

opportunity

Statistics show that young children from low-income families do not receive the same educational opportunities as children from higher income families. In 1996, 45% of low-income children ages three to five went to preschool as compared with 75% of high-income children of the same age. *Source: The Urban Institute.*

Children who are enrolled in quality preschool programs are better prepared to learn and have higher self-esteem and social behavior at school entry. Early education has immediate positive effects on children's socio-emotional development, including self-esteem, achievement motivation, and social behavior. It also provides long-term effects on outcomes such as grade retention and placement in special education, thereby reducing costs to communities.

Black 35%
White 30%
Hispanic 27%

Head Start
A program that provides services designed to foster healthy development in low-income children. Head Start began in 1965 and is run by the Administration for Children and Families.

American Indian 4%
Asian 2%
Pacific Islander 1%

What are the major components of Head Start and who does it serve?

Education
Promotes intellectual, social and emotional development in ways that meet the needs of each child and community served.

Social Services
Offers community outreach, referrals, family needs assessments and crisis intervention geared to each family's needs.

Health
Promotes early identification of health problems through immunizations, medical and dental health and nutritional services.

Parent Involvement
Offers classes on early child development, program planning and operating activities.

Photo: Joe Mikos.

The Child and Adult Care Food Program

CACFP offers federal funding for reimbursing costs of meals, snacks and nutrition education in licensed child care centers, family and group day care centers, family and group day care homes, and Head Start centers.
www.frac.org

Child Care & Development Block Grant

CCDBG provides a block of federal funding to states for use for child care services for low-income families and for activities to improve the quality and supply of child care.
www.hcfa.gov/medicaid/ch-guide.htm
www.acf.dhhs.gov/

TANF Child Care

Temporary Assistance for Needy Familes (TANF) Child Care gives states a block grant, subject to a state match requirement, to pay the cost of child care for low-income families receiving TANF assistance and working or participating in a work or training program.
www.spdp.org/tanf/tanfapps.htm

The At-Risk Child Care Program

This program provides a limited amount of federal funding to states to provide child care assistance for working poor families whom the state considers at-risk.
800.345.KIDS (5437)

In 1999, poor children – those living in three-person families with annual incomes below $26,580 – were more than twice as likely to lack health insurance as were children from higher-income families.
Sources: Census Bureau, Children's Defense Fund.

Childhood immunizations protect children, as well as their communities, from a host of devastating illnesses. Since 1980, all 50 states have been successful in developing immunization requirements for children entering school. This effort has been enhanced by the federal government's Vaccines for Children Program, started in 1994, which has helped bring free vaccines to uninsured children or those enrolled in Medicaid.
Sources: Centers for Disease Control and Prevention, U.S. Department of Health and Human Services.

Asthma

During the past decade asthma rates nearly doubled in the United States, with the greatest increase among children in low-income neighborhoods where air pollution, a leading cause of asthma, is widespread. Other causes of asthma include genetics, allergies and environmental hazards such as smog, cigarette smoke and animal dander.

Lead Poisoning

Lead poisoning is one of the most common and dangerous environmental health hazards threatening our children. Lead poisoning often occurs when dust from lead-based paint in homes and schools gets on toys, clothes and the ground and is then ingested by children. Once absorbed by the body, lead can cause a host of health problems, including learning disabilities, kidney damage, developmental delays and seizures.
Source: Centers for Disease Control and Prevention.

ACTION ITEMS

Learn more about your child's health

Centers for Disease Control and Prevention

Find out how to get immunizations in your area.
National Immunization Information Hotline
800.232.2522 (English)
800.232.0233 (Spanish)
www.cdc.gov/nip

Keep Kids Healthy

Ten things every parent should know, what to do if your child has a reaction, and the ability to create your own vaccine schedule.
www.keepkidshealthy.com

Immunization Action Coalition

Directory of National Immunization Resources, which provides information on organizations, websites, hotlines, and agencies that offer immunization resources.
www.immunize.org
651.647.9009

American Academy of Allergy, Asthma, and Immunology (AAAAI)

Provides information about how to better treat children with allergies and asthma.
www.aaaai.org

80% immunized

Immunization rates jumped 40% between 1992 and 1999. In 1999, 80% of two-year-olds received immunizations against diphtheria, tetanus, pertussis, measles, mumps, rubella and polio. *Source: Centers for Disease Control and Prevention.*

Children's Health Insurance Program (CHIP) and Medicaid.

These programs provide health insurance covering benefits such as immunizations, dental care and prescription drugs, to low-income, uninsured children. Although eligibility and program names may vary by state, most children of four-person families with annual incomes of less than $34,100 will qualify for coverage.

10,800,000 health coverage
In 1999 10.8 million children 18 and under lacked health coverage.

900,000 lead poison
Almost 900,000 children aged one to five have elevated blood lead levels.

4,000,000 asthma
More than 4 million children under 18 in the United States have asthma.

Uninsured children compared with insured children:

Almost twice as likely to have an unmet need for vision care.	Three times as likely to go without prescription medication.	Three times as likely to have an unmet dental need.	More than four times as likely to have an unmet medical need.

2x · 3x · 3x · 4x

The key to giving every child a healthy start in life is providing each child with health care coverage. Programs, such as the Children's Health Insurance Program (CHIP), were recently created to help bring health insurance to children from low- and moderate-income families. More than 3.3 million children were covered by CHIP in 2000.

Sources: U.S. Census Bureau, Children's Defense Fund.

Photo: Joe Mikos.

American Lung Association (ALA)

Help children with asthma understand and manage their illness so they can lead healthy lives.
www.lungusa.org

Asthma and Allergy Foundation of America (AAFA)

Through education, advocacy and research, AAFA seeks to improve the quality of life of children and adults with allergies and asthma.
www.aafa.org

Lead Poisoning

Find out about environmental hazards in your community.
www.scorecard.org

Alliance to End Childhood Lead Poisoning (AECLP)

Initiates to curb childhood lead poisoning.
www.aeclp.org

National Center for Environmental Health (NCEH)

Information about reducing the incidence of environmental health hazards.
www.cdc.gov/nceh

Call 877.KIDS.NOW (877.543.7669) for your state's CHIP or Medicaid eligibility rules and application process.
www.insurekidsnow.gov

Child maltreatment is never a child's fault. However, many abused children mistakenly become convinced that they are to blame by comments made by the abuser. In other instances, children are made to believe that the abuse happened because they angered the abuser or, in cases of neglect, because they have not earned love.

Child maltreatment is any type of child abuse or neglect. Child maltreatment includes physical abuse, sexual abuse, physical neglect, and emotional maltreatment. Children may be subject to a single form of abuse or to several forms of abuse at the same time. In fact, various forms of maltreatment frequently overlap. For example, a physically abused child is often neglected or emotionally abused as well.

Physical abuse is a non-accidental injury or pattern of injury to a child. Physical abuse includes any type of trauma to a child including bruises, burns, fractures and even death, which is inflicted by caregivers.

Neglect refers to a caregiver's failure to provide for a child's basic needs – emotional, medical, safety and educational. It is also the failure to protect a child's health and well being.

Sexual abuse is any sexual act with a child including exploitation of a child for another's sexual gratification.

Emotional abuse includes excessive demands, harassment, severe criticism, rejection and belittlement.

In 1999 there were an estimated 826,000 victims of maltreatment nationwide:
58% suffered neglect
22% suffered physical abuse
12% were sexually abused
7% suffered emotional maltreatment.
Source: U.S. Department of Health and Human Services..

ACTION ITEMS
Understand and prevent abuse

1 **Educate yourself.** The first step in preventing child abuse is to understand the types, signs and symptoms of abuse.

2 **Report suspected abuse.** Do this whether you witness child abuse or simply suspect that a child is being abused. Make sure to file a report with your local child protection agency.

3 **Pay attention.** Be watchful of your child's behavior at all times and the adults that are interacting with him.

4 **Support children.** For the youngest children who can't speak for themselves, you need to be their advocate. Pay close attention and speak up if you see a child is being treated improperly.

5 **Help others in need.** Volunteer to help out friends, family and neighbors who may be going through rough times and could use assistance with their children.

1,100 DEAD

An estimated 1,100 children die of abuse and neglect per year, a rate of approximately 1.62 deaths per 100,000 children in the general population. Children younger than one year old accounted for 42.6 percent of the fatalities, and 86.1 percent were younger than 6 years of age. Maltreatment deaths are more often associated with neglect (38.2%) than with any other type of abuse.

Witness to abuse

Three in ten Americans have witnessed an adult physically abuse a child and two in three Americans have seen an adult emotionally abuse a child. Yet nearly half of these Americans failed to respond to the incident. If abuse is witnessed in a public place, start a supportive conversation with the adult or divert the child's attention if misbehaving.

Perpetrators of abuse

Anyone who has maltreated a child is a perpetrator of abuse. Female parents are thought to be the most common perpetrators of physical abuse and neglect while male parents are identified as the most common perpetrators of sexual abuse.
Source: U.S. Department of Health and Human Services.

Abusive parents typically love their children and don't intend to seriously hurt them. Many parents do not know the basics of child development. Therefore, they cannot set realistic expectations and age-appropriate consequences for their child. Parents mistake their child's inability to comply with a request as disobedience and become frustrated with the child. This type of frustration often can lead to physical abuse.

Reasons cited for child abuse and neglect

A survey was given to American parents on what were the reasons for child abuse:

Increased alcohol and drug abuse by parents	69%
Abusive parents were abused as children	64%
Presence of non-family members living in the home	48%
Lack of spiritual guidance in the parent's lives	2%

Source: Prevent Child Abuse America.

How does maltreatment affect the child?

- Can affect every aspect of childhood development.
- Prevents a child from forming secure attachments with caregivers.
- Distorts a child's understanding of their environment.
- Interferes with a child's ability to interact with others and make friends.
- Encourages inappropriate reactions in social settings.
- Results in poor performance in school.

Photo: Reven Wurman.

Nurture your children. Make your children feel loved, special and secure. Never discipline your children when you are upset. Wait until you calm down and always avoid physical punishment.

Nurture yourself. Taking care of children can be overwhelming and stressful. Set aside a few moments of time each day for yourself. Ask for help when you need it.

Prevent Child Abuse America

This web site contains a link to prevention programs and takes a proactive approach to child abuse with in-depth descriptions of several prevention methods. It also offers resources such as parent training, support groups for new parents, early child and family screenings for abuse, life and social skills training for children and family support services such as crisis hotlines.

www.preventchildabuse.org

The National Clearinghouse on Child Abuse and Neglect

The National Clearinghouse of Child Abuse and Neglect Information provides facts about child abuse and neglect, guidelines for reporting suspecting abuse and toll-free child abuse information.

www.calib.com/nccanch

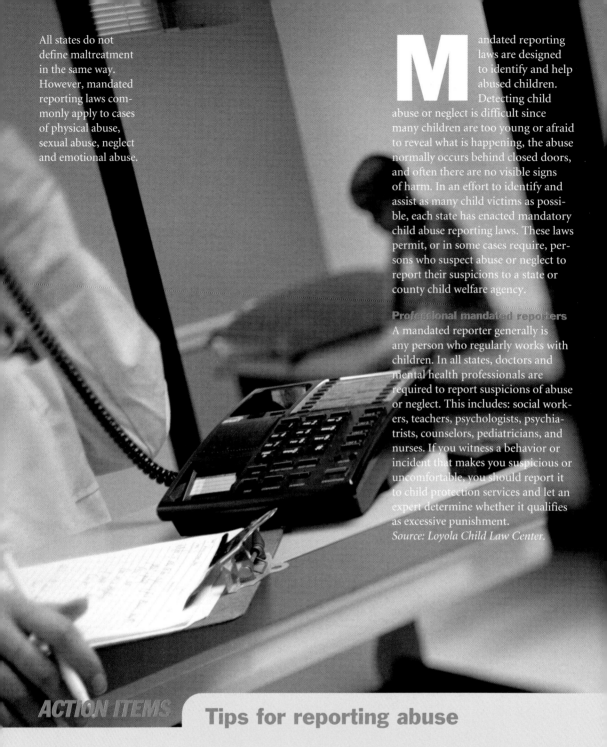

All states do not define maltreatment in the same way. However, mandated reporting laws commonly apply to cases of physical abuse, sexual abuse, neglect and emotional abuse.

Mandated reporting laws are designed to identify and help abused children. Detecting child abuse or neglect is difficult since many children are too young or afraid to reveal what is happening, the abuse normally occurs behind closed doors, and often there are no visible signs of harm. In an effort to identify and assist as many child victims as possible, each state has enacted mandatory child abuse reporting laws. These laws permit, or in some cases require, persons who suspect abuse or neglect to report their suspicions to a state or county child welfare agency.

Professional mandated reporters
A mandated reporter generally is any person who regularly works with children. In all states, doctors and mental health professionals are required to report suspicions of abuse or neglect. This includes: social workers, teachers, psychologists, psychiatrists, counselors, pediatricians, and nurses. If you witness a behavior or incident that makes you suspicious or uncomfortable, you should report it to child protection services and let an expert determine whether it qualifies as excessive punishment.
Source: Loyola Child Law Center.

ACTION ITEMS   **Tips for reporting abuse**

DO:

- Report your suspicions of child abuse or excessive punishment by calling Childhelp's National Child Abuse Hotline 800.4.A.CHILD (800.422.4453) or your local agency.
- Let the individual with the most direct knowledge of the suspected abuse make the report.
- Have some basic information available when you make a report, including names, addresses and ages of the child, his/her siblings, his/her parents and caregivers, details of the suspected abuse, any explanation offered by the child, any other information that may help the investigation.
- Cooperate with the investigators by providing any additional information that may be requested.
- Gather additional information and consider speaking with a supervisor if you believe that the person who took your report made a mistake or if you disagree with the results of the investigation.
- Allow the child to keep communicating with you so that you can continue to collect evidence for the case.
- Be prepared to be a witness if the agency takes the case to court.

Child abuse and neglect cases

In 1998, about 2.8 million reports of suspected child abuse and neglect were filed. More than 900,000 of these were eventually confirmed as cases of abuse or neglect. *Source: US Department of Health and Human Services.*

reports of suspected child abuse and/or neglect

of the reports are investigated

1/3 of these investigations confirm child abuse and/or neglect

1/2 of these children receive post-investigation services

Child Protective Services (CPS)

As suspicions of child maltreatment are reported to CPS, they are either "screened out" or "screened in." After a report is screened in, CPS determines whether to do further investigation on it. Depending on the investigation, it decides whether to take protective action on a child's behalf.

Nearly 55% of the reports were received from professionals. The remaining 45% were submitted by nonprofessionals. *Source: Child Maltreatment.*

45% submitted by nonprofessionals

Remember, you are only required to report your suspicions. You do not need to, and are probably not qualified to, decide if your suspicions are correct or if the actions you witness qualify as abuse. What qualifies as "excessive punishment" is often a matter of individual opinion. If you witness a behavior or incident that makes you suspicious or uncomfortable, you should report it to child protection services and let an expert determine whether it qualifies as abuse.

Who should make the report

When more than one person knows about the suspected abuse, the person with the most direct knowledge of it should make the report. For example, a child care worker may talk to a supervisor about bruises on a child or changes in his behavior. It would be best for the child care worker to report the suspected abuse since she is the eyewitness to the signs of abuse.

What information should I have when I make a report?

- your name, address and relationship to the child victim(s)
- name, address, and age of child victim(s)
- name, address, and age of any brothers and sisters
- name, address, and age of parent(s) or caregiver(s)
- relationship of child victim to caregiver(s)
- details of the suspected abuse or neglect
- any explanation provided by the child or other person(s)

Photo: Joe Mikos.

DON'T:

- Try to decide if your suspicions or the actions you witness qualify as abuse. Report your suspicions.
- Claim that the report is an emergency unless you believe the child is in immediate danger.
- Let another individual make the report of abuse without following up with that individual to ensure that the report was filed. You can be held responsible for failure to report suspected abuse, even if the responsibility was assigned to another person.
- Contact the child's parents or caregivers to ask them about your suspicions unless you are secure in your relationship with them.
- Discuss your suspicions with others, unless necessary for the child's protection.
- Promise the child that you won't tell anybody what she shared with you.
- Examine unexposed parts of a child's body, or otherwise conduct your own investigation, even if you suspect abuse.
- Worry if your suspicions turn out to be wrong—there are no consequences for this as long as you filed the report in good faith.

1 in 6 American children live in poverty. They are at greater risk of stunted growth, lower education and lower earnings. These problems pose consequences for the nation.

In 1997, 2.7 million American children lived in extreme poverty with family incomes below one-half of the poverty line, up by 426,000 from 1996. Most of these children came from families headed by single mothers. This dramatic increase in children living in "extreme poverty" is largely attributed to recent changes in welfare. These changes decreased the amount of welfare benefits like food stamps and cash assistance available to families living in poverty. Although more parents have been able to find work due to a strong economy, the loss in aid has outweighed the gain in earnings.

What is welfare?

The most basic form of welfare for families with children in the United States is Temporary Assistance for Needy Families (TANF), which provides monthly cash assistance to families that meet specified criteria. It is estimated that the federal government will spend approximately $35.8 billion dollars, or 2% of the federal spending budget, for TANF and food stamps in 2001.

Who receives TANF?

In 1999, TANF covered about 2.6 million families and 7.4 million Americans of all ages. Single parents (mostly mothers) headed about 64% of these families. Four percent of TANF family heads were teen parents; 32% were white; 23% were Hispanic; 36% were black; and only about 50% finished high school.

ACTION ITEMS   Resources

Temporary Assistance for Needy Families (TANF)

TANF is a federally-supported welfare program run by the states. Qualifying caregivers may be entitled to medical insurance and food stamps in addition to financial aid.

www.spdp.org/tanf

Earned Income Tax Credit (EITC)

EITC supplements income of working people by giving a tax credit based upon a percentage of earned income and number of children.

www.cbpp.org

Child Tax Credit

Starting in 2001, the Federal Child Tax Credit will provide up to $1,000 per child under 17 for working families earning more than $10,000 per year whether or not they owe federal income tax.

Supplemental Social Security Income (SSI)

SSI is a federal program that gives financial assistance to certain blind or disabled children.

www.ssa.gov

Government research found that poverty poses a greater risk to a child's general health than living in a single-parent family.

Poverty – while the United States became 49 percent richer from 1979 to 1999, the number of poor children rose by 17 percent.

Children born in times of greater family prosperity tend to go further in school than siblings born in times when the family was poor.

A baby of a poor mother is more likely to die before her first birthday than is a baby born to a high school dropout, a mother who smoked during pregnancy or an unwed mother.

What benefits do children receive?

Free or reduced-price school lunches	15.4 million children in 2000
Food stamps	9.3 million children in 1999
TANF	5.3 million children in 1999

Source of information in spread: Children's Defense Fund.

Poor working families

Parents who work don't necessarily escape poverty. In 1999, **3** out of **4** poor children lived with a family member who worked for at least a portion of the year and **1** out of **3** poor children lived with a family member who worked full-time. In fact, the percentage of children from working families who lived in poverty in 1999 was the highest in 25 years of recorded history.

the cost of child poverty
$130,000,000,000

Because American children living in poverty tend to be less educated and less productive workers, it is estimated that for each year they continue to experience poverty, their lifetime contribution to the economy will decrease by about $130 billion.

America's failure to reduce child poverty has been linked to the declining availability of government support (cash assistance and food stamps) and the increase in low paying jobs and single-parent families. Even in 2000, at the height of economic boom, over 11 million American children were poor (with annual family incomes below $13,738). And, American children were two to three times more likely to live in poverty than children in other developed countries.

Photo: Joe Mikos.

Women Infants and Children (WIC)

WIC provides supplemental foods, nutrition, education and healthcare access to low-income pregnant women, new mothers and children.
www.fns.usda.gov/WIC/

Food Stamps

The Food Stamps Program is a federally-mandated program that gives low-income families coupons to buy food from specified vendors. Food stamps are issued to households, not individuals. To qualify, net household income must be below the poverty level.
www.foodusa.org

State Children's Health Insurance Programs (CHIP)

CHIP is a federally-mandated program run by the states to give health coverage to uninsured children in low-income families.
877.KIDS.NOW
www.insurekidsnow.gov

Medicaid

Medicaid is a joint state federal program that provides basic health coverage to people of all ages with low income.
www.hcfa.gov/medicaid/medicaid.htm

About 1,250,000 couples in America divorce each year. In 1999, for the first time in recorded history, more first children were born to or conceived by unmarried women than married women. *Source: US Census Bureau, National Center for Health Statistics, American Demographics.*

Although the ways in which women and men become single parents varies, one concern that most single parents face is how to handle questions from a child about the absent parent. While a "one-size-fits-all" answer does not exist, for most single parents one thing holds true: If you have come to terms with your feelings about single parenting and running a single-parent family, your child will probably feel good about your explanations as well as with being a part of a single-parent family.

Stress for children

With the divorce or death of a spouse, your child may have to adjust to change: new schedules, routines or caregivers. Try to maintain as much normalcy as possible. Your child may lose contact with friends and family. Try to stay in touch and build support for you and your child. Your child may worry about who will take care of them. Try to be attuned to these anxieties and address them as they arise. Your child may blame himself or feel unlovable. Try to listen, validate his feelings and provide reassurance. Children handle loss and express emotions in different ways. Provide opportunities to share memories or create special tributes. Your child may feel the impact of loss without really understanding. Try to offer explanations that are simple and clear and include them in your recovery process where appropriate. Remember that your child will feel your pain. Try to find ways to cope with your feelings so that they don't create issues for your child as well.

ACTION ITEMS — Tips for talking to your child

1. **Be a good listener.** Before you jump in with an answer listen patiently and carefully to a child's questions, concerns and feelings. It is important for a child to feel heard and understood.

2. **Keep it simple.** Provide only as much information as a child needs to know when answering a child's questions. The younger the child, the simpler the answer.

3. **Stay neutral.** Be as objective and factual as possible when discussing the absent parent. Don't let your feelings color your comments. Even the youngest children will perceive your negativity.

4. **Be honest and straightforward.** Don't try to hide the truth to spare a child's feelings. A child will perceive your dishonesty.

5. **Dispel the blame.** Make sure the child understands that he is not to blame for the divorce or other reason for the parent's absence. With time and good parenting, he will heal.

Living with one parent

There are about 11.9 million single parents in the United States raising about 19.8 million children under the age of 18. Of these, 84% live with their mother.

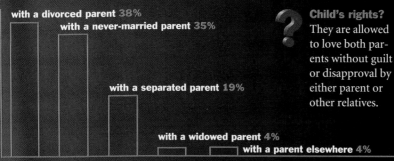

with a divorced parent 38%
with a never-married parent 35%
with a separated parent 19%
with a widowed parent 4%
with a parent elsewhere 4%

Child's rights? They are allowed to love both parents without guilt or disapproval by either parent or other relatives.

Sources: US Census Bureau, Department of Human Services.

Single Teen Parents

Teenage parents are responsible for 13% of births in the United States (highest adolescent birthrate in the world). The teenage pregnancy rate fell 17% between 1990 and 1996, largely due to better contraceptive practice. 1 of 4 teenage mothers will go on to have another child within two years of the first.

500,000 teenage girls give birth each year. 78% of teen parents are single.
Source: Alan Guttmacher Institute.

How to cope with a divorce:

Stage	Child reactions/**Parental strategies**
Infants Do not understand conflict, but may react to changes in parent's energy level and mood.	Loss of appetite More anxious **Keep normal routines** **Maintain warm, safe contact**
Toddlers Understand that a parent has moved away, but doesn't understand why.	More crying May worry **Be reassuring, nurturing** **Spend time alone with the child**
Preschoolers Don't understand what separation or divorce means. Realizes one parent is not as active in his or her life.	Feel responsible May hold anger **Encourage the child to talk**

Source: Karen DeBord, North Carolina Cooperative Extension Service.

Be honest by giving a child straightforward, simple answers and make sure he understands that the situation is not his fault. You may have to remind a young child repeatedly for a couple of years that he is not to blame. When a child expresses his questions, feelings and concerns, give your undivided attention before you respond. Let the child know that it is okay to have such feelings and concerns and that it is safe to express them. Also, reassure a child that he is still loved and safe.

Photo: Joe Mikos.

6 **Talk about it.** Create an atmosphere of open communication so that a child is comfortable asking questions or talking about his feelings toward the situation. Never avoid a child's questions about an absent mother or father.

7 **Give encouragement.** As a child begins to notice that others families have a mother and a father, tell her that all families are different. Let her know it is okay to belong to a family that is headed by only one parent.

8 **Share.** When a child begins to ask questions about a birth parent or parent who no longer is alive or accessible, show the child pictures of the parent and other information or stories you have.

9 **Allow the child to vent.** Let a child know that whatever feelings she has about an absent parent or a divorce are okay and acceptable to express.

10 **Create a support network.** Talk to your child's caregivers, teachers, extended family and friends. Their understanding will help them better support your child.

Early intervention services range from prescribing glasses for toddlers to developing physical therapy programs for infants with cerebral palsy. The goal of these programs is to promote basic learning skills and achieve developmental milestones.

Congress enacted the Individuals with Disabilities Education Act (IDEA) in 1991. It provides educational rights to special-needs children according to their age. It guarantees early intervention services to special-needs infants and toddlers from birth to age two and special education programs to preschoolers (ages three to five) with disabilities. For all special needs children ages three to 21, the IDEA provides certain rights and services, such as free appropriate public education and the right for parents to participate in decisions regarding their children's education. The IDEA covers 13 categories of disability, and the development assessment and evaluation to determine IDEA eligibility is provided to families at no cost.

Thirteen disabilities of IDEA: autism, deaf-blindness, deafness, hearing impairment, mental retardation, multiple disabilities, orthopedic impairment, other health impairment, serious emotional disturbance, learning disability, speech or language impairment, traumatic brain injury, and visual impairment.

ACTION ITEMS

Does your child have special needs?

Autism

Common characteristics of autism include communication problems, unusual play with toys and other objects, repetitive body movements and difficulty relating to people. If you are concerned about autism, contact a child psychologist.

Hearing

A child should have an initial screening at three months. If the child does not show appropriate language skills by 18 months, he should be evaluated for a hearing problem.

Vision

The key to successfully treating a vision problem is early diagnosis. Therefore, a child should be evaluated initially by six months and again at three years. You should report any problems, such as misaligned eyes, or the tendency to cover an eye or hold objects close to the eyes, to your doctor.

Speech

Speech problems are difficult to detect and can be associated with hearing problems. Signs, from birth to four years, that might indicate a problem include:

- **0-3 months:** Failure to listen to speech or make cooing noises.
- **4-6 months:** Failure to look towards the source of noise or respond to a parent's voice.

Disabled school-age children

Learning Disability 51%	
Speech, Language Impairment 23%	
Mental Retardation 11%	
Seriously Emotionally Disturbed 8%	
Other 7%	

Learning disability (LD), defined as disabilities in areas related to reading, language and math, is the most common disability among school-aged children eligible under the IDEA. More than one-half of those enrolled in special education receiving help for LD. Under the IDEA, LDs include conditions such as dyslexia, minimal brain disfunction and perceptual disabilities. It does not include learning problems caused by motor disabilities or emotional disturbance.
Source: The Future of Children, Reid Lyon.

Early intervention is the key to diagnosing and treating young children with special needs. To learn about available early intervention services, contact your local public school, parent support group such as Parent-to-Parent or the proper state agency. Since services are controlled by the states, each state should have a State Resource Sheet listing a contact person for "Programs for Infants and Toddlers with Disabilities." Or, call NICHCY at 800.695.0285.

The First 3 Years

The first three years of a child's life are crucial for spotting trouble signs.
Hearing: most hearing problems are not detected until a child is almost three.
Vision: one in 20 preschoolers has vision problems.
Learning Disabilities: more than 5% of children have learning disabilities.
Autism: one out of 500 Americans may be affected.

 What does "special needs" child mean?

A child with "special needs" often has a delay or problem with one or many developmental areas including:

- Intellectual impairment or thinking skills
- Physical delays or problems with movement and motor skills
- Sensory delays or problems with movement and motor skills
- Emotional disturbances such as communication or behavioral problems, including problems in forming relationships

Photo: Reven Wurman.

- **7-12 months:** Failure to babble, make short groups of sounds or respond to her name.
- **1-2 years:** Failure to ask simple, one or two word questions, put words together or listen to stories.
- **2-3 years:** Failure to string three word sentences, name objects, ask for things or follow directions.
- **3-4 years:** Failure to respond when called by name, understand basic "who?" "what?" or "where" questions, be understood by those outside the immediate family.

Learning Disabilities

Learning disabilities, such as dyslexia, are difficult to diagnosis before the age of three years. Be sure to should report any family history of learning disabilities to your doctor.

Other signs

In addition to the traditional motor and language skills, there are other things to look for that are more subtle, but can help detect problems at an early age.

- **After 4 months:** Does your child related with real warmth and joy? With big smiles and delight?
- **After 8-9 months:** You should expect your baby to engage in back-and-forth communication – returning sound with sound, reaching out with hands, smiling back or initiating smiling.
- **12-14 months:** Your toddler should be able to use back-and-forth communication to solve problems.
- **18-20 months:** Look for the beginning of pretending – kissing dolls, pretending in play.

The key to preventing a child from getting lost in the dependency system is persistence. Keep tabs on where the child is staying, let the court know that you are interested in placement and appear at all the child's court hearings.

When a child becomes a part of the dependency system, decisions regarding the child and the child's family are placed solely in the hands of the juvenile court. Although the goal of the proceedings is to act in the best interest of the child, for a person trying to seek custody of the child, the process has drawbacks. Cases are confidential, so it can be difficult to learn the status of a child's proceedings. Because hearings often get postponed, the process can drag on for years. Also, the system favors biological parents so a third party has very little credibility in court.

Guardianship

Guardianship is the legal and physical transfer of a child's custody to someone other than the child's parents when one or both of the parents are dead, missing or unfit to care for the child. Unlike adoption, guardianship does not terminate parental rights, but it does suspend them. Therefore, second to adoption, it is the most stable arrangement for a person (other than the parent) who is raising a child. A guardian has control of issues such as where the child lives and when she can see her parents (unless a court has ordered visitation rights). The guardian also has power to enroll the child in school, consent to medical treatment and make decisions regarding education, health care and legal actions.

ACTION ITEMS   Don't lose your child in the system

1. **Stay on top of the child's whereabouts and his situation.** If the child gets taken into the system, make sure you locate him and make it known to child protection services that you are interested in placement or visitation. You may be able to aid your cause by having important information on hand like birth certificates or other evidence of the child's relationship to you.

2. **If you are aware of the dependency hearing, be present at it.** Because these hearings are confidential, you may not be allowed in the courtroom. However, you can introduce yourself to the social worker, attorney or court officers and let them know who you are and that you are interested in obtaining placement, custody or at least visitation.

3. **Understand the case against the child's parent(s) at trial.** Based on the testimony and evidence collected from the parents and other witnesses, the court will render a decision as to custody of the child. Make sure you tell the child's social worker everything you know about the child's situation so that you can play a role in and properly influence the outcome of the case.

Issues considered in dependency hearings

A court usually will consider these issues in deciding where to place a child:
- Should the child be removed from the home?
- Where should the child be placed if removed from the home?
- When should the child be allowed to return home?
- What steps must the parents take to regain child custody?
- What type of court intervention is necessary to bring the family back together?
- Does the child need counseling or other services?
- If the child is not allowed to return home, who will take permanent custody of the child? (generally through relative foster care, guardianship or adoption)

Foster care v. guardianship

Foster care differs from court-ordered placement with a relative in that foster parents receive monthly cash benefits and Medicaid for the child and they must be trained and licensed to care for the child in their homes. However, even relative placements have access to certain benefits such as TANF.

the system
at a glance

The Call	The Petition	Mediation and/or Trial	Periodic Reviews
To child protective services about a child suspected of being abused, neglected or abandoned.	The legal document that tells a judge why the social worker thinks the court should intervene to protect a child.	To see if allegations against the parents are true.	These are to review the family's progress.
The Pickup	**Detention Hearing**	**Disposition Hearing**	**Permanency Planning Hearing**
The child will be taken into protective custody if found to be neglected or abused.	The hearing that sets the case in motion.	The Court decides what to do to both protect the child and help the parents regain custody.	A permanent plan for each child who enters the dependency system.

Source: Grandparents as Parents, Sylvie de Toledo and Deborah Edler Brown.

The government created the dependency system to protect children who are suspected of being abused, neglected or abandoned. The system is comprised of a child protective services agency that investigates reports of suspected child abuse and neglect and a court, such as a juvenile court, that hears the dependency hearings. While the hearings take place, the child is deemed a dependent of the court, and the court takes legal custody of the child from the parents.

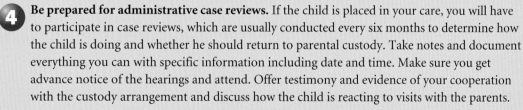

4 **Be prepared for administrative case reviews.** If the child is placed in your care, you will have to participate in case reviews, which are usually conducted every six months to determine how the child is doing and whether he should return to parental custody. Take notes and document everything you can with specific information including date and time. Make sure you get advance notice of the hearings and attend. Offer testimony and evidence of your cooperation with the custody arrangement and discuss how the child is reacting to visits with the parents.

5 **Consider adoption or guardianship as part of a permanency plan.** After 18 months in the dependency system a permanent plan for the child's care must be established. Adoption is the most permanent solution, but not always possible. Guardianship also gives a caregiver full legal and physical custody until the child is 18 years old.

The key to helping a child overcome trauma is to understand what helped other children to recover, such as strong social support and a sense of purpose, and apply that to encourage a positive outcome in the child you are helping.

All people, including children, suffer losses as a part of normal development. For example, it is natural for a five-year-old to experience a temporary loss of security and sadness when he goes to kindergarten for the first time. Although events such as this require recovery and healing, they are not considered clinically traumatic They are simply natural and expected losses that all people feel and can recover from through expression and support. Events may be disturbing but may not necessarily rise to the level of trauma. According to experts, trauma occurs when an individual is exposed to an overwhelming event outside of the realm of normal human experience, resulting in excessive stress to the body, mind and psyche.

Post Traumatic Stress Disorder

The best way to identify whether a child is suffering from PTSD is through a formal psychiatric evaluation. If the child is exhibiting the following behaviors for at least a month, PTSD is a possibility.

- numbing or social withdrawal
- re-experiencing the trauma – "re-living" or playing out the event over and over
- hyper-vigilance or increased hyper-active behavior
- avoidance of situations, thoughts or feelings that are reminiscent of the trauma

ACTION ITEMS

Tips for helping children recover

1. **Provide a safe and secure environment.** Before your child can recover from trauma he needs a safe and secure environment and support from his family, school, community and himself. Make sure to address your own issues.

2. **Understand your child's personality.** Your child's ability to overcome obstacles and adapt under otherwise adverse circumstances depends a lot upon her personality. Valuable character traits include social competence, creative thinking, personal understanding and sense of purpose.

3. **Offer individualized attention.** Efforts should focus on enhancing your child's self-esteem, sense of hope and peer support. You want to send her the message that she is a valuable and worthy person and that you believe in and are proud of her.

4. **Turn to family support.** The family is the front-line resource for helping children overcome traumatic events. All family members can assist a child by offering their trust, friendship and support. The essential role of the parent, or primary caretaker, is to restore order to the child's disrupted life without ignoring the effects of the trauma.

What can I do to help a child overcome a traumatic situation?

Your job as a parent to your child is critical right now. To set her healing process in motion, you should:

· Allow your child to discuss her feelings.
· Make sure that she has plenty of time to spend with friends and socialize.
· Fully explain why the trauma occurred and why it was not her fault.
· Help to resume a regular schedule of normal activities.

Family support: A warm, caring family environment in which people get along provides a safety net for a child suffering from trauma. It offers a child the energy and support to rebuild her inner strength and re-establish her sense of self worth.

Extended family support: Extended family members and friends can help ease the burden of a family member who is struggling with a situation and can help the child of this family member. Such a child will benefit from a relative who cares about her success in school and personal relationships.

Professional support: A professional therapist will observe a younger traumatized child as he interacts with his parents, and will talk with the parents about their concerns in order to provide a thorough assessment of the situation and make recommendations as to the best treatment for the child.

School support: School can often be a valuable outlet for a child recovering from trauma – especially when the trauma is centered at home. A child can benefit from a defined structure, regularly enforced rules and a community that supports students and makes them feel valuable.

Signs and symptoms of PTSD:

Symptoms depend upon an individual's response to the trauma.
Cognitive reactions: the inability to remember details of the event and other memory impairments, poor attention span, lack of goals.
Emotional reactions: bad memories, worries that eventually diminish over time, recurring fear, anger, irritability, helplessness, depression and anxiety.

Behavioral symptoms: withdrawal, aggression, poor concentration.
Somatic-physiological symptoms: low tolerance for stress, startled responses to reminders of the event, and sleep disorders.
Physical complaints: frequent stomachaches and headaches that lack medical validity.

Trauma can occur in reaction to an event that is exceptionally distressing, such as death, injury, violence or the threat of such harm. Depending upon a person's age and individual characteristics, such events can trigger a range of symptoms and responses including intense fear, helplessness or horror. When children suffer from trauma, their ability to achieve their developmental potential is dramatically affected.

Photo: Joe Mikos.

5 **Assure support at school.** A safe, secure school environment gives your child an escape from trauma at home and a chance to focus on healing and developing a positive identity. Nurturing schools can provide many resources to support the healthy adjustment and achievement of their students, such as social support with teachers and peers.

6 **Consider specialized therapy.** Professional therapy allows an objective, trained and trusted individual, often a social worker or psychologist, to join your child and family in their crisis and lend perspective, education and stability.

7 **Seek community support.** Community networks provide children with a sense of belonging and a feeling of safety and security, which are critical to overcoming trauma, especially when families are dealing with their own burdens. Organized programs through churches and local organizations give children valuable attention and positive interactions with peers and adults, which boost self esteem, foster a sense of security and inspire children.

Exposure to violence can have significant effects on children during their development and influence how they form their own intimate relationships in childhood and adulthood.

Violence in America, claims the lives of thousands each year and costs millions in medical expenses and lost wages. Sobering statistics show that an overwhelming amount of violence takes place in the home. About one million violent crimes are committed by former spouses, boyfriends or girlfriends every year. Between 1993 and 1998 about 45% of female domestic violence victims lived in homes with children younger than 12. And, between 45% and 70% of children who witness domestic violence are also victims of child abuse. In fact, experts believe that domestic violence is a leading precursor of child abuse and neglect deaths in the United States.
Sources: The Future of Children, Joy Osofsky.

Supportive homes

Although exposure to violence can have serious consequences for children, they can overcome its effects if certain factors are present in their lives. A child with strong, stable parents or a loving, trusted caregiver who can withstand the stresses of community violence and provide a child with a safe-haven at home stands a better chance of coping and growing into a successful, happy adult. Schools, community centers and recreational programs also can offer children a chance to escape violence, build self-esteem and learn skills to function in the world.

ACTION ITEMS   Tips for eliminating violence

1 **Set a good example.** Children learn how to behave by following the actions of the adults around them. As role models, parents must make an effort to pass on a strong sense of values and morals as well as teach by example nonviolent ways to express themselves. If your child sees you argue, make sure she also sees you make amends and never resort to any type of physical or verbal violence in her presence.

2 **Use nonviolent methods of discipline.** If you hit or spank your child as punishment, he will learn that violence is permissible in certain situations. Plenty of nonviolent means of discipline exist that instill punishment while at the same time teach nonviolent ways to solve problems, such as "time outs." Remember also to reward positive behavior.

TRUE/FALSE "A child aged six months or younger who witness violence, such as seeing his father often hit his mother, will not suffer any long term effects, because children that age have no long term memory."

Parents of children aged 0-6

Definitely false	48%
Probably false	25%
Probably true	16%
Definitely true	7%
Not sure	5%

Source: What Grown-ups Understand About Child Development, Civitas, Zero to Three, BRIO.

Witnesses
The number of children who witness family violence are in the millions.

Answer: Definitely false. Children are like sponges. They soak up the world around them from the earliest ages. They take in anger and violence around them, just as they take in positive and loving interactions from caregivers. For this reason, the nature and quality of a child's earliest relationships and experiences are crucial to his future development.

200,000 violent acts

Did you know that by the time the typical American child turns 18, he will have seen 16,000 simulated murders and 200,000 violent acts through exposure to television, movies and the Internet? It is estimated that television programs geared to children, especially cartoons, contain more than twice the amount of violence than prime-time adult programs.
Source: The Future of Children, Joy Osofsky.

80% aware

Although parents often believe that children are asleep or unaware when domestic violence occurs in the home, studies show that 80% to 90% of such children are fully aware of the violence taking place.
Source: Mediation Quarterly, Mildred Pagelow.

Violence impacts the lives of all who witness or experience it. For children, violence has psychological, emotional and developmental consequences. Even infants and toddlers who witness violence may suffer a range of symptoms, including anxiety, nightmares, regression in language and motor skills and post-traumatic stress disorder. Also, their own self-confidence and ability to trust other people and form attachments with caregivers is often impaired.

Photo: Joe Mikos.

3 **Limit exposure to violence.** Pay careful attention to the television shows, videos, and internet content your child watches, and limit her exposure to violent themes. Toy guns and other such toys that promote violence and aggression should be limited or monitored.

4 **Set clear rules and consistent limits.** Children need to know exactly what is expected of them and the consequences for not cooperating. Therefore, make sure that your child understands all family rules—you might even want to involve him in rulemaking. Also, consistent enforcement of the rules reduces conflict and is essential to maintaining your credibility.

5 **Give your child lots of affection and attention.** Children who feel loved, safe and secure and who have formed a sense of trust with a caring adult are less likely to act violently or aggressively. You can build your child's sense of security and trust by taking an active role in her life, consistently spending quality time with him and offering lots of love, praise and encouragement. Even short periods of special time make a difference.

REVIEW COMMITTEES

The following experts read and reviewed various sections of this book. We thank them for their time, direction and knowledge.

Ages & Stages
Fran Stott, PhD; Erikson Institute

Marc Weissbluth, MD; The Northwestern Children's Practice

Prenatal & Childbirth
Kathryn E. Barnard, PhD, RN; University of Washington

William A. Barnett, OD; South River Eye Care; Bowie Optometric Group

Ida Cardone, PhD; Northwestern University

Cathleen Church-Balin, MHS, MBA; March of Dimes

Ann Corwin, PhD, MEd; Family and Child Development Consulting

Linda Gilkerson, PhD; Erikson Institute

Lisa Kelly, MD; Kelly Eyecare Associates

Rebecca Klein, MS; Erikson Institute

JoAnne Solchany, PhD; University of Washington

Stuff You Need
Jim Scott, BabyCenter

Larry Wilner, Safe Kids Childproofing

Health & Nutrition
Sheila Gahagan, MD; University of Michigan

Betty Lucas, MPH, RD, CD; University of Washington

Jennifer Rosinia, MEd; Erikson Institute

Donald Shifrin, MD; University of Washington

Martin T. Stein, MD; UC San Diego

Sharon Syc, PhD; Erikson Institute

Marc Weissbluth, MD; The Northwestern Children's Practice

Brain
Lise Eliot, PhD; Chicago Medical School

William T. Greenough, PhD; University of Illinois

Megan Gunnar, PhD; University of Minnesota

Charles A. Nelson, PhD; University of Minnesota

Child Care
Kathy Hirsh-Pasek, PhD; Temple University

Edna Ranck, EdD; National Association for Child Care Resource and Referral Agencies

Fran Stott, PhD; Erikson Institute

Faith Wohl, Child Care Action Campaign

Sleep
Rosalind Cartwright, PhD; St. Luke's Medical Center

Linda Gilkerson, PhD; Erikson Institute

Jodi A. Mindell, PhD; St. Joseph's University

Marc Weissbluth, MD; The Northwestern Children's Practice

Meg Zweiback, RN, MPH, CPNP; UC San Francisco

Play
Kathy Hirsh-Pasek, PhD; Temple University

Joan B. McLane, PhD; Erikson Institute

Ellen Metrick, Lekotek

Laura Sanders, LCSW; University of Michigan School of Social Work

Marilyn Segal, PhD; Nova Southeastern University

Behavior
Edward Christopherson, PhD; University of Missouri at Kansas City

Alicia Lieberman, PhD; UC San Francisco

Fran Stott, PhD; Erikson Institute

Amy Susman-Stillman, PhD; University of Minnesota

Financial & Legal Issues
Liz Baer, Solomon Smith Barney

Kara Shadwick; The Hilton Group, Solomon Smith Barney

Wade P. Thomas, Jr.; attorney

Fathers
Michael E. Lamb, PhD; National Institute of Child Health and Human Development

James Levine, EdD; Families and Work Institute

Kyle Pruett, MD; Yale University

Marsha Kline Pruett, PhD; Yale University

Grandparents
Ana Beltran, Generations United

Lillian Carson, DSW; *The Essential Grandparent*

Amy Goyer, AARP

Arthur Kornhaber, MD; The Foundation for Grandparenting

JoAnne Solchany, PhD; University of Washington

Fran Stott, PhD; Erikson Institute

Bernice Weissbourd, PhD; Family Focus

Kathryn & Allan Zullo, *The Nanas and the Papas*

Adoption
Joyce Pavao, PhD; Center for Family Connections

JoAnne Solchany, PhD; University of Washington

Gail Steinberg, PACT An Adoption Alliance

Fran Stott, PhD; Erikson Institute

Challenges
William A. Barnett, OD; South River Eye Care; Bowie Optometric Group

Barbara L. Bonner, PhD; University of Oklahoma

Gregg Haifley, Children's Defense Fund

Hollye Jacobs, RN; University of Chicago

Joy D. Osofsky, PhD; Louisiana State University

Stacey Platt, JD; Loyola University Child Law Center

Barbara Rawn, MS; Prevent Child Abuse America

Arloc Sherman, Children's Defense Fund

Sylvie de Toledo, LCSW, BCD; Grandparents as Parents, Inc.

UNDERSTANDING**CHILDREN** was made possible with special early support from **BRIO**, a trustworthy producer of classic, quality toys with a long tradition of providing the tools for parents to create healthy childhood experiences.

www.briotoys.com

WHAT YOU'LL FIND INSIDE THIS CATALOG:

PRODUCTS
carefully tested and selected by BabyCenter for safety, usability, and value.

PICTURES AND DESCRIPTIONS
to give you a good understanding of what you're buying.

BabyCenter® is here to help.

On the next 15 pages, you'll find a selection of products carefully chosen to help you navigate the first three years of your child's life. See what you need, then go to

www.topbabystuff.com

to order online.

GEAR Shop at www.top.baby....com

🔖 **TOP PICK:** Standard Stroller

Pliko Sherpa by Peg Perego
A strolling dream, the Pliko Sherpa is lightweight and rug...
🖥 Find this product by typing in the sku number etc. Sku#: 1... $249.95
- Holds up to 40 lbs.
- Five-point harness
- Folds easily and compactly for travel. Stands when folded
- Height-adjustable umbrella handles
- Removable safety bar and extension leg rest adjust as your baby grows
- Rear footboard for second child to stand on back
- Removable can... n window
- Basket for sto...
- Softly padd... cushion removes for hand wa...
- Open di... ons: 33 1/2"L x 20"W x 40"H... dimensions: 13"L x 20"W... 1
- ... s 15 1/2 lbs.

🔖 **TOP PICK:** Lightwei... t Stroller

Savvy Z Stroller with Acoustic Canopy by Combi
Durable, maneuverable, and exceptionally lightweight, this is a great stroller for an on-the-go family.
🖥 SKU#: 102414, $199.95
- Partially reclining seat (to 140 degrees) is suitable for babies 6 months and up
- Three-point seatbelt
- Acoustic canopy featuring mini stereo speakers in pocket of canopy
- Opens and folds easily with one hand
- Four-wheel suspension
- Removable front guardrail
- Includes shoulder strap
- Roomy canopy with viewing window, speakers for portable CD or cassette player, and rear pocket for storing small items
- Underseat basket
- Extremely light — 7 3/4 lbs.

🔖 **TOP P...** ...at and Stroller Combination

Primo Viag... ...el System by Peg Perego
This is the to... e car seat/stroller travel system— gorgeous, functional, and con...
🖥 SKU#: 102380, $349...
- Infant car seat / stroller syst... th instant snap-in / snap-out attac...
- Primo Viaggio infant car seat w... base included
- Car seat weighs 6 lbs. and carries a... infant up to 20 lbs.
- Five-point safety harness / restraint system
- Four-position backrest, including
- fully reclined for infants
- All-terrain double wheels in front and back
- Stroller has height-adjustable handlebar
- Deluxe canopy with window, venti... on panel, and rain canopy
- ...rge reinforced seat and backrest ...sh, hand-washable fabric
- ...l weight: 17 lbs.

★★★★★

Choosing a Stroller Here are three popular typ... onsider:

Lightweight Stroller
A lightweight model is great to have when a big stroller is too unwieldy: for fitting in an overhead compartment on a plane or stowing in the trunk of a taxi
- weighs 15 pounds or less
- folds compactly
- easy to maneuver

- ideal for travel an... outings
- for babies at least ... six months old (unless i... eclines)

Standard-Size Strol...
Thanks to more pad... better wheels, a standard st... delivers a smoother ride, espe... n bumpy terrain.
- weighs 12 to 20 po...

Shop online at http://www.babycenter.com/catalog

HELPFUL ADVICE
As in the rest of this book, the bottom section of these catalog pages is filled with tips, advice, and other useful information.

BabyCenter®

is the Web's leading source of information and products for new and expectant parents.

a clear
RATING SYSTEM ★★★★★
that lets you know which products are rated tops by parents.

🔖 **TOP PICK** has received an average rating of five stars (out of five) and represents the best product overall in its category.

🏷 **BEST VALUE** has received an average rating of four or five stars and, in the opinion of BabyCenter editors, offers good value for the price.

🏅 **TOP PICK:** Standard Stroller

Pliko Sherpa by Peg Perego, $249.95
A strolling dream, the Pliko Sherpa is lightweight and rugged.

- Holds up to 40 lbs.
- Five-point harness
- Folds easily and compactly for travel; stands when folded
- Height-adjustable umbrella handles
- Removable safety bar and extension leg rest adjust as your baby grows
- Rear footboard for second child to stand on back
- Removable canopy with window
- Basket for storage
- Softly padded seat cushion removes for hand washing
- Open dimensions: 33 1/2"L x 20"W x 40"H; folded dimensions: 13"L x 20"W x 40"H
- Weighs 15 1/2 lbs.

🏅 **TOP PICK:** Lightweight Stroller

Savvy Z Stroller With Acoustic Canopy by Combi, $199.95
Durable, maneuverable, and exceptionally lightweight, this is a great stroller for an on-the-go family.

- Partially reclining seat (to 140 degrees) is suitable for babies 6 months and up
- Three-point seat belt
- Acoustic canopy featuring mini stereo speakers in pocket of canopy
- Opens and folds easily with one hand
- Four-wheel suspension
- Removable safety bar
- Includes shoulder strap
- Roomy canopy with viewing window, speakers for portable CD or cassette player, and rear pocket for storing small items
- Underseat basket
- Extremely light — 7 3/4 lbs.

🏅 **TOP PICK:** Car Seat and Stroller Combination

Primo Viaggio Travel System by Peg Perego, $349.95
This is the top-of-the-line car seat/stroller travel system—gorgeous, functional, and compact.

- Infant car seat/stroller system with instant snap-in/snap-out attachment
- Primo Viaggio infant car seat with base included
- Car seat weighs 6 lbs. and carries an infant up to 20 lbs.
- Five-point safety harness/restraint system
- Four-position backrest, including
- fully reclined for infants
- Stroller has all-terrain double wheels in front and back
- Height-adjustable handlebar
- Deluxe canopy with window, ventilation panel, and rain canopy
- Large reinforced seat and backrest
- Plush, hand-washable fabric
- Total weight: 17 lbs.

 **★★★★★** **Choosing a Stroller** Here are three popular types to consider:

Lightweight Stroller
A lightweight model is great to have when a big stroller is too unwieldy: for fitting in an overhead compartment on a plane or stowing in the trunk of a taxi
- weighs 12 lbs. or less
- folds compactly
- easy to maneuver

- ideal for travel and short outings
- for babies at least 4 to 6 months old (unless it fully reclines)

Standard-Size Stroller
Thanks to more padding and better wheels, a standard stroller delivers a smoother ride, especially on bumpy terrain.
- weighs 13 to 20 lbs.

Best Value: Standard Stroller

Easy Comfort Plus Stroller by Evenflo, $89.95
This stroller's a breeze to set up and maneuver.

- Reclining seat has two positions
- Folds in one easy step
- Large wheels and full suspension for smooth ride
- T-bar handle for easy steering
- Extended canopy with viewing window
- Heavy-duty frame
- Headrest
- Cup holder
- Snap-on front tray
- Large basket with organizer pockets
- Removable, washable padding
- Weighs 19 lbs.

Best Value: Lightweight Stroller

Reclining Umbrella Stroller by Kolcraft, $29.95
Practical and lightweight, this reclining umbrella stroller makes strolling easy.

- Three-point harness keeps your baby snug
- Seat back semi-reclines for your child's comfort
- Built-in slats for back and neck support
- Folds compactly in one step
- Front-swivel wheels lock to ride smoothly over bumpy terrain
- Cloth canopy shades your baby from the sun
- Lightweight metal frame locks easily
- Upholstery wipes clean
- Weighs 11 ¼ lbs.

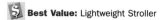

Best Value: Car Seat and Stroller Combination

MetroLite Travel System by Graco, $179.95
This is a terrific car seat/stroller travel system made expecially for urban parents.

- Three-point safety harness in stroller
- Infinite-position stroller seat recline
- Stroller folds easily with one hand
- Front-swivel wheels
- Height-adjustable handle
- Extra-large stroller canopy
- Ultralight aluminum stroller frame
- Large storage basket
- Includes car seat with five-point safety harness in car seat
- Two harness slot positions for growing baby
- Ergonomically designed "M" handle
- Two harness slot positions for growing baby
- Stroller weighs 15 lbs.

Prices subject to change. Visit http://www.topbabystuff.com to see our latest product selection and prices.

- more comfy than the lightweight models
- folds easily; can be bulkier and harder to transport than lightweights
- many recline for infants
- smooth ride, more shock-absorbing

Stroller-Carseat Combo
Many parents love the convenience of being able to move a sleeping baby from car to stroller and vice versa.
- infant car seat snaps into and out of stroller
- seat base remains strapped in car

- more economical than buying stroller and car seat separately
- lets you easily move your sleeping baby from car to stroller and back again
- stroller folds when car seat is out

 TOP PICK: Infant Car Seat

Handle With Care Infant Car Seat by Britax, $149.95
One of the only infant seats with a rear-facing tether for added security.

- Stay-in-car tether secures the seat in rear-facing position
- Built-in lock-off clamps make installation easier than with traditional locking clips, eliminating seatbelt slack for a more secure fit
- Built-in EPS side-impact liners (the same protective material used in bike helmets)
- Height-adjustable five-point harness
- Built-in base converts to a rocker for use outside the car
- Reversible canopy
- Handle has two locking positions
- Approved for use in aircraft
- 21 3/4"W x 16 1/2"D x 25 1/2"H
- Seat weighs approximately 8 lbs.

 TOP PICK: Infant/Toddler Car Seat

Roundabout Car Seat by Britax, $219.95
It sets the benchmark in the convertible car seat category for safety, comfort, and peace of mind.

- Two seats in one: Converts from a rear-facing infant seat to a front-facing seat for toddlers up to 40 lbs.
- Rear facing for infants up to 30 lbs.
- Easily adjustable anti-tangle five-point harness
- Tethers secure the seat in both rear- and front-facing positions
- Built-in lock-off clamps make
- installation much easier, eliminating seatbelt slack (and traditional clips) for a more secure fit
- Built-in EPS side-impact liners (the same protective material used in bike helmets)
- 26 1/2"W x 19"D x 25"H
- Rear-facing for infants up to 30 lbs.

 TOP PICK: Booster Seat

Roadster Booster by Britax, $119.95
A booster seat in fun fabrics that accommodates very tall or heavy children.

- Fits children from 40 to 100 lbs. and up to 56" tall
- Belt-positioning booster
- Built-in hooks ensure correct placement of shoulder belt
- 11 height adjustments allow seat to grow with your child
- Back can be removed and stored once your child reaches 65 lbs.
- Removable, machine-washable cover in fun fabrics
- 18"W x 17 1/2"D x 28"H (with back fully extended)
- Weighs 7 1/2 lbs.

 **Choosing a Car Seat** How to find the right seat for each phase of childhood:

Infant Car Seat
Age range: birth to 1
Weight range: 0 to 20 lbs.
Best for: transferring a sleeping baby into and out of the car.

Either an infant car seat or an infant-toddler convertible car seat (right) will keep a young baby safe; the advantage of an infant seat is that it's more portable.

Infant-Toddler Convertible Carseat
Age range: birth to 4
Weight range: 0 to 40 lbs.
Best for: years of use; grows with your child

Infant-toddler car seats are designed to face the rear of the car when your baby is younger than 1 and switch to front-facing when your child is a year old and weighs at least 20 lbs.

Best Value: Infant Car Seat

Snugride 3pt - Tempo by Graco, $59.95
A safe, easy-to-use infant car seat that's also easy on your pocketbook.

- Rear-facing for infants up to 20 lbs.
- Three-point harness
- Adjustable stay-in-car base lets you lift seat for carrying, rocking, and feeding
- Level indicator insures proper installation
- One-handed release detaches seat from base
- Adjustable padded handle
- Infant head bumper insert offers extra support
- Large sun canopy rotates 180 degrees
- Removable, washable padding and cover
- Approved for aircraft use
- 16 1/2"W x 25 1/2"D x 20 1/2"H
- Weighs 7 lbs.

Best Value: Infant/Toddler Car Seat

Eddie Bauer 3-in-1 Car Seat by Eddie Bauer by Cosco, $149.95
This ample, attractive car seat grows from rear-facing infant seat to booster-size for bigger kids.

- Rear-facing for infants weighing up to 35 lbs.
- Forward-facing for children 25 to 40 lbs.
- Belt-positioning booster for children 30 to 80 lbs.
- Three harness positions
- One-handed release buckle
- Convenient harness adjustment
- Infant insert for snug baby positioning
- Removable pillow for toddlers
- Approved for use on aircraft with internal harness
- Seven-year limited warranty
- 21"W x 17"D x 25"H

Best Value: Booster Seat

High-Back Booster With Arms & Cup Holder by Cosco, $54.95
A booster seat that ensures a comfortable, safe ride—fashioned in cool animal-print fabrics.

- Good from 22 to 80 lbs.
- Adjustable harness
- Polypropylene molded seat shell
- Padded armrests
- Removable cup holder
- Mesh pocket for toys
- Comfortable, supportive sides for napping
- Removable, washable pad
- 20 1/2"W x 15 1/2"D x 29 1/2"H

Prices subject to change. Visit http://www.topbabystuff.com to see our latest product selection and prices.

Booster Car Seat
Age range: 3 and up
Weight range: 40 to 80 lbs.
Best for: extra protection for kids who have outgrown a toddler seat.

Not all states require children to be in a car seat after they reach 40 lbs. But a booster seat positions children more

safely than simply being in a seat belt does. And several states, including California, Washington, Oregon, and New Jersey, have recently passed laws that require children to use booster seats until they weigh 60 lbs. (80 lbs. in New Jersey).

🎗 **TOP PICK:** Front Carrier

Baby Carrier by Baby Bjorn, $79.95

A longstanding parent favorite, the Baby Bjorn carrier keeps your baby close and your hands free.

- Fits babies 8 to 33 lbs.
- Regular size fits adults who wear a small to XL T-shirt.
- New clasp design makes the carrier even more secure
- Enables young babies to face parent and older babies to face outward
- Holds baby upright, providing back and neck support
- Seat adjusts as your baby grows
- Allows parent to lay the carrier down and unsnap the bottom portion for diaper changes or to put down a sleeping baby
- Wide, padded shoulder straps for maximum comfort

🎗 **TOP PICK:** Backpack

Elite by Kelty, $184.95

Kelty's Elite is a real backcountry pack with super weight distribution and great padding.

- For babies who can hold their head and body upright (about 6 months and up)
- Can carry a child up to 45 lbs. with a total load limit of 60 lbs.
- Fits adult torsos 13 - 21" (measure spine from top of hips to top of shoulders)
- Lightweight aluminum frame
- Adjustable, padded five-point child harness
- Folds for easy storage
- Stands on its own
- Generously padded, adjustable cockpit with padded side walls
- Adjustable, padded waistbelt and shoulder straps
- Protective sun/rain canopy

🎗 **TOP PICK:** Jogging Stroller

BOB Sport Utility Jogging Stroller by BOB, $279.95

This is truly the SUV of strollers—gives your baby a cushy ride over the roughest of roads.

- Good for children 10 to 70 lbs.
- Two-position shock absorbers can be adjusted as child grows
- Quick-release wheels
- Easy to fold with wheels attached or removed
- Five-point harness
- Reclining seat back
- Multi-position sunshade
- Storage compartment on seat back
- Large cargo basket under seat
- Seat and canopy detach for washing
- Parking brake on handlebars for easy access
- Assembles without tools
- Weighs 20 lbs.
- Boxy seat is more comfortable for a larger child

BabyCenter ★★★★★ **Backpack Tips** How to get the most from this handy piece of gear:

Tip 1
Choose a backpack that has an adjustable inside seat and an adjustable safety harness for your baby, preferably one that clasps across the chest and shoulders.

Tip 2
Look for a model with a support stand, so you can prop it up on a flat surface as you install or remove your child. The stand should lock firmly and be fairly stable so your child won't tip over.

Tip 3
If you plan to carry your child in a backpack for long periods of time, get a model with a waist belt to take some of the pressure off your back and shoulders.

Shop online at http://www.topbabystuff.com

 Best Value: Front Carrier

Snugli Easy Comfort Front & Back Carrier by Evenflo, $49.95
The Snugli Easy Comfort allows you to carry your little one in three different positions: face-in, face-out, or on your back.

- For babies 6 to 26 lbs.
- Can be used as either a front pack or backpack
- Dual side entry for easy in and out
- Height-adjustable seat
- Fold-down headrest to change seat positions without removing carrier
- Removable infant head and body pillows

- Padded seat, headrest, backrest, and support harness for your baby
- Padded shoulder straps, waist strap, and upper and lower back support for parents
- Internal support system helps distribute your child's weight evenly
- Machine washable

 Best Value: Backpack

Trail Tech Carrier by Evenflo, $69.95
A snappy, low-fuss baby carrier for errands, short trips, or working in the garden.

- For children from 6 months to 3 years, or 45 lbs.
- Five hip belt positions adjust to fit parents 5' to 6' 2" tall
- Three-point harness for your child
- Lightweight plastic frame with padded adjustable straps distributes weight evenly
- Removable storage pack

- Wide-angle stand makes it easy to load the pack
- Mesh back panel lets air circulate so you stay cool
- Machine washable
- 13 3/4"W x 9 3/4"D x 24 1/4"H
- Weighs 7 1/4 lbs.

Best Value: Jogging Stroller

Allterra Jogging Stroller by Baby Trend, $109.95
Lightweight and sturdy, the all-terrain Allterra can handle snow and sand for about half the price of other popular joggers.

- Lightweight aluminum frame
- 12" front and 16" rear bicycle tires handle all types of terrain
- Quick-release wheels
- Front-wheel hand brake and rear-wheel parking brakes
- Five-point safety harness
- Reclining padded seat with strap allows infinite adjustment

- Deluxe canopy with window, a zippered pocket, and an elastic pocket
- Large molded footrest protects child
- Safety wrist strap to keep parent connected to stroller
- Large storage basket
- Comfortably padded grip handle
- Weighs 19 lbs.

Prices subject to change. Visit http://www.topbabystuff.com to see our latest product selection and prices.

 **Carriers & Slings** What's the difference?

Slings
Slings are easier to take off and put on (after a little practice), slip over your shoulder, make it easier to nurse discreetly, and let you put your sleeping baby down without waking him. They're best for newborns, but some parents use them through their child's first year and beyond.

Carriers
Carriers let you hold your baby facing your chest when he's small. Then -- once your baby has sufficient head control -- you can turn him to face forward and get a good view of the world. Carriers are also easier on you as your baby grows, because they distribute your child's weight more evenly so that all the weight isn't on your shoulders.

Shop online at http://www.topbabystuff.com

TOP PICK: Highchair

Prima Pappa by Peg Perego, $169.95

A luxury highchair that makes getting your baby to eat strained yams a pleasure.

- Made of aluminum with a durable finish
- Five-point harness and T-bar
- Four-position seat recline
- Seat adjusts to seven heights
- Side safety shield
- Extra padded seat and fabric cover can be removed for washing

- Large tray is easy to clean
- Tray locks into two different positions or can be flipped up for storage
- Folds easily, and stands when folded
- Open dimensions: 27"L x 22 1/2"W x 39 1/2"H; folded dimensions: 12"L x 22 1/2"W x 37"H

TOP PICK: Baby Monitor

Child View TV/Video Monitor by Safety 1st, $199.00

Watch and listen to your baby sleeping soundly, without being in the same room.

- Camera and monitor run on A/C adapters
- Both pieces are lightweight and compact
- Monitor doubles as 5" black-and-white television
- One-year limited warranty
- Camera is 4"L x 6 1/2" W; monitor is 6"L x 8"W x 6"H

- Up to 300' range

TOP PICK: Humidifier

Germ-Free Warm Mist Humidifier by Slantfin, $79.95

The only humidifier that destroys bacteria with ultraviolet light.

- Medicine cup releases optional inhaled therapeutic remedies
- Quiet fan won't wake your baby
- Stainless steel hot water reservoir
- Steam is warm, but not hot enough to burn your baby's skin
- Replaceable pad absorbs hard water minerals
- Ten levels of humidity to choose from

- Produces no white dust
- Indicator light tells when to replace UV bulb (about once a year)
- 2-gallon tank with water refill indicator light
- Humidifies for 24 continuous hours
- 14 1/4"L x 7 3/4"W x 11 1/4"H

 ★★★★★ **Highchair Options**

Modern highchair
- loaded with features, such as a wide removable tray, a safety belt, and a reliable folding mechanism
- comfortably padded
- reclining seat, so you can use it even before your baby can sit up

Traditional wooden highchair
- visually appealing, wears well, and can be passed down to future generations
- less comfortable for your baby, heavier, harder to use and clean
- most don't fold
Note: Be sure to add a safety belt if it doesn't already have one.

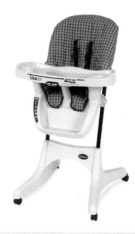

 BEST VALUE: Highchair

Neat Seat High Chair by Graco, $69.95
All the features you really need without the premium price tag.

- Built-in T-bar restraint prevents your baby from slipping under tray
- Five-point safety harness
- Wide, stable base
- Compartmentalized food tray with cup holder
- Built-in footrest
- Seat pad removes for easy cleaning
- Locking casters for easy mobility
- Rear accessory bar keeps bibs and towels handy
- 22 1/4"W x 27"D x 44"H

 BEST VALUE: Baby Monitor

UltraClear Monitor With Dual Receivers by Graco, $49.95
A parents' favorite, this lightweight portable baby monitor with dual receivers offers clear sound and peace of mind while your baby sleeps.

- Two receivers
- 49Mhz bandwidth
- Sound-activated lights on receiver
- Low battery indicator light
- Two channels and advanced sound technology for clear reception
- Receivers can be clipped onto a belt
- Requires two 9-volt batteries (not included)
- Transmitter is 8 1/2"L x 4 1/2"W; receivers are 8 1/2"L x 2 1/2"W (dimensions include antenna height)

 BEST VALUE: Diaper Disposal

Wide Opening Diaper Genie by Platex, $24.95
A simple-to-use, odor-free storage system for dirty diapers.

- Odor-free storage system for dirty diapers
- Wide mouth allows you to insert large toddler diapers
- Holds up to 25 medium-size diapers at a time
- Processes up to 180 diapers before you need a refill
- Easy-Latch safety lid keeps little hands out
- Hinged bottom allows for fast and easy disposal
- Refill units sold separately

Prices subject to change. Visit http://www.topbabystuff.com to see our latest product selection and prices.

Highchair Tip

For meals away from home, an inexpensive portable highchair makes dining out more convenient and hygienic (your child won't be sitting in a restaurant chair used by hundreds of other children). Portable highchairs are lightweight and can even fold down to fit into a large diaper bag.

🔍 **TOP PICK:** Activity Center

UltraSaucer by Evenflo, $79.95

A top-of-the-line portable exersaucer that will entertain your baby while you watch.

- 360-degree swivel rotation
- Adjusts to three heights
- Easy to clean with a damp cloth; seat padding is machine washable
- 28" in diameter; 21"H

🔍 **TOP PICK:** Swing

6-Speed Open-Top Swing by Graco, $99.95

A battery-operated six-speed swing with music, timer, and easy access to your baby.

- Six speeds, including three extra-gentle for infants
- Four automatic-timer settings at 10, 20, 30, and 40 minutes
- Automatic shutoff
- 15 tunes of soothing music and volume control
- Wide, stable base folds easily
- Swings for up to 200 hours on only four D batteries
- Seat reclines to four positions
- Removable infant head support
- Removable washable seat pad
- 37 1/2"L x 23 1/2"W x 34 1/4"H

🔍 **TOP PICK:** Mat Toy

Gymini by Tiny Love, $39.95

Indispensable for new parents, this activity gym keeps your baby happy and occupied while developing his motor skills.

- Folds flat and snaps shut for travel
- Polyester fiber
- Machine-washable mat
- Mat 31"L x 31"W
- Arches 23"H

Bedtime Reading (birth to age 1)

Colorful pictures and rhythmic text will captivate your baby.

1. Goodnight Moon
This soothing bedtime story is a classic.

2. The Big Red Barn
Sweet story of a day in the life of a group of farm animals.

3. Chicka, Chicka, Boom, Boom
The letters of the alphabet race to climb a coconut tree.

4. Boynton's Greatest Hits, Vol. I
Wacky, humorous rhymes are a joy to read aloud.

5. Zoom City
Filled with vivid illustrations and fun noises to imitate.

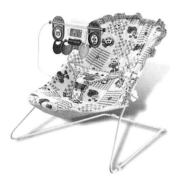

 **BEST VALUE:** Bouncer

Soothing Bouncer Seat With Toy Bar by Fisher-Price, $21.95
This battery-operated bouncer seat has lots of helpful extras, including a toy bar and canopy.

- Bouncer seat
- Battery-powered vibrations simulate a ride in the car
- Three-point restraint holds your baby securely
- Detachable bar with clip-on toys
- Two-position canopy for outside use

- Requires one D cell battery (not included)
- 20"W x 22"D x 23"H

 **BEST VALUE:** Toys

2-in-1 Clutch Ball by BRIO, $12.95
A soft, washable developmental toy that can be grabbed, kicked, shaken, and squeezed.

- Winner of a 2002 Oppenheim Toy Portfolio Award
- Builds motor skills in infants and toddlers
- Fun, easy-to-grasp shapes
- Bright, stimulating colors and contrasting textures
- Awakens senses and encourages exploration

- Machine washable
- 5" in diameter

 **BEST VALUE:** Books

Curious George Board Book Boxed Set by H.A. and Margret Rey, $18.00
In these special editions, the mischievous exploits of everyone's favorite monkey are geared specifically for toddlers.

- Gift set
- Four durable board books
- Classic, well-loved stories
- Specially adapted for toddlers
- Carry-along box
- Illustrated by H. A. Rey

Prices subject to change. Visit http://www.topbabystuff.com to see our latest product selection and prices.

Bedtime Reading (ages 1-2)

Books your toddler will love:

1. My First Lift the Flap Animals Board Book
Dozens of flaps reveal fascinating animal photos and facts.

2. Hop on Pop
A playful gem from Dr. Seuss.

3. Snoozers: 7 Short Bedtime Stories
Tabs on the side let kids flip to their favorite tale.

4. Wheels on the Bus
A comically illustrated rendition of the traditional song.

5. Elmo's Big Word Book
Simple words and colorful pictures featuring furry Elmo.

NURSERY

Shop at www.topbabystuff.com

TOP PICK: Play Yard/Bassinet

Original Bedside Co-Sleeper by Arm's Reach, $159.00
Your infant is within reach at all times with this unique bassinet that attaches to your bed.

- Use as a bassinet for babies newborn to 6 months old
- Attaches to parent's bed with sturdy nylon straps and a resistance plate
- Converts to changing table and portable play yard
- Includes zip-shut nylon carrying bag with handle
- Takes custom-fitted Co-Sleeper sheets (available separately)
- Comes with standard-length liner; longer liners can be purchased separately
- Attaches to twin, full, queen, king, and California King adult beds
- Leg extenders can be purchased separately for beds taller than 24"
- 40"L x 28"W x 31"H

TOP PICK: Crib

Sleigh Crib by DaVinci, $329.00
A great value and beautifully crafted, this hardwood sleigh crib is designed to grow with your child.

- Four-position adjustable spring bottom
- Adjustable side rail can be lowered with one foot
- Castor wheels
- Curved sleigh bed design
- Made from Malaysian hardwood
- Side teething rails
- Easy to assemble
- 2 1/4" slats all around
- Coordinates with DaVinci sleigh changing table
- 54 1/2"L x 30 1/2"W x 52"H
- Weighs 77 lbs.

TOP PICK: Changing Table

Classic Changing Table With Baskets by Badger Basket, $249.00
Rattan storage baskets add style to this sturdy wooden changing table.

- Four fabric-lined rattan storage baskets
- Removable machine-washable basket liners
- Safety strap
- 32"L x 17"W soft waterproof pad
- Some assembly required
- 34"L x 20"W x 39"H

Nursery Essentials The key equipment for stocking your baby's room:

1. Crib
During the first two to three years, this will likely be your baby's primary sleeping spot.

2. Crib Mattress
Choose a firm mattress that fits the crib snugly with no space for little fingers to become trapped.

3. Mattress Pad
A good waterproof pad extends the life of the mattress and makes cleaning up leaks easier.

4. Crib Sheet
Make sure it fits the mattress snugly so it stays safely tucked in.

5. Crib Bumper
Tied inside the crib, it prevents bumping against the rails or getting an arm or leg caught in the slats.

6. Changing Table
Makes diaper changes easier on your back.

Shop online at http://www.topbabystuff.com

BEST VALUE: Play Yard/Bassinet

Fold 'N Go Plush Bassinet by Century, $119.95

A soft padded bassinet that converts to a portable play yard.

- Removable padded bassinet
- Converts to play yard
- Folds into carrying bag (included)
- Bassinet can be used solo
- Bassinet pad doubles as play yard floor mat
- Pad wipes clean with damp cloth
- Play yard has padded corners and mesh sides

- Weighs 28 lbs.
- Dimensions: 39 1/2"L x 30"W x 28"H

BEST VALUE: Crib

Jenny Lind Crib by DaVinci, $229.00

A true classic, the Jenny Lind remains a favorite year after year.

- Single drop side with steel stabilizer bar
- Fully turned spindles
- Made of hardwood
- Converts to daybed with the addition of a safety rail (sold separately)
- Teething rails to soothe achy gums
- All hardware included; assembly required

- Mattress and bedding not included
- Matches Jenny Lind changer
- 54 1/2"L x 30 1/2"W x 44 1/2"H

TOP PICK: Changing Table

Monterey Changer by DaVinci, $124.00

A strong, sturdy changer with ample shelf space and contemporary good looks.

- Includes 1" thick changing pad
- Safety harness
- Matches the DaVinci Monterey crib
- 35 1/2"L x 20"W x 37 3/4"H
- Weighs 33 lbs.

Prices subject to change. Visit http://www.topbabystuff.com to see our latest product selection and prices.

7. Changing Table Pad
Comfortably cradles your baby while you're changing his diaper.

8. Changing Table Cover
Keeps your baby warm and comfortable during changes and removes for washing.

9. Monitor
Enables you to hear your baby's cries even if you're in another room.

10. Diaper Pail or Disposal
An odor-free place to toss diapers during changes without leaving your child's side.

11. Bassinet
Having your sleeping baby close by makes nighttime feedings more convenient.

12. Nightlight
Soft lighting lets you see your way around the nursery without disturbing your baby.

🏆 **TOP PICK:** Breast Pump

Pump In Style by Medela, $259.65

Extremely efficient and discreet, this pump is the number-one choice of back-to-work moms.

- Durable motor lets you pump four or five times a day
- Variable speed settings mimic your baby's nursing pattern
- Adjustable suction pressure
- Four freezer- and microwave-safe bottles with lids
- Two bottle stands

- 20 bags for collecting, storing, and freezing breast milk
- Three cooling packs to chill expressed milk for about four hours
- Discreet carrying case with insulated compartment holds up to four bottles
- Takes about 10 to 15 minutes total to pump both breasts

🏆 **TOP PICK:** Compact Breast Pump

Mini Electric Breast Pump by Medela, $79.00

This pump works well for mothers who need to pump only once a day.

- Can be used manually
- Uses two AA batteries (not included) or an adapter
- Includes one 150 ml. bottle
- Attaches to any standard baby bottle
- Takes about 15 minutes per breast to express milk

🏆 **TOP PICK:** Manual Breast Pump

Isis Breast Pump With Reusable Bottle by Avent, $39.95

An extremely efficient, comfortable, and discreet manual pump ideal for occasional use.

- Discreet manual pump
- Mimics your baby's suckling
- 4-oz. reusable bottle
- Nipple and sealing disc
- Can be sterilized in boiling water
- Top-rack dishwasher safe

 ★★★★★ **Breastfeeding** Which pump is right for you?

Whether you use it several times every day or only occasionally, there's a model to suit your needs:

Manual
An affordable choice for moms who need to use a breast pump once in a while.

- quiet
- inexpensive ($20-$36)

- lightweight
- requires no power source
- can be used in the shower to relieve engorgement

Our top pick: Isis Breast Pump With Reusable Bottle by Avent

Mid-Range Electric
Best for mothers who are away from their babies only a few hours a day.

Breast Pump Conversion Kit by Avent, $7.15
Allows you to pump directly into an Avent bottle using almost any breast pump.

- Breast pump adapter
- Two 4-oz. feeding bottles
- Two newborn nipples
- Dome cap
- Four disposable breast pads

Medela Storage Bags - 50 Count by Medela, $19
Freeze breast milk for months in these high-quality pre-sterilized nylon bags.

- Fifty breast milk storage bags
- Attach to any Medela breast pump
- Pre-sterilized
- Made of medical-grade nylon
- Pump directly into bag

Car Adapter for Breast Pumps by Medela, $15.00
Essential for on-the-go moms who use the Medela breast pump.

- Plugs into car's cigarette lighter
- For use with the Medela breast pump

Lansinoh by Hollister, $11.95
Clinically proven to soothe, heal, and protect cracked nipples associated with nursing.

- Hypoallergenic
- Endorsed by La Leche League International
- Totally natural, pure, and safe
- The purest form of lanolin, it need not be removed before nursing.

Round Back Glider by Dutailier, $239.00
Has rounded back and circular arms.

- Made of solid wood
- Assembles quickly with a screwdriver
- Angled back for excellent support
- Patented gliding mechanism
- 27"W x 31 3/4"D x 40 1/2"H

Round Back Glider Cushion by Dutailier, $120.00
A comfortable and stylish four-piece cushion.

- Polyester cushion
- Covered with Scotchguarded cotton or cotton/polyester fabric
- Roomy armrest pockets
- Snaps easily onto Dutailier's Round Back Glider frame
- Dutailier ottoman also available

Prices subject to change. Visit http://www.topbabystuff.com to see our latest product selection and prices.

- semiautomatic
- moderately priced ($75-$150)
- faster than manual pump
- portable
- double-pumping capability

Our top pick: Mini Electric Breast Pump by Medela

High-End Electric
The way to go for women who work full-time and others who need to pump more than once a day

- fastest

- expensive ($150+)
- fully automatic
- simulates natural sucking rhythm
- adjustable suction pressure
- double pumping
- comfortable
- maintains good milk supply

Our top pick: Pump In Style by Medela

THE **BABY**CENTER **STORE**
Products parents love. Answers parents need.

We make it **easy and worry free** to shop online for the pregnancy, baby, and toddler products rated tops by new and expectant parents.

Great Gift Ideas
Browse our gift center for terrific ideas for showers, newborns, birthdays, and more.

Parents' Picks
See which strollers, car seats, breast pumps, activity centers, and other essentials get the highest ratings from BabyCenter shoppers, and read customer comments for helpful insights.

Recommendations and Advice
You'll find must-have checklists, helpful buying guides, and detailed product descriptions to help you choose the best products for you and your family.

To get started, go to

www.topbabystuff.com

BabyCenter®